The Speaking/Writing Connection: A Rhetoric

Revised Edition

David Ryan | Fredel Wiant

FOUNTAINHEAD
PRESS

Cover and text design: Ellie Moore

For information, please call or write:
1-800-586-0330
Fountainhead Press
Southlake, TX 76092

Web site: www.fountainheadpress.com
E-mail: customerservice@fountainheadpress.com

ISBN: 978-1-59871-554-5

Printed in the United States of America

Dedications

For my parents, Tom and Harue, brother Michael and sister Angela.
—David Ryan

To our students and colleagues.
—Fredel Wiant

CONTENTS

Preface for the Revised Edition

RHETORICAL INSTRUCTION: A CLASSICAL AND MODERN PERSPECTIVE

With more college and university programs combining the instruction of public speaking and college composition, we offer this revised edition of *The Speaking/Writing Connection*. This edition offers a freshly modern but decidedly classical approach to teaching rhetorical communication. We synthesize the instruction of speaking and writing because we believe that learning speech and composition is best achieved when they are taught together. This combined approach is based on a premise that language exists as a continuum and recognizes that literacy has its roots in orality.

Students who learn rhetorical communication this way better understand the dialectical relationship between speaking and writing, and, based on our experience, they learn each discipline more thoroughly because they gain an enhanced linguistic and rhetorical perspective of language and argument.

In many ways, we favor classical approaches to teaching and learning rhetoric, but our enterprise is decidedly modern. Though we model our book on some classical approaches to teaching speaking and writing, we approach communication as an integral part of human growth and helpful in explaining human behavior.

Historically, the practice of argumentation and the study of persuasion began as an oral discipline in preliterate societies. The discipline of rhetoric grew in significance when classical Greece shifted from the rule of monarchs to the earliest forms of democracy. In democratic societies, ordinary citizens became increasingly responsible for governing their communities. Citizens, not always accustomed to having a public voice, engaged in active dialogues and made persuasive speeches about issues, topics, policies, and laws.

Teachers, called sophists, seized upon this social need and focused on teaching the skills of argumentation. Of course, there were competing claims as to what a rhetorical education should encompass. These sophists taught the discipline of rhetoric as a set of skills to be used by their students in their political, legislative, and judicial battles. However, Plato,

Aristotle, and Isocrates re-visioned rhetoric as philosophical, ethical, and civic endeavors. Their collective effort further systematized rhetoric into a broader social and educational discipline.

As literacy grew out of social necessity, rhetoric moved to a literate-based communication. This transition allowed citizens who lacked the confidence in public speaking, such as Isocrates, to use writing to argue their points. Other orators used writing to help prepare speeches or hired *logographers* (speech writers) to teach them how to act and speak in front of a critical audience of listeners. The advent of writing allowed politicians and political commentators to transcribe and preserve their oral performances for people to read. In one sense, rhetoric nourished the development of public speaking and, after the advent of writing, nurtured the development of argumentative writing.

From a modern perspective, we all understand that writing can help us with speaking; we use outlines, notes, or scripts because speaking from a written text allows us to be thorough and accurate by relying on writing rather than our memories. This relationship can lead to giving good speeches. But we also understand that our inner voice assists us when we compose our papers. Quite often, teachers and students will converse about papers in all of the stages of writing, from drafting and composing to editing and revising.

SPEAKING AND WRITING: A DIALECTICAL APPROACH

Exploring, analyzing and understanding the dialectical relationship between the spoken and written word is the premise of this book. This premise affirms and acknowledges the rhetorical undergirding that is fairly consistent in public speaking and college writing courses. However, most university and college composition and public speaking programs do not explicitly teach this approach. Rather, rhetoric instruction is split: public speaking is taught by the Communication Department and argumentative writing is taught by the English Department. This bifurcation has many organizational benefits, but this approach teaches students about discontinuity and dissonance, and for the most part tends to emphasize the differences between speaking and writing.

There are, of course, important differences, but such differences are studied with more intention in classes that examine speaking and writing together.

Both disciplines, however, recognize the importance of the other. Composition teachers encourage and depend on a range of oral or speech-related activities in their classes, such as individual and group responses, class discussions, and oral reports. These oral components are part of the norm of learning writing and strongly indicate an intuitive understanding that oral discussions can lead to an enhanced understanding of reading and writing. This social and rhetorical dynamic is universally understood as a fundamental part of learning writing.

Additionally, speech teachers understand that writing plays an integral role in the production of speeches, so teachers often require evidence of preparation, such as annotated bibliographies and outlines or copies of note cards. Speech teachers often require their students to write analytical papers that demonstrate a rhetorical understanding of different speech acts.

In many ways, there is great commonality in spirit and purpose related to teaching language in its wonderfully varied forms. Despite this encouraging and promising pedagogical practice of bringing together speaking and writing, the unfortunate result is there are few, if any, modern examples of a textbook that offer a historical and rhetorical approach to teaching speaking and writing together.

Because our project bridges the institutional divide between public speaking and college composition, our book may appeal to the rhetoric and composition instructor looking for a modern context to teaching writing and argument, or a speech teacher looking for alternative content beyond the standard technique-based speech textbook.

This book, however, is dedicated to those small but growing number of faculty who opt to teach speaking and writing together.

CONNECTING SPEAKING AND WRITING

It is evident that there needs to be a different kind of text given our premise that students will learn more effectively when they approach rhetoric as an epistemological system rather than seeking out rhetoric's significance in its current state of disjointedness. In this textbook, our primary goal is to reunite the discipline of rhetoric in an undergraduate context, so that students may gain a better understanding of the continuity associated with speaking and writing, listening and reading—and to better learn the rhetorical theory and skills necessary to engage in rhetorical exploration and analysis.

Our approach is different, for we are concerned with teaching a body of knowledge rather than merely teaching students transitory skills and techniques. In chapter 1, we begin with our students and highlight the numerous rhetorical situations in which they find themselves. In chapter 2, we move into a historical understanding of the speaking-writing connection to discuss the origins of rhetorical education. Chapter 3 focuses on the work of rhetoric—the *whys* and *hows* of communication. Chapter 4 discusses communication anxiety while chapters 5, 6, 7, and 8 analyze the process of rhetorical inquiry and argument in clearly delineated sections. Chapters 9 and 10 prompt students to think substantively about how to persuade their audience by marshalling evidence through research, organization, and attribution. Chapters 11 and 12 dig deeper into the intricacies of performing their work as a public act.

These chapters explore, explain, and analyze the best way to communicate to an audience and to overcome potential and real blocking mechanisms in this process. Finally, we conclude the book with a chapter on rhetorical criticism that synthesizes the knowledge students have gained into application for the public and academic spheres.

We hope our theoretical and practical approach helps students and teachers hear the consonance and see the continuity of language, and that this convergence of thought, labor, and argument adds to the belief that speaking and writing is best learned side by side.

ACKNOWLEDGMENTS

For our revised edition, we are indebted to our teachers, colleagues, students, friends, and families for their continued support, insight, inspiration, and patience. In particular, we thank Michael Rozendal, who piloted several of the early chapters in his courses; colleague David Holler who guided our first edition and contributed to this revision; and our gratitude extends to Chris Ames and Ellie Moore, both of Fountainhead Press, for shepherding this revised edition; and, finally, we reserve our deepest gratitude for our own Oral and Written Communication students who read our book and responded to our instruction.

David Ryan
University of San Francisco

Fredel Wiant
University of San Francisco

SECTION ONE

The Word and You

CHAPTER 1

Oral and Written Communication: A Rhetorical Tradition

The relationship between speaking and writing is complex . . . My own research and studies, as well as my personal experiences, suggest that exposure to writing and reading affects speaking. My accent changes, it seems, with every book I read. We don't have to give voices to students. If we give them pen and paper and have them read aloud, no matter what their grade, they'll discover their own voices.

—Victor Villanueva, "Whose Voice Is It Anyway?"

FOCUS ON THESE WORDS. As your eyes move from left to right (and right to left), your brain is using your "inner voice" to process what you are reading. You recognize that these letters are arranged in chunks called *words*, and these words create sentences charged with meaning. The center left cerebral region of your brain coordinates these external elements (words, syntax, rules of grammar) with your internal life, particularly your memory, to comprehend what you are reading. This mental coordination connects social and cultural objects with your very own biological and cognitive ability to analyze words.

Because you are reading along, you are using your inner voice to speak these words. As these words cross your mind, we are influencing your thoughts and feelings. This connection—between the printed word and your inner voice—is achieved only because you learned the phonemic differences between sounds and the alphabetic differences between the letters that correspond to those sounds. This process of linguistic education still influences you because language is a significant part of your life.

The above excerpt by Professor Victor Villanueva touches upon an important aspect of the verbalization of reading. As readers, we are influenced by the printed word, for these written patterns affect our way of thinking and speaking. Though no one is quite sure about the extent to which this influence takes place, it is certainly a factor in how we use writing to develop our own voices. This interactive connection between the printed word and the spoken word not only assists in developing our own inner voices, but helps us develop our public voices in a culture that demands both oral and written competence.

As theorist and theologian Walter Ong S.J. argues, the impact of writing on the development of our minds is quite profound. In pre-literate societies, people didn't "study" in the sense we do today. They couldn't pick up a book, sit in isolation, and pore over writings. Rather, in order for a non-reading people to engage in study, they had to talk to people—listen to and converse with them. This activity did promote social bonds and helped develop strong communal identities; however, as Ong argues, important mental activities such as critical reflection and introspection didn't occur in oral cultures to the extent that they do in literate societies. Reflection and introspection happen only when writing is deeply involved in a person's sphere of activities.

Writing, Ong claims, helps us become more reflective thinkers by developing more dimensions of ourselves. When we read, our mental horizons confront complex poetry, philosophical treatises, and scientific theorems. As we grapple with these texts, our minds become engaged, enriched, and enlightened. And when we arrive in class after reading Homer, Shakespeare or a theory on quantum physics, we consult these works, and our teachers. Then, perhaps, we write about them by summarizing, paraphrasing, and critiquing. This kind of recursive act is how we deeply interiorize knowledge, and this process is the basis of academic learning.

What is obvious is that language is the medium by which this kind of substantive learning takes place. Studying and understanding language in its varied forms, then, must be the primary goal of writing and speaking classes.

LANGUAGE, IDENTITY, AND CULTURE: A MODERN CONTEXT

Most of us would have great difficulty going a single day without speaking, reading, or hearing language used in some way. Language plays a vital role in connecting us to things, places, ideas, and people, for we use language in our notes, emails, letters, essays, and most importantly conversations. Our sensory receptors (eyes and ears) are confronted by language at every turn: on radios and billboards, in magazines and newspapers, on television, and in our classrooms. We use language to establish friendships, buy products, get jobs, and teach our children.

Of course, language is more than just a helpful tool that allows us to be more developed and refined social beings. We use language to develop our inner lives. From our very beginnings as infants, we heard sounds permeating our environment: voices of parents and siblings helped us become familiarized with the varied universe of sounds. We internalized the building blocks of language when we began listening to others singing the ABCs and nursery rhymes—and then we imitated them. Our parents, older siblings, and extended caregivers used language to teach us what to say and how to behave. They corrected our mispronunciations and imprecise use of words so we could speak correctly. They used language to warn us not to run into the street or pick up dangerous things. In our infancy, our caregivers read myths, fables, and stories to teach us about the dangers and values of real life. In many ways, language is a moral instrument that teaches us right from wrong, so we can contemplate the mistakes of the past and inherit the great wisdom of previous generations.

Our intellectual inheritance is important. As children, we are assimilated into a society that agrees on many things, such as the value of literacy and the importance of mathematics. There is little doubt that learning how to read, write, speak, and listen has immense personal and social benefits. That is why our culture insists that children learn how to spell and count. Although we rarely think of it as such, language is a marvelous technological system that compels us to make meaning of circumstances and people, allowing us to categorize our ideas and communicate our thoughts.

As Ong argues in *Orality and Literacy: The Technologizing of the Word,* technology is defined as any artificial instrument that allows its users to extend their knowledge, ability, and experience. Clearly, learning the alphabet enables us to spell words, compose paragraphs, and read papers. Using language allows us to organize and refine our thoughts and modify our behavior. Oral language, Ong writes, is a natural instrument; written language, however, is an artificial construct. The artificiality of our written language does make learning to write difficult for many students, for they can't always make the transition between speaking and writing. However, in every generation, we take this technology and forge new and interesting ways to use language.

More often than we realize, we use language to entertain ourselves, for we are a nation that loves to tinker with words and ideas, stretch our elocution, and enunciate in varying ways. Creative minds—from

Different dictionaries boast a vast range of words: the *American Heritage Dictionary* lists 65,000 entries, the *Oxford English Dictionary* has more than 200,000 words, and *Random House Webster's Unabridged Dictionary* contains 315,000 entries.

young people to artists and scientists—love to invent new words, experiment with new phrases and consider new ways of saying old things. Without being too internet-savvy, most of us could probably figure out the meanings of such a word as *dot-conned*. But what about *schmick* or *femtosecond?* If we took stock of an average day, we might discover that we use language to direct and guide ourselves through our activities. However, we do use language to ward off silence or boredom.

More socially, we use language to lift the sagging spirits of friends and family by responding to their experiences and stories. We even use language as a display of showmanship and as an expression of romance.

In an academic setting, we read, write, converse, and listen not only to meet the demands of our professors, but to gain more knowledge, and, as many of our students indicate, become smarter and improve our lives. Language is an important instrument by which we learn more about ourselves and the changing world.

Using language also signifies generational and regional differences. To some degree, today's youth speak differently than the youth of the 1960s, 70s, and 80s. The style of expression often shifts and changes between parents and their children. Additionally, choice of language and style of speech often depend on where you live. Linguists have demonstrated that Americans who live in different parts of the country often pronounce their words differently; folks from the South often speak differently than people from the East Coast.

Regional dialects are important features of learning language. We do not, however, have to go back generations or travel great distances to notice different ways of speaking. In what ways do you speak differently than your cousins? Is your style different than that of your friends? Most of us shift our style of speech based on audience. For example, we speak slowly and, perhaps, repetitively to our younger brothers and sisters; we speak respectfully to our grandparents; and we speak passionately to our beloved. Hence, our style of communication is very important because we understand that we use different ways of communicating (words, techniques) for different audiences. When we use language to meet the varying needs of different audiences, we are using language rhetorically.

LANGUAGE AND COGNITION

Throughout our lives, we have been instructed in language, and by the time we become adults, we have internalized language to the extent that we cannot escape it—even if we isolate ourselves by studying alone or going for long walks. Why? Even in our isolation, we use language to process and analyze feelings, impressions and tasks. In essence, we use language *to think*. Ask yourself this question: To what extent are linguistic operations (speaking and hearing, writing and reading) involved in thinking? Can you think without using language? The answer seems to be simple: although we can account for impressions and feelings, the relationship between thinking and language is by far the most important mental operation we have because we are constantly thinking—about the people we love, about ourselves, about our jobs, about quizzes and exams, and about having fun. These thoughts and tasks are often achieved primarily within the structure of language.

Because language permeates our mental lives and stretches our cognitive horizons, studying language should be our central concern. Certainly, to the average middle schooler, however, "language" is a befuddling subject governed by a series of tedious rules that besmirch the fun we have at school. To this student, "language" is synonymous with "grammar," a perception that views language merely as a series of abstract rules that are punitive in nature when the rules are fumbled.

When this student reaches high school, "language" falls into the province of poetry, fiction, and drama: language becomes Emily Dickinson, Jane Austen, and Shakespeare. In high school, students are asked to demonstrate some critical regard for their learning in the form of individual answers, group discussions, short essays, or brief speeches. Then, students are assessed, evaluated and graded by the language they use—in both speech and writing—by making important distinctions between the right and wrong answers and between valid and invalid claims.

For most of us, language is our constant companion. (Even in our sleep, we cannot fully escape language.) Language informs our consciousness, decisions and actions. In many respects, we use words to define ourselves: we are tall, short, slender, smart, challenged, nervous, and confident; we are women and men; we are African-Americans,

European-Americans, Asian-Americans, Arab-Americans, and Latino-Americans. We are Arab, Dominican, Filipino, French, German, Irish, Israeli, Italian, Palestinian, Polish, Serbian, Ukrainian, and Vietnamese. We are students, sorority members, psychology majors, research assistants, resident advisors, tutors, and library assistants. We aspire to be nurses, engineers, teachers, police officers, or business leaders. We use these categories to communicate who we were, who we are, and who we want to be.

RATIONAL ANIMALS AND RHETORICAL BEINGS

In fact, language is so important to our lives and vital to our prosperity that our goal must be to understand the personal and social significance of language—in both its spoken and written forms. As we know, language is implicated in our memory, creativity, ethics, morality, learning, and behavior. Philosophers often argue that language is what separates us from other animals. Aristotle (ca. 384–322 BCE), in his *Metaphysics*, called humans "rational animals." His reasoning was simple: we have much in common with tigers and apes—we have eyes, ears, and noses; we bleed, sweat, procreate, and rear our young. Animals have basic emotions: fear, confusion, and contentment.

We can compose a longer list of commonalities, but we must make some important distinctions. Aristotle's point was that what distinguishes us from the other animals is our ability to think abstractly, rationally, and reflectively, all of which can be achieved by using language. Our mental ability to think reflectively, assess our place in the world, and develop complex feelings such as remorse, shame, and gratitude is what further distinguishes humans from other animals. As we can guess, tigers feel no remorse for killing a young gazelle; apes probably feel no shame for eating too many bananas; and elephants feel no sense of gratitude for park rangers who protect them from poachers. As far as we know, animals are incapable of these kinds of deep, sophisticated feelings. Why? Because these complex feelings are formulated by and are dependent on language.

Though animals and insects are able to pass information to each other in complex ways, humans are able to create multifaceted social relationships, vast civilizations, and cultural phenomena such as art, music, and poetry. The social use of language is important because we also use language to exercise persuasive power over other people, from persuading people where to eat, what film to see, which music has value, and what political action is desirable and feasible. We employ a system of rhetoric when we use language persuasively to help govern society—particularly in democratic societies—and to help people overcome their differences. Rhetoric, then, is the study of argument and the art of persuading people in specific situations and contexts. More specifically, as Donald C. Bryant argues, rhetoric is "adjusting ideas to people and people to ideas" (Bryant 413). Rhetoricians, then, are teachers who teach the system of rhetoric, an art based on persuasion.

As a result, language constitutes our laws, business contracts, and university mission statements, all of which were created by people who wish to persuade you to live safely, prosper, and earn a good education. In essence, language is an instrument of the intellect, a tool for inquiry, and a means of expressing passion and reason. We cannot deny our own ability to understand our own internal processes for making meaning. Rhetoric is also a means by which we understand our own mental processes of thinking, learning and evaluating. We try to understand concepts, theorems, and arguments within our own linguistic sphere. The best and highest use of language, beyond developing yourself, is to use language as a unifying force, a way of compelling different people to work together, learn together, argue together, and live together.

◆ QUESTIONS FOR CRITICAL REASONING, DEVELOPMENT, AND DISCUSSION

1. In this section, we assert that language helps us understand our experiences and the experiences of others. In this respect, we use language to tell stories and listen to "what happened." In what ways do you see language as an extension or a part of yourself? If you were asked to compose a linguistic portrait of yourself, how would you compose this portrait? Are you "good with words"? A better writer than speaker?

2. We claim that language is a moral instrument. Restate what this assertion means, then elaborate on its meaning with your own examples. Can language be used in immoral ways? How?

3. Sometimes language fails us. There are ineffable qualities and chaotic experiences that evade easy explanation. Consequently, we are either stumped by our own inability to express certain feelings or experiences, or we try to explain them by creating new

words or new metaphors. What experiences of yours have evaded explanation?

4. What new words have you come across? Here's a challenge: create at least three new words with corresponding definitions to share with your classmates. You determine how to spell these new words. Be prepared to explain your choices.

5. Bryant defines rhetoric as "adjusting ideas to people and people to ideas." What other definitions can you find?

Language and Identity:
A Historical Context

PRIMARY ORAL CULTURES—ORAL ROOTS OF WRITING

As we stated in our introduction, our goal is to focus on rhetorical studies by understanding the relationship between speaking and writing. Instead of merely presenting this discourse in its modern context, we believe in looking critically at the origins and evolution of communication in order to understand the modern relevance of rhetoric. This framework poses some difficulty because the origin of communication—particularly rhetorical discourse—is unclear. Despite our best efforts to understand our beginnings, we lack some fundamental knowledge regarding our own linguistic development as a species. We have neither any records for when human beings began to speak, nor any specific knowledge as to when humans first used language. We do know, however, that cultures existed without writing. Preliterate cultures, according to Walter Ong, are primary oral cultures, cultures in which no system of writing existed. These cultures, Ong further theorizes, developed specific habits of communication and ways of thinking.

SOCIAL POWER OF SPEECH: FAMILIES, POETS, AND POLITICIANS

In the pre-literate Greek world, speaking was ascribed great importance because speech was instrumental in bringing communities together. In practical terms, speakers require the presence of a listener. Because talking and listening give people a great sense of interpersonal and communal participation, most oral interactions are conversational; speakers and listeners face each other and, typically, take turns speaking, listening and reacting rather than talking over each other. This oral interaction is quite different from when a writer composes something for an audience he may never have to face; a speaker faces a dynamic social context because this speech performance or conversation can never escape the influence of an audience of hearers as they respond to or interact with the speaker's message.

Certainly, we can never fully know how people functioned in preliterate societies. Oral transmissions and spoken records, by nature, suffer from a predictable fate: they evaporate as soon as they are spoken. In the oral world, words do not survive in literary form because people could not jot down notes or use recorders; therefore, knowledge wasn't preserved in journals, textbooks, or DVDs. Rather, knowledge was stored in the only way it could be preserved—in the human mind—and passed on using the only reliable means of communication—by word of mouth. Therefore, knowledge in an oral culture was preserved in the personal memories of its people and the rituals the culture performed.

Attending public festivals and epic recitals, singing in choruses, and acting in dramas helped people learn and remember social norms and cultural customs. According to Ong, the oral mind was one that focused on memorizing and storing information, rather than analyzing information, because the survival of cultural values and knowledge depended solely upon individual memory retention. The absence of writing explains why speech was the key to all authority in the community and the nation-state. Therefore, communities held speaking contests and competitions to train their citizens: these became customs in which people would orate and sing from their memories as a way of fostering speaking skills and strengthening memories.

Because speaking was so important, interpersonal relationships were quite strong among families in preliterate Greece because these ties were built on the bonds of spoken words. Having regular mealtime conversations, sharing common speaking times, having long public dialogues (à la Plato), and praying communally not only compelled people to form strong familial bonds, but also helped to create a strong community life, according to Ong. Most significantly, speech held great social power in council meetings, town gatherings and assembly debates because public speaking was the means by which communities were governed.

THE HOMERIC MYSTERY: THE SPEAKING/WRITING CONNECTION

Modern audiences are familiar with the *Iliad* and *Odyssey* as thick, lengthy books, but over the last century, scholars have investigated the Homeric Question with great curiosity. Because these twin tales were two of the first written stories to emerge in western culture, most scholars assumed these stories were solely the creation of literate minds. However, scholars asked some basic questions: Why were these long tales composed as poems? Who was Homer, and was he solely responsible for writing the *Iliad* and *Odyssey*? How did these tales, created 2,700 years ago, survive? After much analysis and debate, scholars now believe these epic tales were originally conceived as oral tales composed by poets for largely preliterate audiences. The evidence regarding the oral roots of these books is quite compelling.

Scholars believe that these tales were crafted somewhere between 1150 and 800 BCE, roughly several hundred years before the advent of the Greek alphabet. Though the books vary in length and there is great coherence among the sections, there are some problems with thematic continuity. Moreover, many of the written sections were recorded in different Greek dialects. These clues led scholars to believe that different people at different times—rather than one original author—may have been responsible for composing these tales. Additionally, the verse-like nature of the writing and the sheer length and voluminous nature of this enterprise led scholars like Milman Parry and Eric Havelock to believe that these tales were composed originally by a collective effort of several generations of poets and singers, most of whom could not read or write. Because Homer was reputed to be blind (the word *homeros* means "blind man"), it is difficult to imagine that he wrote these verses himself, so scholars have concluded that Homer may have been one important figure among a professional guild of poets who took these oral tales and transposed them into writing when writing became socially necessary.

TRAVELING POETS: THE FIRST POP STARS?

In early Greece, poets originally performed in royal courts for sovereign audiences, but they made their living traveling from town to town singing their tales to eager crowds ready to hear exotic stories of the past. These poets sang their verses accompanied by musical instruments, such as the lyre or the beating of staffs. This fusion of lyrics and music engaged ancient audiences. Crowds gathered to hear these poets tell tales of gore, glory and grandeur—to hear in the *Iliad* how the enraged Achilles slew armies of Trojans and destroyed his rival, Hector.

In these mythic tales, the noble heroes are smart but make mistakes, and they use language in eloquent and inventive ways to manage personal conflict and public strife. These tales taught audiences

> In Greek mythology, the golden-haired muse, Mnemosyne, is the goddess of memory and reason. She was the goddess who named all mortals and gave them the power to remember.

the moral virtues of the nobility, so common citizens could understand the heroic ideals and the valorous actions of the aristocracy who fought and perished for their nation. What the Homeric tales imparted was an understanding of the aristocratic pursuit of *aretē*, or divine virtue. These tales taught *demos* (or ordinary citizens) that they were an inferior, but nevertheless privileged, group that formed an important part of the kingdom's social framework.

Interestingly, none of the characters in the *Iliad* have knowledge about writing, but they do give a number of speeches, many of which are didactic in nature. Scholars Milman Parry, Eric Havelock, and Albert Bates Lord argued that because there was no writing to help audiences remember what was learned, these professional poets crafted their verse in ways their audiences could understand. Havelock theorized that there were two ways to aid the primary oral memory: (1) knowledge should take the form of a narrative or story, using set or familiar themes—because our memories are helped when information is told to us as a story, particularly a dramatic story; and (2), the language should be cast in mnemonic form by using metaphoric and rhythmic language to give the story a poetic and memorable rhythm—stylistic devices, such as tropes and schemes, for example. (See chapter 12 for more about tropes and schemes.) Over the span of many years, the poets' verbal performances evolved into a high degree of artistic virtuosity when they sang their elaborate tales at public events, ceremonies and festivals—many years before writing was ever conceived.

Furthermore, improvisation was an important part of a poet's performance as he relied on his own memory not only to recall earlier parts of the stories, but to create new tales to add to the ones that were previously told. Groups of poets performed sections of the *Iliad* and *Odyssey* over a period of days or weeks to eager audiences willing to involve their imaginations with these epic stories. Scholars speculate that poets would get together and sing an entire Homeric epic with each singer expected to fulfill his role. What also helped spark the memories of the audiences was the dramatic spectacle of the stories that were told. For young people of this era, listening, memorizing, and repeating what they learned was their way of getting involved in their own cultural education. A public education was a poetic education that taught the highest cultural values of aristocratic life, so people could understand how their leaders were supposed to behave.

The Oral-Literate Transition:

The Rise of the Alphabet

For 100,000 years or more—up until 3,500 years ago—human culture was dominated solely by an oral tradition. Our earliest estimates reveal that the Greek alphabet was recorded between 725 and 625 BCE. The creation of the Greek alphabet did not occur in one instant, but evolved slowly over a period of hundreds of years. This alphabet was derived from many antecedent forms of writing, from *Linear B*, *pictographs*, and *logograms*.

So how and why does an oral culture invent an alphabet? What is the need for writing? We must not forget that in the totality of human history, writing is a relatively new phenomenon. In many ways, even the best-trained minds forget things, so writing was created to meet some basic practical needs, most of which were economic transactions.

Greek merchants, traveling abroad, used a simple form of writing to keep manifests of inventory as they traveled between different destinations. Bookkeepers and priests used writing to keep records of wages and sacred rituals in order to preserve knowledge *accurately*. This need to preserve information illustrates a culture's desire to preserve itself through writing. However, in this transition from primary orality to literacy, people still held onto their custom of memorizing knowledge.

According to Ong, "Only long after the invention of writing did it occur to man to record in writing a performance of a storyteller, speechmaker, or singer, and finally to make up songs and tales and other such literary works with writing instruments in hand" (331). This transition from primary oral culture to a literate one was quite difficult given how strongly people identified with the oral nature of language. Scholars agree that in the seventh, sixth, and into the fifth centuries BCE, what few examples of writing that existed were viewed with great suspicion and prejudice—even hostility—partly because of the impractical nature of writing itself (inscribing on stone, wax, or parchment). For many people, writing was a sign of cultural decline.

THE STIGMA OF WRITING?

Because we live in a literate culture, we tend to think that the idea of a stigma being attached to writing is a bit strange—perhaps even bizarre. However, in the transition from primary orality to a literate culture, the majority of people who could not read and write viewed writing as a mysterious process. But the primary reason why writing was stigmatized was because writing offered an alternative yet highly specialized way of communicating apart from the established norm of speaking.

This new, radical technology called writing created great cultural tension and personal anxiety because writing signified a movement toward a different kind of life, a different kind of living, a new way of thinking. In many ways, writing offered freedom from memorizing rituals, customs, and experiences. Because the oral state of mind was psychologically connected to memorization, oral cultures viewed writing as a process that would alter relationships among people and significantly change social customs. Nevertheless, the transition to literacy-based consciousness created a new generation of minds who were free to contemplate other patterns of consciousness and intellectual habits of mind, such as abstract philosophy and higher forms of math.

For Havelock, "The creation of the Greek alphabet (and it alone) was able to bring about widespread literacy, which in turn radically and permanently transformed human consciousness. Alphabetic literacy enabled thought to transcend the limitations of the 'oral mind,' represented by Homer, to become the instrument of logic, philosophy, and science" (148). How did the invention of writing give birth to higher forms of thinking? Looking at math problems helps us make this point. We can compute simple math problems ($5 \times 5 = 25$) silently and rapidly because we memorized the times table when we were in elementary school. However, more complicated equations pose some problems. What is $5,333 \times 519$? Certainly, math *savants* can compute this equation without writing the question, but most of us require the tools of literacy (paper and pencil) to figure out the answer (2,767,827).

Clearly, contemplating higher forms of math and complex philosophical questions can compel us to move on to even more complex equations, most of which require us to write to determine their significance. As a result, literacy-based cultures are able to build complex machinery (computers, cars, etc.) and find cures to diseases by writing down the sequence to their problem-solving schemes, preserving this knowledge, and adding to this body of knowledge. Keeping records of our successes and cataloging failures add to the substance of our collective knowledge.

THE RHETORICAL POWER OF LANGUAGE

In the 5th and 4th centuries BCE, Athens was a city at the height of its cultural influence and social power. In this era, philosophy, politics, and higher education were formally born because of the growth of democracy and emergence of literacy. Because all citizens were members of the assembly, ordinary citizens were expected to speak in front of an audience. In this era, the assembly could number up to 40,000–50,000 members. Because of social reforms, ordinary citizens were allowed to examine and challenge laws and were expected to make these challenges in speeches.

Because the Greeks loved to debate in the open market, the courts, and the assembly, oral exchanges could be highly charged, inspirational and even combative. For instance, politicians used oratory to impassion their audiences about war and peace, about domestic and foreign policy, and about civil and criminal matters.

Democracy fostered a new era of openness, but this era also initiated the frequent practice of litigation. Because no lawyers existed, ordinary citizens represented themselves in court. Litigants marshaled evidence, interrogated witnesses, and presented arguments. Unfortunately, the consequences for losing a case were severe—sometimes ending in exile or death. Therefore, the need for persuasive public speaking and open advocacy was significant. Even with the advent of writing, speech was still the primary means of exerting and obtaining social power. Inexperienced speakers, if they could afford one, hired professional speechwriters—called logographers—to help rehearse their speeches and prepare their cases for court.

Logographers were experienced speakers and writers, and they often tutored their clients on how to behave, prosecute, and defend themselves in court. They would often write their statements for their clients, but litigants were expected to speak without a written text because writing still suffered from a heavy stigma, and at this time, speakers who had prepared written texts gave the appearance of giving extemporaneous testimonies, because litigants would often accuse each other of preparing ahead of time if their speeches sounded too rehearsed. Highly stylized oral performances were still the desired norm of public presentation, and rhetorical appeals were the primary means of persuading people in the *agora,* or open market, the assembly, and the court system.

✦ QUESTIONS FOR DISCUSSION

1. Scholars assert that rituals are ways of preserving and practicing cultural and familial knowledge. Beyond our national customs (Christmas, Thanksgiving, Fourth of July, etc.), what family-based rituals do you practice? What do these customs preserve? Are these customs designed to entertain and teach? If so, how? Why?

2. In what sense does the information related to the ancient poets relate to modern rock/pop/rap bands? What is the rap phenomenon of "freestyling"? How does this approach rely on set themes and formulas? Explain how you memorize music lyrics. Of the songs you can recall, to what extent is your memory aided by formulaic language?

3. Are there areas of the world in which the value of literacy is questioned? Even subverted? If so, for whom? Why?

Language and Communication:
Translation and Compromise

In human cultures, language serves many important functions. A common language is a social instrument that unites different people in conversation, contemplation, and decision-making. Based on these social actions, one may conclude quickly that the primary purpose of language is communication. There is no denying the communal value of language, and because we agree to use language for most functions, language takes on a shared and important property. However, common sense dictates that in order for language to be communicative, in order for information to be transmitted, received, and understood, many things have to happen first before communication can take place. We must understand that certain building blocks of communication must be in place before we can engage in the process of communicating. Therefore, according to John Ellis, categorization—not communication—is the primary purpose of language.

CATEGORIZATION: GENERALITY AND SPECIFICITY

Language, as an organism, plays an organizing role in terms of how we think about our world and ourselves. Language is geared toward identifying objects and then placing them in useful categories, so that we can make better sense of these objects. For example, individual words (*cat, tree, green,* etc.) lend themselves to specific definitions and associations. These definitions often specify a category to which the word belongs. We associate *cat* with a specific kind of furry animal, but we also understand that this general category breeds numerous yet specific kinds of associations because, *cat* is a general term while *Siamese* or *Persian* is a specific kind of feline.

Language not only allows us to make close associations among similar categories, but also allows us to find similarities among different categories (Ellis 30). For instance, we understand similarities between dogs and cats—whiskers, four legs, nose, eyes, fur, and tails—but we also understand the differences between canines and felines. Thus, language allows us to better understand the similarities and differences, and we try to teach children to use language to make these meaningful distinctions first.

But before any kind of oral or written communication can happen, we must come to some agreement on terms, because when we use language we are entering a domain of consensus. As a society, we agree about what the word *cat* relates to before we communicate our thoughts about the cat. Furthermore, we must agree to learn and use the building blocks of words— the alphabet—before we can instruct our children to communicate with us. In fact, parents and caretakers spend a lot of their time teaching their infants to understand these building blocks. Clearly, of course, these linguistic norms were established long before we ourselves were born. We inherited these linguistic principles without much debate.

ALPHABET AS TECHNOLOGY

Rarely do we give the alphabet much thought, because we have internalized— since a very young age—the alphabet within our consciousness. The alphabet has been embedded so deeply within our minds that we rarely recognize these characters as *technology*. Broadly defined, technology is anything that allows us to extend our activities and knowledge. Clearly, knowledge of the alphabet allows us to do many things, such as spelling, writing, and reading. We often underestimate the complexity of our own linguistic knowledge because we have been using written language for some time.

We use language to think rationally in words, to categorize our thoughts and feelings, to reflect on language, and to express our thoughts and passions. Our ability to engage in reflection should not be taken for granted, for learning this process began even before we were born. Language instruction begins when infants are in the womb. Parents and caregivers speak to infants in utero to help familiarize them with the sounds of their parents' voices. After babies are born, they use their vocal cords to signify their hunger, and after about eight to ten months of child rearing, infants exhibit the first signs of intentional non-verbal communication when they use gestures and vocalizations to influence their caregivers—whether they are expressing joy or frustration (or the desire for a certain toy).

After a year or so of familial teaching, infants are able to initiate communication by saying some simple words and associating them with objects and people. *Dad* becomes associated with the father, *momma* with the *mother,* and *dog* with a particular pet. This kind of categorical association is a shared experience, one that occurs between the infant and caregiver. The genesis of communication begins with teaching and learning the building blocks of language—of filling young minds with phonemes, words, and, indirectly, syntax, sounds that relate to external objects and patterns of speech—before more formal kinds of instruction about writing takes place.

COMMUNICATION AND CONFUSION

We understand there is both great ease and great difficulty in understanding people and their messages. For the most part, we tend to understand better those people who are within our peer groups, and we tend to misunderstand people who are outside of our peer groups. Quite often, different groups of people share different values, concerns, and perspectives, but we use language to overcome these barriers. Beyond personal disagreements or social misunderstandings, the subject of language itself is often a cause of misunderstanding.

Why? In metaphorical terms, language is often considered a living organism. For instance, language relies on the steadfastness of words and syntactical rules that have been around for generations. This linguistic stability can be interpreted as the roots of language. As we know, the roots of a large tree provide a firm base, one that nourishes and helps maintain the tree. But we also know that language grows and changes. It sprouts new branches and leaves. New technology and shifting cultural norms quite often demand new words and innovative modes of expression. Despite this fertile, linguistic growth, language also changes out of ignorance and neglect. Just like biological organisms can be genetically altered or invaded by other species that damage the organism, language is often permeated by bad grammar and confusion.

Generations of people have grown up without understanding some basic rules of grammar and principles of style. Many speakers and writers abuse language in ways they do not understand, ways that go without much detection or protest from their teachers. When students say or write, "I should of" rather than "I should have," they are repeating a mistake based on phonetic confusion. Or when people write: "Everyone should move their cars," instead of "Everybody should move their cars," they are violating a simple principle of noun/pronoun parallelism. Quite often, people will utter "between you and I" to elevate their style when grammatical correctness dictates "between you and me" as the proper way of speaking.

Either out of politeness, ignorance, or loss of nerve, people rarely correct these usage errors in speech. After all, why should anyone care about these blunders, especially when the meaning of the words isn't lost? The problem, as the critic John Simon reminds us, is that one grammatical error can induce others. Misunderstandings about grammar and style can eventually create misunderstandings in communication among people, particularly between students and teachers. A young audience unaware of grammatical violations, Simon warns, will merely repeat these mistakes again and again.

These challenges can be overcome by helping speakers and writers understand certain rules of syntactical propriety. Understanding proper grammatical expressions can help students overcome potential problems, such as misspeaking at a job interview, anguishing through a revision based on poor grammar, suffering through the embarrassment of revising memos and business letters at work, or paying the expense of recalls due to mistakes in a publicity campaign.

Communication Involves Translation: Differences Between Speaking and Writing

The basis of elementary, middle, and high school education is teaching young people how to demonstrate their knowledge through speaking and writing. In the day-to-day activities of the typical student, conversing in class (asking and answering questions) and turning in written homework or class work are the primary means by which students are evaluated. Because of these experiences, when most students come to college they have a strong intuitive understanding of the differences between speaking and writing. For instance, students understand that writing is a process that often creates a material object, an object that can be seen and touched. In this sense, an essay is a static organism—an organism that freezes our thoughts and the expressions of others.

When we read written texts, we are translating alphabetic characters, words, and syntax so that we can understand what is being communicated. Because we have been reading and writing since we were young children, we tend to underestimate this complicated process. Writing, as we have learned, is an artificial process, one that we must learn—sometimes with great difficulty. Spelling, word choice, syntax, sentences, and punctuation are all partners in writing. For the average writer, orchestrating these choices can be a difficult enterprise—one that becomes easier through repeated use, practice, and helpful instruction.

Many of us find informal speaking more comfortable. After all, our primary means of linguistic communication is conversational in nature. Conversations are based on the principles of taking turns between two or more people. Our social norms dictate that we listen and respond. This human activity depends on each person's desire to talk within different kinds of social contexts with different people.

By definition, conversations are dynamic interactions between individuals, small groups, and large groups, requiring different sets of communicative skills related to listening, interpreting, and speaking. Good conversations can be direct, colloquial, warm, and colorful. Good listening requires interpreting phonic sounds, sounds that evaporate once they are spoken, so *repetition in speaking is significant*. Repeating points—particularly important ones—is a feature of linguistic coherence that isn't used as often in writing. In speech, repetition can be used tactically to emphasize points; repetition is used also as a stalling tactic (exclusive to speaking) when we are searching for an appropriate response. Quite often, such repetition can sound clumsy and awkward because forcefulness of thought is sacrificed for excessive coherence.

Writing, however, has different dynamics. Repetition of points is not always valued in writing, particularly because stalling within an essay risks losing conciseness. Certainly, we can stall and delay in the process of drafting an essay (waiting to write your paper until the night before it is due can compromise your paper's effectiveness); however, repetition of thematic points should be used sparingly in order to retain forcefulness.

These differences between speech and writing are clear and useful. There are, of course, many other differences. Quite often, when we translate our voices into writing, we lose and gain certain things. For certain, a conversational style of speaking normally is lost when writing an argumentative essay.

People understand that moving between speaking and writing is a process of negotiation based on the rhetorical situation, a situation that calls for you to consider your message, your audience, and your environment (see chapter 6 for more on rhetorical situation). As communicators, we realize that we gain and lose something when moving between the spoken and written word because of the context of each situation.

WHAT WE LOSE WHEN WE WRITE

1. When we write, we lose an intimacy or immediacy with our audience; when readers look at our papers, and when they read the work of others, they substitute their own voices for the author's. This vocal substitution means we can sometimes (though not always) lose the explicit tone and attitude of the writer.

2. When we write, our physical presence is lost; given our own gestures (hands, arms, facial, bodily, etc.) often support what we say, the physicality of our presence is lost when we write. In addition, when we read, we lose our ability to "read" the physical habits of speakers—to detect whether they are nervous, confident, dissembling, or telling the truth.

3. When we write, there is no spontaneous response to our writing that we witness; when we converse, what we say is always interpreted—and we respond to our audience in order to carry on conversations. When we turn in our essays, we do not see how the teacher reads the essay or grades the paper.

4. When we write, we lose our pace. For instance, when we speak, we control the pace of transferring information, whereas the pace of reading is controlled by the reader. Essentially, when we write, we often lose control of how the reader will read what we write.

WHAT WE LOSE WHEN WE SPEAK

Conversely, when we speak instead of write, we lose many important things. When we write a 10-page paper for class or a lengthy report for our supervisors, sometimes we are asked to give a brief presentation of our report. When we engage in such a transaction, we lose a few things, and when we have ordinary conversations, rather than writing a letter to someone, we lose a few things.

1. Normal conversations are often spontaneous and not well-planned. Consequently, when we speak, we may forget to convey many important points and may lose the fullness of our thoughts because speeches or presentations rarely capture every detail from

our essays, so our speeches tend to summarize written findings. Writing is often copious while speaking is brief. For example, our written reports may make ten important points about a product, but in a five-minute presentation, we have to summarize the most important points to meet the requirements of time.

2. We often try to craft our speeches in a literate style—long sentences full of copious details and lush imagery. If we fail to memorize the written text, coupled with any kind of lingering nervousness, our comfortable, conversational demeanor is lost when giving a speech. In these circumstances, students lapse into a public reading of their paper. When speakers lapse into reading their papers, although they ensure an accurate presentation of their ideas, their monotonous drone and their lack of engagement with their audience will lose the audience.

3. Sometimes we lose our composure. New or inexperienced public speakers often lose control over their bodies; our nervousness can induce uncontrollable shaking, trembling, and quivering. Although our nervousness can force us to focus on the task at hand, it can also manifest itself in embarrassing ways.

WHAT WE GAIN WHEN WE WRITE

When we sit down to write a paper, we typically have some time to craft our prose. This time may be a few minutes for an in-class assignment or a few days to a few weeks for a paper for class. But this period gives us the time to do some research, whether jotting down ideas, plotting an outline, or crafting a draft. Typically, we read and re-read what we have written in order to smooth out our sentences and complete our thoughts. This time can be used to make long, elaborate papers with complicated and sophisticated arguments. What we gain from writing is a process where we try to cohere our thoughts and make them reader-friendly for our intended audience.

1. Writing creates a greater sense of permanency to our thoughts and feelings. Though we have all lost or mistakenly deleted electronic files, writing gives our thoughts a lasting record. Letters, poems, books and even wills outlive us; therefore, writing can transcend death.

2. Writing imposes a coherence on our thoughts—we often take our random thoughts and write them down; and when we write them down, we *visualize our thoughts* and meditate on their implications and revise them—typically before we show them to other people. Revision allows us to refine thoughts that may be unclear or tentative in their oral forms.

3. When we write, we often purposely integrate our writing with the writing of others. We paraphrase, summarize and quote our sources. Using attribution and citation helps qualify and substantiate our research. Though we do use quotations in our speeches—and give attribution—we are not required to give detailed parenthetical citations or provide a bibliography for our audience—unless your teacher requires a written one as evidence of research.

4. Writing presents a different perspective; we use phonemes, words, and syntax. Punctuation, of course, is a significant difference in the distinction between speaking and writing. Space, or spatiality, of course, is also a necessary distinction. When we speak, we do not ordinarily pause between each word and insert a space. We use spaces in between our written words and write commas and periods to denote the visual boundaries that are required between certain written words.

5. Writing provides control and consistency. For instance, if a corporation or government agency creates a policy that must be disseminated to employees or a new policy meant for the public, this written policy must be consistently delivered to everyone. Department heads, public information officers or even the President of the United States often speak from a script to ensure a carefully controlled consistency of information, because accuracy is supremely important to ensure clarity regarding a decision of political significance.

6. Writing helps us create an argument that has a beginning, middle, and end—and allows us to see the totality of the product. We can flip through a book and skip to the end without reading the

middle. We do not have this kind of control when we speak (unless we are viewing a video of a speech).

7. Quite often, jobs that require writing have a higher status, while work that does not require writing (or where writing is incidental) are socially devalued (gas station worker, retail clerk, food attendant, etc.).

WHAT WE GAIN WHEN WE SPEAK

When we speak to an audience of hearers, we create an important social interaction. What we often gain from speaking is a sense of immediacy where we can measure how our words can affect people. When we speak, we interpret their verbal and non-verbal cues in our minds to measure their level of comfort or discomfort.

1. We gain a greater sense of propriety when we enunciate words. When writing, we do not have to pronounce words, yet this responsibility is important when we speak. We have a social obligation to our audience to pronounce names and technical terms correctly—particularly if we are speaking to a group of peers. An audience of nursing majors, for example, will expect proper pronunciation of specialized medical terms.

2. When we speak, we gain a spontaneity that allows us to break certain grammar and style rules based on the rhetorical situation. Certainly, different neighborhoods and communities have different ways of speaking. Normally, if you're accustomed to saying "y'all," you would revise this southern expression when writing a formal paper.

3. If we use a manuscript to read from in a formal speech, we gain a sense of safety by having the written speech in front of us.

4. When we speak, we gain an opportunity to support our words physically. Our gestures can support what we say in meaningful and illustrative ways. Combining verbals with gestures can create memorable and powerful messages.

5. When we give speeches, we gain a public venue for our thoughts and ideas, whether we present our speeches in class, in workshops, or at conferences.

PROCESSING DIFFERENCES BETWEEN SPEECH AND WRITING

The above list, although by no means exhaustive or definitive, is important because it recognizes the significant differences between speaking and writing. Many of these distinctions are explicitly understood; other differences are not always easily distinguished. There is ample evidence to point to further differences in how the brain processes writing/speaking and reading/listening. Despite intense study, scientists and researchers are still not exactly sure how the brain processes these different linguistic modalities. However, there is consensus to make some important general comments about the psychological and neurological differences between speaking and writing.

Both speaking/listening and writing/reading trigger different electro-chemical responses in our brains. Because the majority of people are right-handed (about 85% of the population), most kinds of language processing occur in the left hemisphere of the cerebral cortex because the left hemisphere controls the right side of our bodies. In fact, the brain is stimulated differently when we hear sound waves and when we read letters. Furthermore, our memory retention differs when we read as opposed to when we listen because our brains encode information differently in relation to auditory and visual stimuli.

The reasons are simple enough. When we read, we are looking at objects arranged in sequence that, for the most part, appear the same every time we see them. Most writing systems have standard syntax and respect a standard spacing between letters and words (as evidenced by these sentences). This consistency accounts for a uniform approach to writing and a fairly consistent manner of "reading" visual stimuli. On the other hand, when we listen, we are listening to variable speech signals that are spoken or sung with variable acoustical patterns. Meaning, even though people use the same language, they often speak at different speeds, pronounce common words differently, possess different accents, and have varying voices. These differences are distinct enough to slow our comprehension down. Studies have shown that expert readers can take in more information at a higher rate of speed and retain this information far better than good listeners do.

Simply stated, our brains retain written information far better than acoustic-based information. For this reason, most classes have textbooks—particularly speech classes. In classrooms, teachers employ lectures or discussions to add to substance of the readings. For students, the most common approach is to take notes to record spoken words. When studying, the best way to retain information is to read the information, say the information out loud, and re-read what was just said. This dialectical method, where speaking reinforces reading and vice versa, is one of the best ways to retain information in your short- and long-term memories—particularly in preparing for tests and preparing for speeches.

WORKS CITED

Aristotle. *Metaphysics. Books I–IX.* Trans. H. Tredennick. Cambridge, MA: Loeb Classics, 1979.

Bryant, Donald C. "Rhetoric: Its Function and Scope." *Quarterly Journal of Speech.* 39.4 (1953): 401-24.

Ellis, John M. *Language, Thought and Logic.* Evanston, IL: Northwestern UP, 1993.

Enos, Richard Leo. *Greek Rhetoric Before Aristotle.* Prospect Heights, IL: Waveland Press, 1993.

Gleason, J.B. *The Development of Language.* 6th ed. Boston: Allyn and Bacon, 2005.

Havelock, Eric. "The Coming of Literate Communication to Western Culture." *Journal of Communication* 30.1 (1980): 90-98.

_____. *The Muse Learns to Write: Reflections on Orality and Literacy from Antiquity to the Present.* New Haven, CT: Yale UP, 1986.

_____. *Preface to Plato.* Cambridge, MA: Harvard UP, 1963.

Jahandarie, Khosrow. *Spoken and Written Discourse: A Multi-Disciplinary Perspective.* Stamford, CT: Ablex Publishing, 1999.

Ong, Walter. *An Ong Reader.* Eds. Tom Farrell, and Paul Soukup. Cresskill, NJ: Hampton Press, 2002.

Ruehlen, M. *The Origin of Language: Tracing the Evolution of the Mother Tongue.* New York: John Wiley and Sons, 1994.

Simon, John. *Paradigms Lost.* New York: Viking, 1981.

Villanueva, Victor. "Whose Voice Is It Anyway?" *Conversations: Readings for Writings.* 5th ed. Ed. Jack Selzer. New York: Longman, 2003. 166-174.

CHAPTER 2

The Citizen–Rhetor

It has been said that rhetoric is the handmaiden of democracy. Whether in the courtroom, the legislature, or the public forum, free and intelligent speaking and writing are the lubricants that keep democracy running smoothly.
—Richard A. Katula

Rhetoric and the Origins of Democracy

THE TRUE ORIGINS of rhetoric and the citizen–rhetor are not clearly defined. What we do know is that persuasive tactics were first evident in the speeches and dialogues of the *Iliad* and *Odyssey*; Homer, then, stands at the earliest horizons of rhetoric studies as the first teacher of literature and rhetoric. In Homer's world, the citizen–rhetor was an aristocrat and not a commoner, for the nobility possessed great political power; everyone else, unfortunately, was merely a subject. For the lower classes, there was little upward mobility because a strict class system was enforced.

Though Homer offers us an uncertain but essential starting point, rhetoric has a clearer origin point several hundred years after Homer, one predicated on teaching rhetoric not as a companion to the high ideal of noble virtue, but as a practical tool of the middle class. Our most popular account of the origins of rhetoric gives us Corax and Tisias. They began teaching a legal or forensic rhetoric in the Greek colony of Syracuse, Sicily, around 467 BCE. During this time, the Syracusans had deposed a tyrant and established a democracy similar to Athens, creating a situation that allowed citizens to enact lawsuits to recover confiscated property taken by the former ruler. Because there were no lawyers, people had to argue in court for themselves.

Reportedly, either Corax or Tisias wrote a technical manual on argument, but it is lost. Scholars aren't too clear about the specific contributions of Corax or Tisias to rhetorical theory, but we do know that many of their students went on to accomplish a great deal, including some prominent Sicilian sophists, such as Lysias, a logographer, and Isocrates, the civic rhetorician who opened his own school in Athens. Because legal claims are a complicated matter, Corax and Tisias taught their students how to navigate through a court system and argue in front of a jury. For these reasons, they are considered to be the founders of the discipline of rhetoric. This relationship between rhetoric and civic activism helped create the notion of the citizen–rhetor as a common person. Carried further, this connection between rhetoric and an active citizenry plays out in a clearer context in Athens rather than Syracuse.

RHETORIC AND CIVIC POWER

In early antiquity, people were not afforded the same rights and legal recourse because great social distinctions were made between citizens and non-citizens, free men and slaves. Modern ideas of democracy (in which people have equal protection under the law) were completely alien to Athenians. However, democracy evolved gradually and often violently over a period of two to three hundred years when political reforms in Athens broadened to include different social classes that assumed more political power.

Prior to the birth of democracy, ancient Greece was constituted of tribes ruled by kings, most of whom legitimized their power by claiming to be direct descendants (or a particular favorite) of the gods. These kings relied heavily on a number of councils that served the interests of the monarchy. Staffed by an aristocracy of princes, priests and warriors , these councils made decisions, legislated codes, served as judiciary members, and made plans for war and peace by arguing, conversing, debating and even dissenting.

Within these councils, important rhetorical principles were practiced. For instance, social issues about taxation, war, and peace were debated, contested, and voted on. Sometimes policy or judicial rulings were made by *consensus*; other times councils would recommend actions— particularly matters related to warfare—but the final decision was made by the monarch. The key here is that aristocratic councils used dialogue, debate, proofs, reason, and appeals. Rhetoric, then, was an important tool of the ruling class. Modern audiences understand that consensus-building is an important part of the political process—even in elite circles—and creating consensus means achieving understanding and agreement, practices that are the very foundation of civic society.

The ruthlessness of aristocratic rulers is well documented. They made unfair and unjust demands on the underclass by taking a large share of their products and agricultural goods. Part of the problem for this kind of power lay in the oral nature of the laws. In some preliterate Greek societies, such as Sparta, memorizing laws was part of the elementary curriculum. In most cities, however, laws were rarely written down, so special council members were appointed to memorize laws. Because of the persistent state of war during these times, the political climate was chaotic and dangerous. Therefore, councils were given to secrecy with little accountability from their subjects.

Etymology:
The word *aristocracy* is derived from *aristoi*, which literally means "the best people." The common people were later called *demos*, the root word for *democracy.*

Under these conditions, political abuses were unfortunately common, creating deep resentment and extreme bitterness among citizens and non-citizens, forcing many of the working poor to flee and seek their livelihood elsewhere. Although certain small yet powerful administrative bodies often ruled with an iron fist, over time, a wealthy growing middle class flexed their political muscles and demanded more of a stake in the governance of Athens—particularly in the military affairs of the city. Because an oral tradition relies on specially trained aristocrats to recall laws, we can never discount the role of human nature in the court system. As we know, oral memories are fallible. And because spoken words are always personalized, living words uttered by prophetic storytellers or charismatic speakers often carry more weight and persuasive power than the words spoken by low-keyed, poorly trained, or inarticulate people.

Furthermore, oral testimony or oral transmissions of laws can never escape the influence of an audience or social circumstances, because what is spoken (particularly in criminal cases and judgments) rarely fully represents all of the information available. What is spoken in a court to a jury is that which can be understood in the moment. In addition, even specially trained noblemen were not immune from undue political pressures of party politics, corruption, and out-and-out threats. Consequently, a society that relies on the oral memories of elite judicial specialists is a society that concedes that laws will not be equally applied.

In many ways, creating written laws not only gave councils and magistrates a fixed and faithful record of laws to reference, but these written documents compelled people to seek something outside of themselves on which to focus—an authentic written code that was exteriorized, visible, and probably open for inspection. Rather than giving judicial specialists sacred status, people began to give written laws more authority. A written body of laws helped develop a consistent understanding of criminal laws and helped reduce opportunities for corruption, because these written laws could help authenticate the oral representation of these laws in courts and the assembly. For example, people could hold up a written document rather than rely only on the memory of an official court member. This transformation from oral memory to writing gave laws (criminal laws, in particular) a more stable continuity and clarity.

RHETORIC AND SOCIAL ORDER

These gradual reforms instituted in Athens leads eventually to a limited form of democracy. What is important is that rhetorical practices—such as dialogue, discussion and debate—were used by the upper classes, and when these political reforms occurred, all citizens were expected to use these practices as well. Though rhetoric was routinely used by the aristocracy, the lower classes were not at all unfamiliar with persuasion. By modern standards, Athenian democracy had several critical shortcomings. Like many cities derived from tribal life, Athens had slaves. In fact, slave labor was an essential part of rural and city life, for these slaves—men, women, and children, whether privately owned or belonging to the king—underwrote the material freedoms of Athenians by serving in homes, fields, silver mines, and even battlefields. Slaves freed Athenians to tend to civic affairs and had great material value, but had neither political rights nor a voice in the assembly.

Eventually, laws were created to protect slaves from abuse. In Athens, slavery was not based on ethnicity or perceived racial inferiority; rather, slavery was based on bad fortune and military defeat. Defeated armies and villages were prizes to be sold and taken. Prior to the fifth century BCE, slavery was a permanent condition, but with the advent of the fifth century, slavery became more temporary. In this time, slaves were liberated by their masters for exemplary military service, were made citizens as the population declined, or were freed by the death of the master.

Like slaves, women were forbidden to speak in public because they too were excluded from citizenship. However, there were some remarkable exceptions. There is evidence that women did study at Plato's Academy; women such as Diotima and Perictione were very active, and Aspasia served as one of Socrates's teachers.

Though female public figures were rare in Athenian public life, female figures evinced a strong presence among myths, religious stories, and art. For instance, female divine figures (Aphrodite, Athena, Hera, etc.) were common in myths and religious stories. Strong and bold women appear in Greek literature: Clytemnestra slays her husband, King Agamemnon, for sacrificing their defenseless daughter to gain favorable winds at the start of the Trojan war; the beautiful and reasoned Helen of Troy was the "face that launched a thousand ships" in the *Iliad*, and the brainy Penelope was admired for her domestic wisdom and chastity in the *Odyssey* because beauty and elegance represented the apex of womanhood. In the mythical arts, the Greeks cast the erotic Peitho as the goddess of persuasion.

Though women were socially honored for their domesticity and spiritual dignity, Athens excluded this wisdom from the halls of power—even though women could hold property. In some other cities, such as Sparta, women even had limited legal rights. The situation in Athens, however, fails our modern expectations of a liberal democracy. Scholars are uncertain why women were excluded, but hypothesize that because politics were so intertwined with warfare, men wanted to protect women from the perils and nastiness of war. Other scholars argue that a Middle Eastern or Asian practice of excluding women from public affairs influenced Athenian consciousness. Either way, women were consigned to manage the household and raise children. They were excluded from formal education and were muted in public affairs.

As we stated earlier, rhetorical practices first appeared in the Homeric tales. Scholars believe that these tales were used primarily to teach audiences about aristocratic *aretē*, the excellence of the warrior ethic. However, it is no surprise that the rise of rhetoric as a form of public education coincides with the emergence of democracy. The growth of democracy was a slow and even violent political process—with the ruling class acquiescing power when the lower classes threatened and even engaged in violent acts. To a similar degree, the discourse of classical rhetoric is a pedigree of intellectual torrent, a tumultuous record in which different teachers led rival schools of rhetorical education and argued against each other for the hearts and minds of the young Athenians.

The educational climate in fifth-century Athens was very competitive and even politically nasty. The old Homeric school of teaching young Greeks about the aristocratic values of *aretē* and *paideia* was replaced by a new demand for people who could argue in the courts and assemblies. As more and more people became involved in the political affairs of their city, new social norms and civic needs were created. Democracy fostered a craving for multiple political perspectives and a strong thirst for competitive political power.

Different teachers had different ideas of how to use rhetoric to best meet this growth. Because of democratic reforms, ordinary citizens desired to have more say in the governance of their societies, and this kind of labor required knowledge and training in oral skills beyond singing poetry and telling epic tales. Therefore, oral performances by nomadic poets were eclipsed by a new oral tradition of rhetorical education taught by the earliest group of rhetoricians, called *sophists* ("wisdom-pliers").

The sophists were a band of loosely affiliated teachers who traveled from city to city teaching rhetoric to students who could afford their services. Public speaking was the primary means of influencing the civic affairs of society, so the sophists made a living preparing people for public engagement and verbal combat. Popular accounts of this sophistic movement describe the Sicilian teacher Gorgias and his student, Protagoras, as skilled and influential teachers who taught rhetoric so that their students could gain political influence. The sophists believed that persuasive speechmaking in an open culture was an important means of gaining individual power. For Gorgias, a rhetorical education was one that helped improve the circumstances of the individual. He believed that an effective political performance—based on speaking and leadership—was an important means for ordinary citizens to gain social power.

Gorgias believed that knowledge was created by individuals coming together to form a consensus of beliefs. Therefore, he believed strongly in the importance of public opinion because opinions figured prominently in the making of laws, in rendering decisions in the assembly, and in determining guilt and innocence in courts. Understanding public opinion and comprehending the desires and needs of the average citizen were paramount to understanding how to argue in front of an audience. Why? The greatest force that moves a democracy is the will of the majority, and persuading people requires great oratorical skill and a deep understanding of the passions of the audience.

Critics have noted that the sophists, though influential, merely emphasized a sense of individuality in their instruction. Missing from their teaching practices was a moral philosophy that said that people should use their skills to work together and prosper together—to be good stewards of the community. The sophists' primary concern was teaching individuals the skills of argumentation, so their students were well prepared for court or the assembly, because citizens were expected to represent themselves in court. To the unskilled litigator, the chances of not knowing what to say, what to do, and becoming nervous and tongue-tied were very real factors.

Understandably, there was a great need for teachers who prepared people for this new kind of public responsibility, and teachers who taught the skills and techniques of argumentation dominated education in an era that demanded overt acts of self-assertion and human agency. To their critics, the sophists taught techniques (or in modern parlance, *vocational skills*), but didn't emphasize an explicit moral philosophy that taught their students to use their skills to improve the civic welfare of Athens or to think beyond winning arguments.

The result was an Athenian society gripped by the students of the sophists who enflamed passions and exploited people's emotions in order to rouse the populace. For many reformist critics, Athens wasn't necessarily ruled by the democracy, but was governed by mobs of people. For them, the sophistic use of rhetoric was predicated on achieving a quick victory, a tactic which often emphasized exploiting their audience's emotions rather than using good reason and logic.

PLATONIC RHETORIC: SEEKING *SOPHIA*

One reformist critic, Plato, disdained the sophists, and he openly attacked their use of rhetoric in his text, *Gorgias*. Plato's attack stemmed from some fundamental differences regarding the nature of knowledge. Whereas the sophists believed in creating consensual knowledge among people, Plato believed in the existence of higher forms of knowledge outside of the realm of public opinion, a divine sort of wisdom or heavenly truth called *sophia*.

Peitho, Greek goddess of persuasion

Plato recognized that in the world of public opinion, opinions varied, shifted, and changed—that people were often fickle, and their allegiances changed often and quickly. Therefore, people were better off seeking a more permanent and truer kind of knowledge, the kind of knowledge that existed outside of the domain of public opinion and outside of the realm of human perception—divine wisdom. Plato believed in transcendence because he believed that the human spirit preceded human form—that the human soul is immortal.

For Plato, the human spirit existed perfectly in a divine place called the *world of ideas* or *world of forms* before we took human shape. In this world, our minds were pure, understanding everything clearly and explicitly. Before we left this ethereal dimension, true knowledge imprinted itself on our minds before we became corporeal. Once we became human, our bodies and sensory receptors (eyes, ears, nose, and our sense of touch) were but crude instruments used to perceive these truths. Therefore, Plato used a rigorous process of questioning—called the Socratic method—to dig deeply into the minds of his students so that they could remember the ideas that existed perfectly in the *world of forms.*

Plato's belief in a higher form of knowledge put him at odds with Gorgias and the rest of the sophists. Gorgias denied the possibility of attaining and comprehending objective truths beyond the sphere of human communities and saw any labor to seek divine truth as impractical. For the most part, the sophists believed strongly in only what they could prove to an audience. In the *Gorgias*, Plato condemns sophistic rhetoric as mere "cookery"—simple skills devoid of any philosophic labor. Although Plato continues to attack the sophists in the *Phaedrus*, he concedes and acknowledges that rhetoric could be used to seek higher forms of knowledge such as divine wisdom.

Platonic rhetoric, then, is the use of argument and inquiry to search for divine knowledge and heavenly truths. Plato was interested in a rhetorical perspective outside of the courts and assemblies because he believed rhetoric could help individuals, not to win debates or court cases, but to find personal truths. Most important, rhetoric could help "implant justice in the souls of its citizens" (*Gorgias*). For Plato, a rhetoric that aids in the search for divine virtue is a far more worthy use of analysis, argument, and inquiry than merely winning arguments and getting elected to office. Many students and scholars have noted some contradictory notions in Plato when he uses a rhetorical approach to argue against rhetoric. The problem with this critique is that Plato in the *Gorgias* and *Phaedrus* was not arguing against all forms of rhetoric. He was arguing specifically against the prevailing rhetorical practice of the time: sophistic rhetoric.

PLATO ATTACKS WRITING

This era of change and reform brought together two educational traditions: (1) the old-world oral education of Homeric poetry and (2) the emerging education of sophistic rhetoric. In this era as well, the notion of secondary orality was taking shape. Students entering sophistic instruction expected to learn speaking as well as writing. Walter Ong defines secondary orality as an oral consciousness that was influenced by writing. In this era of change, the majority of people still were illiterate and clung to oral customs and rituals. Consequently, many people held great suspicion of literacy. According to Tony Lentz, Plato's belief in the social dynamism of primary orality and his conception of divine knowledge led him to attack poetry and writing (15). Plato believed that the mind had to actively engage in pursuing divine knowledge, and the only genuine way to do this is through an active and direct engagement with people *by speaking directly to them.*

Conversations and dialogues, then, were the best way to discover *sophia*, so Plato, speaking through Socrates, advocated speech as the only legitimate means of learning. He favored the living intelligence of the speaker and sought to directly engage with the substance of a person's mind rather than read a person's writing. For Plato, writing is deficient because a piece of writing cannot engage in a conversation, cannot respond to questions from readers, and cannot always explain its own meanings. Writing, then, is not only a poor imitation of a person's knowledge, experience, and wisdom, but may even betray the writer's intent as well. For instance, a reader may interpret a text contrary to the intent of the author. However, if the writer were present, then the writer could explain what was meant in clear, definitive terms.

With some irony, Plato chose to write down his attack on writing and did so in the form of conversations or dialogues, an approach that best represented the spoken word. The paradox is simple: he criticizes the written word by using the written word. For scholars such as Eric Havelock, Plato's written record functions not as a sign of intellectual hypocrisy but signifies a pivotal transition between an older oral world and an emerging literate world. Plato argues in the *Phaedrus* that the best use of writing is to preserve lists and archaic forms of knowledge. Perhaps Plato concedes in his argument that his method of oral instruction was being eclipsed by the sophistic method of teaching—where speaking and writing were taught together—and his writing was meant to record his oral teachings.

ARISTOTELIAN RHETORIC: AN APPEAL TO ETHICS AND LOGIC

Plato dedicated his Academy to studying divine wisdom. His student, Aristotle, studied there for approximately twenty years before starting his own school, the Lyceum (which literally means "gymnasium"). At around 358 BCE, he began teaching rhetoric at Plato's Academy, and he left because, as a Macedonian, he could not assume leadership of an Athenian school. In essence, Aristotle believed in creating a true knowledge brought about by employing a methodical system based on *ethos*, *logos,* and *pathos*. This systematized approach reflects his scientific, empirical approach to discovering and cultivating knowledge.

In his *Rhetoric*, Aristotle presents rhetoric as a system of thought and as a method of rigorous activity. Concerned about rhetoric's relationship with human discourse, he would not merely accept rhetoric as a method concerned only with the mechanics of language and the art of persuading an audience. According to William Grimaldi, both Aristotle and Plato were interested in teaching rhetoric as a form of critical analysis. In order to engage in this kind of activity, students were required to learn a kind of knowledge rooted in philosophical and ethical convictions and logical processes. Aristotelian rhetoric is not concerned with just the vocation of making arguments; Grimaldi points out that Aristotle combined *philology* (love of words) with *philosophy* (love of wisdom) in which students were always engaged in learning about language and knowledge. For Aristotle, his love of language and wisdom was expressed in his argument for the centrality of the enthymeme to rhetoric, a process that centralized *logos* or logic to persuasion.

According to Grimaldi, once we understand the enthymeme and its implications for human discourse, we can begin to better understand a rhetorical structure that involves the speaker, audience, and subject matter as well as a discursive methodology that involves inductive and deductive reasoning. For Aristotle, teaching a rhetorical methodology was meant to teach more responsible social acts, acts that were based on good reason. Aristotle's argument about the importance of rational inquiry and the

> The difference between *sophists* and *philosophers* is that sophists made public claims to possess wisdom while philosophers, by contrast, claimed not to possess but to seek wisdom.

accumulation of good evidence allows reason—rather than passion—to dictate moral choices.

The enthymeme's centrality to rhetoric has been explored and analyzed by scholars such as William Grimaldi, James Kinneavy, and Lloyd Bitzer. We'll present more on Aristotle's contribution to rhetoric throughout this textbook.

ISOCRATEAN RHETORIC: A CIVIC CONCERN

Isocrates was an Athenian who knew Plato and Aristotle; he was a former logographer and sophist who looked beyond his beloved Athens and saw immense value in uniting all of the Greek states into one unified state he called *Hellas*. Whereas the sophists were concerned primarily with improving the circumstances of the individual, Isocrates argued that individuals had a solemn duty to improve the conditions of their immediate civic environment, their cities, and their nation. The notion of the civic-rhetor begins to take a stronger shape in Isocrates's work, and his arguments regarding the moral qualities of the rhetor are later championed by the Romans Cicero and Quintilian.

In his often-read essay, *Antidosis*, Isocrates claimed that rhetorical training was meant to prepare students for a meditative and active civic life. He believed that rhetoric should be used rationally and ethically so that active citizens could make reasonable and ethical judgments regarding politics and public policy in order to improve the social circumstances of citizens. Though he did not discount emotions, Isocrates argued that rhetoric should function as a unifying force of reason, a force that brings people together and binds them in contemplating difficult civic solutions through a process of decision-making. Consequently, Isocrates, much like Aristotle, believed that rhetoric was a moralizing and civilizing activity.

In many ways, modern audiences find many of Isocrates's perspectives socially relevant. Given education's emphasis on citizenship, Isocrates's arguments relating education to the civic culture has made communication and rhetoric scholars examine his work more closely, for he cared deeply about how education impacts society. His students profited immensely from his emphasis on teaching writing and speaking together, and many of his students went on to become prominent civic leaders.

ROMAN RHETORIC: THE GOOD PERSON SPEAKING WELL

As a form of government, democracy lasted approximately 140 years in Athens. Once Athens was overrun by the armies of Alexander the Great (or, as the Persians called him, Alexander the Cruel), democracy gave way to older models of rule: monarchies and aristocracies became politically dominant. Rhetoric, as well, returned to its origins as an instrument of the ruling class. The transition between early and late antiquity happened when Greek powers declined and when Latinate powers grew in influence. Tribes such as the Etruscans dominated southern Italy until Roman tribes grew in influence and power. The Roman Empire grew beyond its tribal borders by conquering old Greek colonies and by absorbing much of its cultural teachings.

The history of Rome is inextricably linked to Greece, and the phrase *Roman rhetoric* is used quite frequently to delineate the Latinization of Greek rhetorical education and its civic uses. As we know, rhetoric was introduced in the Homeric tradition, initially systematized in Sicily, and matured in Athens, a process that occurred over several centuries before Rome ascended to power. Despite some attempts to outlaw rhetoric, the Romans gradually built a greater structure on a venerable Greek foundation. There is a temptation to heap praise on the shoulders of Cicero and Quintilian for creating Roman rhetoric, but this adoption of Greek rhetoric was neither conceived at a single moment nor was one person responsible for introducing this persuasive force to the Roman world. In fact, many complex variables account for Rome's introduction to and assimilation of Greek rhetoric, so many that any brief explanation omits many details. However, two important reasons require exploration: (1) Greek imperialism and (2) Roman expansionism.

After some initial resistance from Roman censors and the Senate, rhetoric became a social force in the Republic because of its civic benefits and its support from Roman patricians. Once we understand that rhetoric was a social movement created by many minds working together, we can briefly study the contributions of two important Roman figures: Cicero, the Roman rhetor, and Quintilian, the Roman rhetorician.

KAIROS: THE POLITICAL ENVIRONMENT

Important as these two men are, we must pay close attention to understanding the *kairos*, or the political environment, of Roman political culture. The political environments of Athens and Rome were quite different. Consequently, these varying political structures placed a different kind of civic responsibility on the citizen. Because of these different needs, Athenians and Romans functioned differently in their respective eras, and rhetoric was used differently in varying degrees of emphasis.

These distinctions, however, begin with a general understanding of the *kairos* each society created. For instance, Athens, in essence, was a selective democracy that favored political parties, assemblies, and citizen-courts. To participate actively in these venues, citizenship was required. According to Cheryl Glenn, "Citizenship was determined by birthright; thus, citizenship was awarded to any adult male who could establish his Athenian heritage, whether he was wealthy or not, aristocratic or not. These were very inclusive requirements for the time" (19). Consequently, Athenian citizens "participated directly in making political and judicial decisions, rather than acting through elected representatives" (20). Because Athenians, concerned with fraud, "scorned elections" (20), they "met in the assembly to make policy decisions" (20) and served as jurors on trials.

However, during the fifth century BCE, a remarkable policy was developed and implemented in Athens called *isegoria*. This policy allowed all citizens the equal opportunity to speak in the assembly. Although the logistics of public discourse were uncongenial to having all assembly members speak during an assembly session, deliberative oratory, therefore, eventually fell on professional *rhetors*, people who not only introduced legislation but who were trained in the art of public speaking. Although public speaking was a necessary condition of governance in a time when orality was still the dominant form of communication, the art of speaking became even more important after this policy was implemented. Clearly, Athens saw public discourse as a necessary condition of governance. Because the statecraft for a democracy requires some kind of consensus for governance, and consensus is often established by persuasion, knowledge of persuasion and an education in persuasive tactics became increasingly important. For these reasons, rhetoric became the animating and organizing principle of Greek political life.

The Roman Republic, however, was not a selective democracy. Instead, Rome established an *oligarchy* after the overthrow of its last king. This aristocracy consisted of wealthy families who held social influence and shared political power with the Senate. According to George Kennedy, Roman "power most of the time lay in the hands of a small number of members of noble families, often rich, working through their clients, but popular leaders, or demagogues, often using the office of the tribune, arose to demand change and at times completely disrupted the government" (105). Any assemblance of citizens was normally accomplished in the Senate or in the courts.

As noted, a male citizen in Athens was expected to participate in the civic affairs of his home. In Rome, however, the power to govern civic affairs was the responsibility of the powerfully connected, the aristocratic minority. In Athens, a rhetorical education became increasingly important because of the civic duties of the citizen. However, when rhetoric was introduced in Rome by Greek sophists, rhetoric was greeted with scorn from the ruling class. Why? According to Kennedy, "skill in speaking constituted a possible threat to the dominant senatorial oligarchy" (100). Threatened by this power, the Roman elite banned rhetorical education and the practice of rhetoric on a few occasions; however, as Kennedy explains, "none of these efforts seems to have been successful, and by the middle of the first century rhetorical schools, and the practice of declamation, were central features of Roman education" (100).

The oligarchy's animosity toward rhetoric was an attempt to preserve its power because, as Richard Leo Enos explains, a non-aristocratic citizen might use rhetoric to gain political status and earn social mobility as well. History acknowledges a strong class consciousness and sentiments regarding the consolidation of power in Rome, but a powerful and eloquent oratory could allow middle-class subjects to gain influence and power through their fame as public orators, a dimension of rhetoric not directly discussed or accounted for by the Greeks. Figures such as Gorgias, Protagoras, Plato, and Aristotle were, by all accounts, progeny of wealth, and, perhaps, considered relatives to the ruling class.

Their social standing might help explain why rhetoric as a source of social mobility was rarely discussed in the rhetorical literature of Greece. For these reasons, the subject of rhetoric as a force of social transcendence seems to be more unique to Roman rhetoric than Greek rhetoric, a circumstance that reflects the *kairos* of Rome. For example, a brilliant Roman orator could bring fame to himself by establishing a popular reputation that would gain the favor of a stingy electorate: "The conservative Roman voter could seldom be induced to elect a man whose name had not been known for centuries as part of the history of the Republic" (Syme 11). Hence, new political leaders outside of the politically connected nobility were rare figures in Rome. But, as we have seen, Roman political life teaches us that there were only two ways for a common citizen to gain power—through his military prowess or through the oratory (Enos 52).

Because Rome was an oligarchy and not a democracy, civil procedure was structured differently than in Athens. An important difference between Greek and Roman courts was that Greek litigants were ordinarily expected to speak on their own behalf, and the teaching of forensic rhetoric assumed this condition. Conversely, by the time of the later Roman Republic, most members of the upper Roman classes may have been able to speak in court, but they regularly got their more eloquent friends to help them. Kennedy explains:

> In practice, major cases were pleaded by professional orators, called 'patrons.' The procedure was an extension of the patron/client relationship of the early republic. Originally a patron was a patrician who had certain responsibilities toward a number of 'clients,' who might be citizens or freedmen in Rome or in allied states . . . much of the law was not published or well known, with the result that clients were ignorant of procedure in cases in which they might be involved, and they also lacked the social prestige to defend their own rights in a society heavily dependent on personal authority. (103)

This quotation is important in recognizing another difference between Greek and Roman rhetoric. Although the merits and validity of each court case were presented and debated, Roman patrons also used their own social standing—their own *ethos*—to persuade juries to their side (102–3).

As Kennedy explains, the personal authority of the client was not only an issue, but the patron frequently used his standing (sometimes patrons held important public offices) as an artistic proof in his case. For example, "a patron like Cicero took advantage of this, often speaking about himself and his opponents as well as about his client and his opponents, and sometimes exploiting the differences between himself and his client as a way to strengthen his case" (104). These situations leave Kennedy to conclude that "the most characteristic feature of native, early Roman rhetoric was heavy reliance on *ethos* and *pathos*, the latter taking the form of moral outrage" (103).

Interestingly, although deliberative and forensic rhetoric were integral to Roman life, *epideictic* (ceremonial) rhetoric was not. Some scholars have suggested that Rome's governing class saw the epideictic as impractical and apolitical—relegating ceremonial rhetoric to the arts instead of politics and, in particular, to funeral orations. Surprisingly, however, epideictic rhetoric did allow women a public platform for artistic expression. As Kennedy notes, women had more influence in Roman society than in

Athens. "Though they could not vote, hold office or plead in law courts," noble women "were accorded funeral orations equally with men" (106).

Although writing in the Western tradition began in Greece, Roman rhetoric played an important role in the *literaturization* of rhetoric. With increasing frequency, rhetoric becomes part of the literary discourse of Roman life. In his fascinating observation, M.L. Clarke believes that rhetoric served as an organic influence on the language of Latin: rhetoric "developed the capacities of the Latin language as an effective instrument, disciplined its rough vigour, modified its stiffness, taught it new rhythms and turns of expression. [Rhetoric] encouraged a care for form and artistry, and discouraged waywardness and eccentricity and incoherence" (Clarke 158). Rhetoric, then, fostered a new and heightened sensitivity toward both spoken and written language.

As we have seen throughout rhetoric's dynamic early history, the rhetorical situation—and the need for rhetoric—is created by the environment, or *kairos,* of a particular culture. Because the statecraft for open societies (both democracies and republics) requires some kind of

Two Key Figures of Roman Rhetoric

Cicero (106–43 BCE): Born in a small village outside of Rome to a moderately wealthy family, Marcus Tullius Cicero became one of the most prolific orators in Western history as a statesman and practitioner of rhetoric in the days of the Roman Republic. Because he lacked considerable social status, Cicero built his public career as public advocate and rose to prominence after he prosecuted the corrupt Roman governor Gaius Verres in 70 BCE. Though he prospered in private practice, Cicero was elected as Consul (or a Roman Attorney General), where he successfully suppressed a conspiracy to overthrow the government. After an active political career, he turned away from politics to concentrate on his writing as a champion of freedom and ethical statesmanship—and a teacher of rhetoric. His most influential books include *De Inventione, Rhetorica,* and *De Oratore.*

Quintilian (35–95 CE): A Spaniard by birth, Marcus Fabius Quintilianus gained fame and wealth as an advocate and public speaker. He became tutor to the eventual Emperor Galba and became the first state-sponsored teacher of rhetoric under Emperor Vespasian. As a teacher, he wrote the *Institutes of the Oratory,* which contained his ideas on the proper education of a Roman citizen.

consensus for governance, and consensus is often established by persuasion, and persuasion is the primary goal of the rhetorician or rhetor, rhetoric became the animating and organizing principle of Greek political life and, eventually, in Roman civic life. Finally, one important characteristic of Roman rhetoric must be underscored. As Richard Leo Enos pointedly emphasizes, rhetoric education would not have been successful if Roman citizens did not find this education appealing, desirable, and necessary. Furthermore, if Roman patricians did not endow schools, teachers, and students with the extensive funding necessary to sustain rhetoric education, rhetoric would not have made the pervasive inroads that it did in Roman culture. As a result, Rome assimilated Greek rhetoric, and Roman rhetoric became a cornerstone of Roman civic life and Roman education.

◆ QUESTIONS FOR CRITICAL THINKING

1. Anthropologist Jack Goody once argued that writing helps facilitate democracy by allowing ordinary citizens to read laws and take part in elections. Is this argument valid? If so, how?

2. Is there some sense of irony that the principles of democracy come from the aristocracy? Why or why not?

3. In what sense is the definition of history tied to literacy? Why is recording events or writing things down important to creating a public record? In what ways does writing help develop a sense of community?

4. Because political campaigns are staggeringly expensive, is the United States a *timocracy*? Can you form an argument that the poor have access to political or civic power?

5. In Rome, fame and notoriety could give a Roman citizen a platform to influence social policy. How is this circumstance similar to celebrities in America? Are there any credible and not-so-credible examples of celebrities involving themselves in politics or political issues? If so, explain.

6. Why do athletic shoe companies use celebrities such as Michael Jordan and LeBron James instead of orthopedic doctors to pitch

sneakers? What does this circumstance say about American audiences?

7. Plato argues that writing makes your mind weak. In what sense is this statement valid? Can relying on written documents compel you not to memorize important information?

RHETORIC THROUGH MEDIEVAL, RENAISSANCE, AND MODERN TIMES

Around the fourth century CE, rhetoric and the idea of the citizen–rhetor take on an even more limited shape. Emperor Constantine (274?–337 CE) transformed the Roman Empire in 313 CE when he declared that Christianity was the official religion of Rome. However, Christian elders were initially suspicious of rhetoric and tried to ban it in the early stages of the Holy Roman Empire. Christian clerics and church leaders, such as St. Jerome, held a strong distrust of rhetoric because it was tangled with pagan themes. However, when a former teacher of rhetoric, Augustine of Hippo (354–430 CE), wrote *De Doctrina Christiana* (*On Christian Doctrine*) between the fourth and fifth centuries CE, he argued that rhetoric, once pared of its paganism, could help clerics strengthen their religious messages and help deliver providence to the masses.

Augustine believed that Christians could use rhetorical training to help reinforce their faith and help their flock discover biblical truisms. His intellectual stance regarding the relationship between persuasion and religion gave church leaders good reasons to incorporate rhetoric into the bedrock of Christian education. For Augustine, rhetoric's primary purpose was to discover truth in biblical scriptures, and he believed that a mutual understanding of scripture could help build stronger, more unified Christian communities. Because rhetoric was meant to serve faith, Augustine did not emphasize rhetoric's practical application in the courts or assemblies. Rather, rhetoric was used by skilled bishops to rouse crowds to put public pressure on imperial leaders to show public support for church policies.

During the Middle Ages, rhetoric grew as a monastic discipline in which religious monks translated many of the ancient texts by hand, and letter writing became an important genre, not only as a means of correspondence but as a means of record keeping. After the decline of the Holy Roman Empire, Christian and rhetorical education were fostered predominantly in Europe by emperors such as Charlemagne, who built Christian schools within the province of every church that was built. In this era, rhetorical education ebbed and flowed, with different emphasis placed on linguistic studies by different teachers. Sometimes grammar was the primary aim of an education; at other times, rhetoric education concerned turning students' attention to civil matters. Charlemagne appointed the English monk Alcuin (730–840 CE) to better establish a liberal arts system of education based on the seven arts (the trivium and quadrivium), with a rhetorical education central to these liberal arts. However, this educational system was not organized under a Greek or Roman system; rather, this rhetorical education was superintended over by a Christian monarchy. The purpose of learning these arts was so students could better comprehend the salvation of the soul and improve their understanding of how Christian morality leads to an improved civic environment.

> *The child who is not yet old enough to love his studies should not be allowed to come to hate them. His studies must be made an amusement.*
> —Quintilian

During the Renaissance (roughly 1300–1600 CE), rhetoric was a clear feature of humanistic education and religious teaching and enjoyed great prominence, particularly in England and Italy, for this time was of renewed interest in antiquity. For clerics, sermonic rhetoric came to the forefront of study, while intellectuals embraced ancient rhetorical and historical texts to further their professional lives as historians, lawyers, grammarians and teachers. In a broader sense, the nobility studied rhetoric to improve their personal circumstances as eloquent letter writers, courtly speakers, and shrewd statesmen. There seems to be little connection between rhetoric and the common citizen during this era, particularly the working and lower classes. If the majority of the lower and middle classes were not engaging in commerce or farming, they were fighting in many wars that constituted this violent period of human history.

In England and continental Europe, much of public discourse was relegated to well-heeled aristocrats and courtiers who sought business relationships with ruling monarchs. In practice, rhetoric was used sweetly and stylistically to polish a young man's learning in order to prepare him for his civic duties as a scholar-statesman. For instance, Leonard Cox's *The Arte or Crafte of Rhetoryke* (1524) was the first English book devoted exclusively to rhetoric studies, a work derived from Cicero and other ancients. In sixteenth-century England, style gained an even stronger emphasis. Ornamentation, the study of tropes and schemes, was a strong component of rhetoric and helped speakers become more eloquent. This emphasis on eloquence brought about great experiments in the variances of style in poetry and prose, where writers such as Francis Bacon and Ben Jonson experimented with different styles of writing.

During the Renaissance, communication theories were focused on grammar, rhetoric and logic, disciplines which constituted the trivium. The trivium dominated much of a young man's education during the Renaissance, and in this era, rhetoric became fragmented due to curricular reforms: what was systematized by Aristotle and Cicero was broken up by reformers such as the French teacher Peter Ramus (1515–1572), who relegated the academic study of rhetoric to the study of style and invention. For him, logic became associated with scientific inquiry, and invention was confined to the creation and dissemination of factual data. Ramus' reform of education affected generations. His reclassification of rhetoric coupled with the resonance of Plato's attack on sophistic rhetoric endures today in popular and journalistic definitions of rhetoric, definitions that merely refer to rhetoric as "all style," conveying empty, even bombastic, language—often defined in antithesis to logic and reason.

In the seventeenth and eighteenth centuries, it was the preachers, particularly the great Scottish preachers, who practiced and wrote about rhetoric. Most notable were the works of George Campbell (1719–1796) and Richard Whately (1758–1859). This religious tradition traveled to the American colonies, where the earliest rhetoricians were Jonathan Edwards and Cotton Mather of the early New England churches. It was not until the ferment of revolution that political causes once again emerged as the primary subject of rhetoric. The broadsides of Thomas Paine, the impassioned speeches of Patrick Henry, and especially the stirring words of the Declaration of Independence reasserted rhetoric as the key element of America's intellectual independence. In Europe, and especially in Britain, the Age of Eloquence was brought about by a number of practitioners and teachers when rhetoricians became interested in the works of Hugh Blair (1718–1800), who focused on ornament and eloquence. His influence became known as the *belles lettres* movement, and the resulting rhetoric was called *belletristic*. The rise of the elocutionary movements saw the decline of rhetoric as university discipline in England (Foss 11).

In America as well, the earliest universities emphasized style and elocution. Ornamentation was taught to help students better understand their Latin studies (Connors 1), but after a while, rhetoric studies waned and declined until new departments of speech began to flourish on American campuses in the earliest part of the twentieth century. Classical rhetoric studies were revived with the growth of debating societies and with rise of English departments. While literary instruction became the eventual focus of English departments, communication studies focusing on classical rhetoric began to gain academic attention after World War II.

In the middle part of the twentieth century, rhetoric became, if not a lost art, at least a lost term until in 1958 two books were published that revitalized the study of rhetoric and argument. The first was *The New Rhetoric* by Chaim Perelman and Madame Lucie Olbrechts-Tyteca. This treatise reinterpreted the classical theories of rhetoric for a modern world. The second was *The Uses of Argument* by Stephen Toulmin, which attempted to design a new method of logic that, unlike Aristotelian formal logic, could deal with the uncertainties of society. Toulmin's method of logical argument is what many composition texts emphasize today. (See chapter 8 for more on the Toulmin method.)

At this time, rhetoric studies re-emerged in many universities as singular departments. Other universities couched rhetorical studies in language or communication studies departments. For many rhetoric programs, a strong emphasis on teaching a civic-oriented rhetoric has come to the forefront of rhetoric studies, an Isocratean kind of rhetoric that imparts reason and fosters a care for the civic community.

✦ QUESTIONS FOR DEVELOPMENT AND DISCUSSION

1. To what extent has your education been sophistic? Should colleges and universities focus exclusively on improving the knowledge and skills of students? If so, how does service learning relate to improving the individual knowledge of students?

2. Does your university have a role in improving its surrounding community? Is this role derived from your college or university's mission statement? If so, how? Why?

3. Look up the term *rhetoric* in a search engine. Based on what you locate, to what extent is rhetoric used negatively? Positively?

WORKS CITED

Clarke, M.L. and D.H. Berry. *Rhetoric at Rome: A Historical Survey.* 3rd ed. London: Routledge, 1996.

Connors, Robert, Lisa Ede, and Andrea Lunsford. "The Revival of Rhetoric in America." *Essays on Classical Rhetoric and Modern Discourse.* Carbondale, IL: Southern Illinois UP, 1984.

Enos, Richard Leo. *Greek Rhetoric Before Aristotle.* Prospect Heights, IL: Waveland P, 1993.

Foss, S. K., K.A. Foss, and R. Trapp. *Contemporary Perspectives on Rhetoric.* 2nd ed. Prospect Heights, IL: Waveland P, 1991.

Glenn, C. *Rhetoric Retold: Regendering the Tradition from Antiquity through the Renaissance.* Carbondale, IL: Southern Illinois UP, 1997.

Grimaldi, W., S.J. "Studies in the Philosophy of Aristotle's Rhetoric." *Landmark Essays in Aristotelian Rhetoric.* R.L. Enos and L.P. Agnew, eds. Davis, CA: Hermagoras P, 1998.

Howell, W.S. *Poetics, Rhetoric and Logic: Studies in the Basic Disciplines of Criticism.* Ithaca, NY: Cornell UP, 1975.

Jaeger, Werner. *Paideia: The Ideals of Greek Culture. Vol. I, Archaic Greece, the Mind of Athens.* 2nd ed. Trans. Gilbert Highet. New York: Oxford UP, 1967.

Katula, Richard A. "The Origins of Rhetoric: Literacy and Democracy in Ancient Greece." *A Synoptic History of Classical Rhetoric.* 3rd ed. New Jersey: Lawrence Erlbaum Associates, 2003. 3-19.

Kelber, Werner H. *The Oral and the Written Gospel: the Hermeneutics of Speaking and Writing in the Synoptic Tradition. Mark, Paul and Q.* Bloomington, IN: Indiana UP, 1997.

Kennedy, George. *A New History of Classical Rhetoric.* Princeton, NJ: Princeton UP, 1994.

Lentz, Tony. *Orality and Literacy in Hellenic Greece.* Carbondale, IL: Southern Illinois UP, 1989.

Murphy, James and Richard Katula, with F. Hill and D. Ochs. *A Synoptic History of Classical Rhetoric.* 3rd ed. New Jersey: Lawrence Erlbaum Associates, 2003.

Pierre V. *The Origins of Greek Thought.* Ithaca, NY: Cornell UP, 1982.

Syme, Ronald. *Roman Revolution.* Oxford: Oxford UP, 1939.

Waterfield, R. *Athens: A History: from Ancient Ideal to Modern City.* New York: Basic Books, 2004.

CHAPTER 3

The Communication Process:
Why and How We Communicate

Communication works for those who work at it.

—John Powell

The single biggest problem in communication is the illusion that it has been accomplished.

—George Bernard Shaw

Why We Communicate

THE ANSWER to the question "Why do we communicate?" seems self-evident, because communication is such a central feature of our lives that we take it for granted. However, as rhetors we need to understand the human needs that impel us to strive for more effective communication. We suggest there are three: the need for human contact, the need for social interaction, and the need for understanding.

The Need for Human Contact. We are social beings who cannot thrive, or even survive, in isolation. We rely on others at all stages of our lives. As infants, we require constant care from parents; as adults, we require both affection and support from friends and relatives. Imagine for a moment, a person who has absolutely no contact with any other human being. Even the hermit, living apart from civilization, clearly has had, at some point in his life, human contact. But most of us are not antisocial hermits, and the level of contact we desire, even those of us who are quite shy or introverted, is far greater than the hermit's self-imposed isolation. We achieve that contact largely through communication, both verbal and nonverbal. Just as a baby cries out in hunger or discomfort, we all make some attempt to let others know that we have needs, that we are present, that we have being.

The Need for Social Interaction. Beyond simply asking for an acknowledgement of our basic human needs, we all yearn for community. The community not only responds to basic needs for hunger and protection, it also provides affection and affirmation. We enter into a social contract that allows for mutual action to attain security, stability, and happiness. This contract is achieved through communicating our needs and desires to others, and by the efforts of others to communicate ways in which these aims can be achieved. We, as a community, act together for the common good. The problem then becomes deciding on what is in the common interest. This is done through communication. We debate, discuss, deliberate, and finally decide. The decision takes the form of laws or principles by which the community agrees to live. Those who abide by the rules continue to be supported by the community; those who choose to break the rules are punished by that community. All of this is a function of human communication.

The Need for Understanding. From aboriginals huddled in fear during a solar eclipse, to the Freudian search to fathom the workings of the mind, to the quest by particle physicists to understand the origins of the universe, humanity has struggled with the great philosophical questions: "Who am I?" "What is the purpose of life?" and "What is our place in the universe?" Communication is central to the search for meaning. It allows us to share and record experiences and events, allows us to debate the meaning of the events, and allows us to prepare for the future.

Again imagine, if you can, where the search for knowledge would be without communication.

How We Communicate

HOW WE COMMUNICATE: LANGUAGE

Although why we communicate may be almost self-evident, *how* we communicate is a complex question that may be answered in a number of ways, depending on how we define "communication." If communication is seen as any gesture, picture, word, touch, or anything else that imparts meaning, then our task is huge. For our purposes in this book, however, we are going to limit the definition of communication primarily to the use of language to interact with ideas or persons. This, however, inevitably raises the question, "What is language?"

We define language, again for the purposes of this book, as a system of signs and symbols that both point to and show the relationship between things, people, and ideas. The use of signs and symbols, we argue, is a fundamental distinction between human and nonhuman communication. Rhetorician Kenneth Burke, in fact, asserts that "man is a symbol-using animal." But what does that mean? For this we must look to semiotics and semantics. Semiotics is the study of signs or symbols and their interpretation; semantics is the study of meaning. If you ask someone to give you a book, the word *book* is a sign or symbol that denotes the meaning you attach to the word *book*. You might think of meaning or the definition as the bridge between the sign or symbol and the object itself. Problems arise when the bridge we make between symbol and definition is constructed differently than the bridge someone else might make. To avoid this, of course, we could simply point to the object. However, this would seriously limit our ability to carry on any sort of conversation. This is aptly illustrated in part III, chapter 5 of the satirical *Gulliver's Travels*, in which Jonathan Swift describes Lemuel Gulliver's visit to the imaginary Academy of Lagado, where he discovers professors who have developed a new method of communication that would abolish the use of words. (You may judge for yourself the appropriateness of the stereotype.) Swift's professors argue:

> Since Words are only Names for *Things*, it would be more convenient for all Men to carry about them, such *Things* as were necessary to express the particular Business they are to discourse on. . . . [I]f a Man's Business be very great, and of various kinds, he must be obliged in Proportion to carry a greater bundle of *Things* upon his Back, unless he can afford one or two strong Servants to attend him. I have often beheld two of those Sages almost sinking under the Weight of their Packs, like Pedlars among us; who, when they met in the Streets, would lay down their Loads, open their Sacks, and hold Conversation for an Hour together; then put up their Implements, help each other to resume their Burthens, and take their Leave.
>
> But for short Conversations a Man may carry Implements in his Pockets and under his Arms, enough to supply him, and in his House he cannot be at a loss: Therefore the Room where Company meet who practise this Art, is full of all Things ready at Hand, requisite to furnish Matter for this kind of artificial Converse.

Among other problems, limiting discourse to the availability of actual objects, besides being tremendously burdensome and impractical, would negate the possibility of speaking about abstractions. How does one, for example, point to love, or freedom, or philosophy? We must, therefore, communicate using signs and symbols that are, at best, only a representation of reality. As we shall discover, the way in which we assemble and organize these symbols determines how effective we will be as communicators. That organization of symbols into larger units—phrases, sentences, paragraphs, speeches, essays, and all other forms of oral and written expression—brings us to the next step in our understanding of communication: the process.

HOW WE COMMUNICATE: PROCESS

Even the earliest rhetoricians recognized that there were three factors involved in any act of public communication: the rhetor, the audience, and the presentation. When Aristotle discusses *pisteis* (proofs or means of persuasion) in Book I of *The Rhetoric*, he speaks of *ethos* (the character and credibility of the rhetor), *pathos* (the emotional responses of the audience), and *logos* (the argument or message).

Scholars since that time have used this basic concept to develop a number of models of the communication process. Many students may be familiar with the "communication triangle" that describes the basic elements of a communicative event:

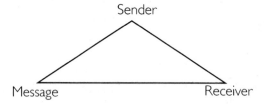

Shannon and Weaver (1949) proposed a more linear model:

Information Source	→	**Transmitter**	→	**Noise**	→	**Receiver**	→	**Destination**
(Message)		(Signal)		(Received Signal)		(Message)		

The words with arrows represent the stages of transmission; the words in parentheses indicate what is happening between each of those stages. This model, though somewhat outdated, is helpful in several ways. First, it incorporates the necessity of message creation by acknowledging that messages come from somewhere (an information source) as well as from someone.

Second, the Shannon and Weaver model recognizes that there can be interference with the message. As you might guess from the language and the linear nature of the model, Shannon was an engineer with the telephone company who was primarily concerned with finding ways to improve telephonic communication, particularly issues of noise or static that interfered with reception. Weaver expanded the concept to apply to human communication as well.

Many factors can create interference, including inattention, emotional state of the audience, cultural or language differences, antipathy toward the speaker or the message, physical environment (heat, light, furniture arrangement, or décor), and a host of others. Rhetors should always consider the amount and types of message interference they are likely to encounter.

Finally, and most importantly, the Shannon and Weaver model reminds us that the message the audience receives is not necessarily that one that we, as speakers, intended. That is, we may think we are being perfectly clear; our listeners and readers may, on the other hand, take away an entirely different message. This, as we discussed in the previous section, is one of the problems with a language of signs and symbols rather than of artifacts—not everyone will interpret the symbols in the same way.

Imagine, for example, the opportunities for misunderstanding that might arise from the simple act of making a grocery list. Suppose you need a few items from the store and ask a friend to pick them up for you. The items you write on the list are oranges, hamburger (which you intend to use to make chili), butter, and soda. Your friend returns with oranges, a hamburger from the deli, a pound of margarine, and a box of baking soda. What happened? First, you did not specify a quantity of hamburger and did not use the butcher's term "ground beef"; second, many people use "butter" as a generic name for margarine and will buy whichever is least expensive; third, if your friend is from the Midwest, he probably calls soft drinks "pop," not "soda." As far as he is concerned, he bought exactly what you had on the list, and is probably a little angry that you seem unappreciative after he did your shopping for you. Clearly, 75% of the message you intended to send was not the message he received.

In this case, you still have a hamburger and you have oranges, so although your friendship may take a minor hit, you at least have lunch, and no lasting damage has been done. Consider a more significant example of interference and miscommunication from the 2004 presidential campaign. At a West Virginia rally in March 2004, Senator John Kerry answered a question about his vote on a military appropriations bill with the unfortunate response: "I actually did vote for the $87 billion before I voted against it." Within 48 hours, President Bush's campaign staff had mounted a national ad campaign reinforcing their image of Kerry as someone who tried to take both sides of an issue. The few audience members who were familiar with the complex negotiations in the Senate understood exactly what Senator Kerry meant; most listeners, however, took away the clear impression that he had indeed changed his mind. Kerry's lack of clear phrasing, and the noise (to use Shannon and Weaver's term) provided by the Bush campaign ads, distorted Kerry's message into a convoluted maze from which many election analysts felt he never recovered.

MESSAGE PREPARATION (THE COMPOSING PROCESS)

Whether simple or complex, ancient or contemporary, all of these models refer in some way to the actual performance of the oral or written communicative act. In this chapter, though, we want to focus on the preparation of the message, since that is the first step in ensuring clarity. In particular, we will discuss at length a concept that writing instructors often call the writing or composing process. This concept, which is equally applicable to speaking, involves all elements of the composing act, from invention to performance, but focuses on message production. There are five elements to this process:

- Planning / Prewriting
- Drafting
- Revising
- Editing
- Presenting / Publishing

These elements should be conceived of not as a linear progression but as a circular process that is recursive; that is, they may be re-enacted in almost any order at any time in the process. A model of the process might look something like this:

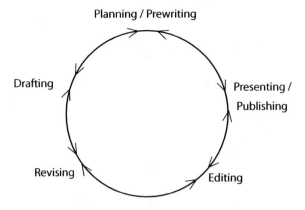

PLANNING (INVENTION)

*You've got to be careful if you don't know where you're going,
because you might not get there.* —Yogi Berra

When Aristotle asserted that rhetoric is "the discovery, in any given case, of the available means of persuasion," he summarized in one simple sentence the complex and vitally important role of invention. To understand the invention process, we must unpack that statement and discover the implications for rhetors. The phrase "any given case" means that you must first discover *the rhetorical situation*, which, according to rhetorical scholar Lloyd Bitzer, consists of three elements: audience, exigence, and constraints (*Philosophy and Rhetoric 1.1*).

Audience. The first element, audience, is more complicated than simply figuring out who will be receiving your message. You need to think about the beliefs, values, biases, and presuppositions that your audience is likely to have, so that you will not alienate them with your message. This is one reason political candidates do a great deal of polling before determining the approach they will take in their campaign speeches.

Consideration of audience can be critical in determining how your message is received. Suppose, for example, you are an ardent advocate of anti-smoking laws, and decide you will give a speech urging that all smoking on your campus be banned, outdoors as well as indoors. You work very hard on message preparation and are on your way to speech class when you notice your instructor, who will be grading your speech, is huddled behind the classroom building taking the last few puffs of a cigarette. We call this an "Oops!" moment. However, if you had remembered that your audience is likely, on a college campus, to contain both smokers and non-smokers, you will have made sure to anticipate that by focusing on the problems caused by smok*ing*, not by smok*ers*, your audience will understand your concern without feeling you have attacked them personally.

Student speakers are not the only people who suffer from an occasional "Oops!" In January 2005, Lawrence Summers, then President of Harvard University, addressed an academic conference on economics, an audience that included several notable women in mathematics and the sciences. During his remarks he opined that some women were genetically less capable in math and science than men. A predictable furor erupted, which could easily have been avoided had he spent a bit more time analyzing the audience to whom his remarks were addressed. (Of course, in this case all he really had to do was look around the room.)

Often, though, audience analysis is more complex. You can't simply look at your classmates to judge their beliefs and values. Whether college students are liberal or conservative, religious or secular, capitalists or socialists, they all look pretty much alike. You can, of course, determine some features: sex, height, weight, fashion preferences, and sometimes age and ethnicity. However, these are superficial characteristics that may play a role in, but not fundamentally determine, a student's value structure.

What, then, is a rhetor to do? While you might be able to administer surveys, do polling, or engage in conversation with your classmates to determine their predilections, there are many times when that is not practical. Whether you are speaking to a civic meeting, making a sales presentation, or writing an op-ed piece for the newspaper, anticipating how the audience will react is often not possible. Here then are some guidelines for analyzing this larger, more general concept of audience:

1. *Learn what you can about your audience.* Do some research. If you're speaking to the city council, check voting records and public statements. If you're making a sales presentation, research the company and try to determine who will be making the decision. If you are writing an op-ed piece, read similar pieces from past issues of the paper to get a verbal picture of some of the readers.

2. *Find common ground.* Try to determine something—almost anything—you have in common with the audience. Perhaps you are from the same geographical locale as some of them; perhaps you are the same age as the audience, or in the same profession (and we consider being a student a profession for this purpose). Whatever the commonality is, use it to establish rapport with your audience.

3. *Assume they disagree with you.* This will be covered later in the chapter dealing with organization, but essentially the advice is to always lay the groundwork for your argument first unless you are absolutely sure that all, or almost all, of the audience agrees with your position.

4. *Acknowledge the opposition.* Even if you think most of the audience agrees with you, you would be wise to make concessions to the opposing side. This will show you have carefully considered all opinions before taking a position.

While completely knowing and understanding your audience is almost never possible, following these guidelines will at least minimize the difficulties encountered in speaking or writing for a general audience.

Exigence is a term that encompasses two very important rhetorical considerations: **purpose** and **occasion**. Just as audience considerations address the "Who?" question, exigence addresses the questions "When?" "Where?" and "Why?" Traditionally, purpose has been divided into generic categories: to inform, to persuade, and to entertain. A true understanding of purpose, however, is much more complex.

Aristotle spoke of three rhetorical genres that are directly related to purpose: forensic, deliberative, and epideictic. *Forensic* rhetoric was used in the courts to determine the facts of the case and advocate for guilt or innocence; *deliberative* rhetoric was used in the assembly to determine a course of action; and *epideictic* rhetoric was ceremonial, used to mark an event or person. We can apply these categories to our own communicative acts: forensic rhetoric may be seen as an effort to determine the facts of any matter. For example, a science experiment, an informative speech, or a research paper are all designed to discover some fact or truth. Deliberative rhetoric attempts to persuade the audience that a particular policy or idea should be pursued. The end of deliberative rhetoric is decision-making.

Examples might include advocating support for a homeless shelter, persuading your teacher to reconsider your grade, or trying to convince your parents you need a car. Epideictic rhetoric is designed to elevate or celebrate a person or event. Commencement speeches, wedding toasts, roasts, eulogies, and sometimes even demagoguery generally fall into this category. Understanding the differences among types of speeches is important, because each suggests certain conventions and requirements that should be followed.

The genre categories suggested by Aristotle are related to the general purposes that a message might fulfill: for example, to inform, to persuade, and to entertain. But beyond the general purpose, you must consider the specific purpose, particularly in seeking to inform or persuade. This is particularly important because finding the specific purpose forces you to focus on your intent—what you are trying to accomplish. It helps frame your thesis and also acts as a check against irrelevance. For example, suppose your assignment is to give an informative speech and your topic is American jazz masters. Simply reading a list of famous jazz musicians would fulfill the general purpose—your audience would then presumably know who you consider to be the leading figures. But, in addition to being a relatively uninspiring speech, what would that accomplish? Why should the audience know this material? Furthermore, why should they care? On the other hand, there are a variety of specific purposes that would give focus and meaning to this speech. You might choose to inform the audience about:

- the struggles of jazz musicians to gain recognition in the cultural landscape
- the debt owed to jazz musicians by rock-and-roll or rhythm-and-blues or hip-hop artists
- why so many jazz masters have classical training
- the loss of many leading jazz masters and the implications for the whole genre of jazz

Now, having chosen one of these specific purposes, you have a direction and focus that tell you what to include and, just as importantly, what not to include, and you have some ideas forming about why your audience should care about this. And caring about your subject is very important.

If you want the audience to be engaged, and to remember what you say or write, they need to feel some connection to it. We call this the "So what?"

question, and this, too, is a consideration in exigence. Why this particular message? Why now? Who cares? If you do not anticipate and answer these questions, your audience will raise them for you, at least in their own minds. Deciding on the "So what?" question is not terribly difficult when you are, for example, writing an op-ed piece urging a new stoplight at the most dangerous intersection in town, or speaking to a group of high school students about the importance of good study habits. In the classroom setting, however, this is perhaps one of the most difficult tasks. Let's face it—you're giving a speech to get a grade; you're not trying to change the world. Or are you? Even in the artificial communication situation that a classroom suggests, you can still talk or write about something that is important to you. This is possible even with an assigned topic. All you have to do is make the topic your own. One of our students turned in an assignment to give an informative speech into an opportunity to inform the class about *Femicidio*—the deaths and disappearance of some 400 women in Mexico—a problem about which she cared very deeply, but was new information to the class, including the instructor.

Constraints. Students often assume that once they graduate they will be able to speak or write about anything they choose. Here is the bad news: you probably have more freedom in topic selection and development in your classes than anywhere else. Nearly all communication situations are subject to constraints, the third element of the rhetorical situation. A constraint is any consideration that limits or dictates the circumstances of your performance. Constraints may include the occasion for the speech, the length of the speech, the type of audience, the purpose, the setting, and a number of other factors. Whether you are making a sales presentation, writing a research paper, or writing a State of the Union address, these constraints must be carefully considered.

The occasion for the speech or essay, although included under exigence, is better considered here, we think, because the occasion dictates several important communicative features, the first of which is subject matter. In most cases, even if the subject matter is not pre-assigned, you will need to choose an appropriate topic for the occasion. This seems fairly obvious: you would neither speak about your visit to Alaska at a funeral, nor about your own divorce when giving a toast at a wedding. Sometimes the demands are more subtle, however. Imagine you are chosen to give the commencement address at your graduation. Your audience will have certain expectations, based on the occasion. The speech should be congratulatory and, at the same time, inspirational. If you do not fulfill their expectations, your audience will go away disappointed and will feel that somehow the occasion has been demeaned. This is not the time to criticize those classmates with whom you have had disagreements or to lodge complaints about the cafeteria food, the high tuition, or the losing football team.

TAKING OWNERSHIP OF YOUR TOPIC

Earlier we suggested that you must choose a topic and make it your own. That seems like a difficult task, though, especially if the topic has been assigned by an instructor rather than chosen by you. The key to getting your head around a topic is not by looking for answers, but by asking the right questions. Questions that explore any topic are called *heuristics* and have their root in Aristotle's *topoi* (topics). Heuristics are a series of questions we can routinely ask about anything, including: What is it? What is its importance? What are its causes/effects? What should be done about it? What is its history/future? What is it similar to?

You can exercise these questions by both internal and external dialectic; that is, you can question or talk to yourself or to others. Comedians and others have asserted that "talking to yourself is no problem, but when you start answering, you're in real trouble." We heartily disagree. We believe that conducting internal question-and-answer sessions is one of the best ways to explore a topic, at least initially. After you have conducted this internal dialectic, you may want to bounce the ideas off others as a check on your thoughts. But here's a caution: if you get ideas from a source, a book or newspaper for example, you must be sure to give credit to the source. To use ideas from others without giving them credit is plagiarism.

Pre-writing. Once you've spent some time thinking about your topic and exploring ideas with others, you must more formally address the issues involved in message preparation. There are some preliminary steps you should follow:

1. *Define and analyze the rhetorical situation.* What is your audience? Purpose? Occasion? What are the constraints?

2. *Narrow and focus your topic.* This step is extremely important. Consider the time or length that you want to achieve. You cannot cover much material in five minutes or five hundred words. For example, suppose you want to address the issue of HIV/AIDS policy. That is a vast topic.

You might decide to look at US policies towards AIDS in Africa or Asia. That might work for a twenty-minute speech or a twenty-page essay, but that is still too much for most classroom situations. In a five-minute speech, you could probably critique the policy as it has evolved in one particular nation, or you could trace the changes in policy from one administration to another, or you could briefly sketch the scope of the problem and suggest a solution, but you cannot do all of these. Choose one and develop it.

3. *Make it your own.* What do you actually know about the topic? Why are you interested? Do you have any special knowledge or personal experience that might help the audience view the topic in a new or unusual way? If not, perhaps you ought to do some reading and find out what insights others may have. Be sure to cite the sources, however.

4. *Record your thoughts.* Nothing is more frustrating than having some clever insight on a topic then, when you begin to write, forgetting what that insight was. Whether you make a list or an outline, record them, or do some freewriting, get those thoughts down on some sort of recording device! You might not remember them later.

Planning. Now that you have followed these preliminary steps, you can begin planning in earnest. The first step is to decide on an operational thesis, that is, a thesis statement (also known as a claim) that may be modified as you continue to work on the speech or essay. The purpose of the thesis is both to act as a map for your speech/essay and to clarify your position or stance on the topic. The process for formulating a thesis also involves several steps. We will follow these steps using a sample topic—a proposed hike in tuition at your university. You decide to formulate a pro or con speech on the issue to deliver to your class.

1. *Think of a thesis question.* Go back to the list of heuristics we discussed above and see how some of these might fit with your topic. For example: What is the current tuition? (This is not a good topic because it can be answered with a single fact.) How is our tuition money spent? (This falls short because it also can be answered fairly easily. In addition, although the question may support some of what you have

to say later on, this question is not directly relevant to the issue.) How much will this tuition increase affect me? (A good question, but it fails to involve the audience. It is self-centered, or solipsistic.) What effect will a tuition increase have on the diversity of the student body? (Now here's a question you can work with—it is complex and directly affects your audience.) This will be your thesis question.

2. *Think of possible answers to this question; be sure to include answers that both proponents and opponents might suggest.* Feel free to go a little far afield here; later you will select from among the answers those that are most relevant and that address the question most effectively. For example, you may decide that the following answers are possible:

> a. Diversity will decrease because fewer disadvantaged students will be able to attend.
> b. Increased fund-raising will be needed to maintain diversity through increased scholarship aid.
> c. More students will have to take outside jobs.
> d. Economic diversity may decrease because wealthier students will choose to go to other, more prestigious schools since the tuition is equalized.

3. *Select the best opposing answers.* Since the issue of outside jobs is marginally irrelevant, and the issue of increased diversity is highly speculative, we think the two choices that will make the best thesis lie somewhere within statements A and B. Perhaps through careful phrasing we can use these two for the next step.

4. *Formulate the operational thesis.* Although we ordinarily do not favor prescribing formulas for composition, in this case a formula consisting of three parts can be very useful. The three parts are the qualifier, the claim, and the reason. For example:

> **qualifier:** *unless* the university makes more and larger scholarships available
>
> **claim:** an increase in tuition will decrease diversity on campus
>
> **reason:** because fewer economically disadvantaged students will be able to attend

There seems to be something missing here. There is no link between economically disadvantaged students and diversity, so we need to add a link: Economically disadvantaged students are frequently ethnically more diverse than the population at large. We can then modify the reason: because fewer economically disadvantaged students, who are often among the most diverse, will be able to attend.

Discovering Arguments. Now that you have a complex, interesting, and arguable claim, you should think of what arguments you might make in support of that claim. Your thesis serves to get you started; at this point, beginning an outline will help. Always begin your preliminary outline with a reminder that you need an introduction, including at some point an attention-getter, a context statement, the claim, and a preview of the main arguments you will be making. You may also need to define some of the terms you will be using. A sample draft outline might look like this.

I. Introduction
    A. Attention-getter
    B. Context (The University Board of Trustees has proposed a tuition increase.)
    C. Claim or Thesis (Problem: Raising tuition will decrease diversity) [*Remember—you must define "diversity."*]
        1. Subargument 1. (Fewer economically disadvantaged students will attend.)
        2. Subargument 2. (Economically disadvantaged students are more diverse.)
    D. Solution Argument: The University must increase the number and size of scholarships.

Now, pull your subarguments down to complete the body of the speech. For example:

II. Subargument 1. (Fewer economically disadvantaged students will attend.)
    A. First main reason supporting this point (*topic sentence*)
    B. Evidence supporting the reason
    C. Link between evidence and main reason

We will discuss formulating arguments in much more detail in chapter 9. The point here is to show how your thesis lends itself to sketching the entire outline of the speech or paper.

At this point, you are ready to begin gathering evidence to support your arguments. In academic speaking and writing, evidence collection is generally a matter of research. Often, particularly in the sciences, social sciences, and business, this involves original research—a project you design and run yourself. However, most academic papers and speeches also involve library research. As you will discover in the chapter on evidence, there are a number of possibilities here. As you develop your paper, though, the most important thing to remember is to give credit to the sources of your evidence. To do otherwise is to commit an act of academic dishonesty, plagiarism, that usually carries severe penalties.

DRAFTING

Drafting means exactly that—writing a draft, not a final copy. The goal is simply to get your ideas and arguments on paper so that you have something concrete to work with. Up until now, the ideas have been spinning around in your head and percolating; now it is time to begin putting them into writing. That doesn't mean, however, that the speech or paper is now cast in stone. In fact, this first draft will probably be one of several as you work your way through the text.

In her book *Writing Down the Bones*, Natalie Goldberg presents a somewhat mystical vision of writing, but one that is useful for preparing this first draft. She envisions our brains as divided between the "creator mind" and the "editor mind" and suggests that when we worry too much about format, spelling, mechanics as we write the draft, we may find ourselves with what is commonly called writer's block. Goldberg argues that when we are drafting we must separate these two "minds" and simply get the ideas down on paper. Just as a sculptor first studies the clay or stone and roughs out a crude image before coaxing the statue into shape, the ideas are your raw materials, and once you rough them out, you can go to the next step—revision.

REVISION

If you are used to doing a quick read of your speech outlines or papers to check for spelling and grammar, then announcing that they have been "revised," this section is definitely for you. Revision is not editing; revision can best be thought of as "re-*vision*," that is, seeing your work from a different perspective or through new eyes. Once your first draft is complete, lay it aside for a bit—a few hours or a few days—then take the draft out and look at it as the reader might. Here is a handy list of things to ask yourself as you read:

- Does the introduction grab the audience's attention and interest? If not, what can I do to make it more interesting?

- As a reader, do I know what this speech or paper is about? If not, how can I improve my preview of the main arguments?

- Is my position on this issue clear? If not, how can I recraft my thesis to announce my stance?

- Does the order of arguments make sense? Do they go from least to most important, or from earliest to the most recent example? If not, how should I reorder them to help the listener/reader follow my chain of thoughts?

- Have I included sufficient transitions and signposts to help the readers and listeners find their way from one sentence/ paragraph/argument/piece of evidence to the next?

- Do the arguments make sense, both internally and externally? (Many writers and speakers overlook this fundamental question; make sure that you don't!) Have I avoided faulty reasoning (logical fallacies)? Can I follow the chain of reasoning in each case? If not, how can I relate the arguments to the thesis so they do make sense?

- Is there sufficient and credible evidence to support each argument? Does the evidence really say what I think it does? If not, should I do more research, or do I simply need to rethink the way I've presented the evidence?

- Have I cited the source of every quotation, summary, paraphrase, or idea that I've used from someone else? If not, now is the time!

- Is the style appropriate for the subject and audience? If not, what devices and language might I use to make it more formal/informal, age appropriate, specialized/general?

- Does the conclusion tie the argument together without being boring and repetitious? If not, how can I make the ending memorable?

These are the questions of revision. You will notice that we haven't mentioned spelling, grammar, or punctuation. That comes later. First, you must make the changes suggested by the answers to your own readerly questions.

One commonly used way to envision the revision process is to think of the phrase "HOCs, MOCs, LOCs" (Sharber). HOCs stands for **Higher-Order**, or global, **C**oncerns, including whether arguments make sense, whether the overall organization is clear and logical, and whether the paper has a sense of purpose and focus expressed in the thesis and conclusion. MOCs, **M**iddle **O**rder **C**oncerns, include such items as evidence, transitions, paragraphing, and style that is appropriate to audience and purpose. By now you have probably concluded that LOCs stands for **L**ower **O**rder **C**oncerns: grammar, punctuation, and spelling. If you revise your paper beginning with the HOCs, then the MOCs, you will avoid the temptation to simply look for mechanical problems and overlook some of the larger issues. When you've completed the HOCs and MOCs process, the next step in the journey toward essay (or speech) excellence is rewriting.

REWRITING

"Back in the day," rewriting was a horrendous job, because it was literally that—rewriting. Every word would have to be scratched out on a legal pad or typed on a manual typewriter. To change a word, the hapless student often had to retype the whole page; the alternative was an ugly erasure that many professors refused to accept. To move a paragraph, the student had to completely retype the paper. Those were *not* the "good ol' days!" The computer has made much of that effort obsolete, so if you are not familiar with all the features of your word processing program, you should make every effort to become familiar. They are your best friends. You can "cut and paste" paragraphs in any order you want; you can add extra evidence, sources, or ideas; and you can rewrite the introduction or conclusion—in short, you can exercise complete control over your manuscript.

But before you get carried away with this newfound power, you need to remember this important point: the pieces of a jigsaw puzzle each have their own special place and are not interchangeable—neither are the pieces of your message. There is a "best" fit for your organization, a best choice for language, and a best use of evidence. Notice we do not say "right fit" because many of the options may be right—what you must do is look for "best." After all, when you've become frustrated at finding just the right puzzle piece, you can, by sufficient force, make a reasonably similar jigsaw piece fit in the wrong place—but you are then likely to end up with a small lime-green square in the middle of an otherwise rosy-pink sunset.

As we go through the chapters of this book, we will discuss how to make the choices of what is "best." For now, just be thankful for your computer—not only does it make the task of rewriting much less burdensome, it also is indispensable in the final step of the process: editing.

EDITING AND PROOFREADING

At last—we've reached the final step in this communication process. Editing is last, but certainly not least; it is also usually the only part of the process that most students bother with, especially if they're in the habit of writing papers or planning speeches the night before the assignment is due. We hope that by now we have established the bankruptcy of that habit, and that you realize that speeches and papers are long-term projects. We hope you have also discovered that the spelling and grammar error detection features of word processing programs are not infallible. In fact, there are two specific areas in which they are of almost no help: first, they do not detect such common errors as the confusion between *to* and *too, their* and *there,* or *its* and *it's;* second, they often note grammar errors that are not really errors. One program, for example, frequently flags sentences as run-ons when they are not, simply because the sentences are complex and longer than average.

So, if you can't rely on your computer to do your proofreading and editing, what can you do? First, equip yourself with a reliable, easy-to-use handbook of grammar and usage. If the project you are working on involves research, make sure your handbook has an up-to-date style manual, or buy the style manual appropriate to your subject matter (e.g., MLA for humanities, APA for social sciences, and Chicago Style for history). Style manuals generally also have a grammar and usage section, but these are frequently not complete.

Now, with handbook nearby, you can begin to proofread. Here is the most important advice we can give you about proofreading: READ YOUR WORK ALOUD, ONE SENTENCE AT A TIME, EXACTLY AS YOU HAVE WRITTEN IT. If you are preparing a speech to be given extemporaneously, read the outline, notes, or whatever aid you are using aloud, and don't forget to proofread your visual aids, too.

Reading the work exactly as you have written it is not easy; we generally tend to read a piece as we *intended* to write it, not as it is actually written. Look quickly at the following sentences:

> Marsha swallowed thirteen jelly beans, on her thriteenth birthday. Her favorite flavor is bubblegum but she likes blueberry and marshmallow too.

Most readers, having been provided the context clue *thirteen,* would not notice the misspelling of *thirteenth;* instead they would pass over it and go immediately on to the next sentence. They also would not be likely to notice the comma after *beans* or the lack of a comma before *too.* However, if the sentences are examined separately, the misspelled word will become more apparent, and if the sentence is read aloud, pausing (or not pausing) as indicated by the commas, there will be an unnatural pause after *beans* and none after *marshmallow.* This will sound "wrong" to the ear and can be corrected. That is why reading aloud one sentence at a time is the key to establishing excellent proofreading skills. You will be amazed at the number of typographical errors and other mistakes you discover simply by reading the text out loud.

If reading aloud is the key to improving your proofreading skills when writing an essay, it is absolutely essential to proofreading the outline or manuscript of a speech. Almost nothing will trip up a speaker as badly as an unexpected misspelled word or a missing or extra punctuation mark. One way to avoid that mishap is practice—a word you will encounter frequently in this book—and the very first practice session should be devoted to a thorough point-by-point or sentence-by-sentence proofreading of your speech.

"IT AIN'T OVER TILL IT'S OVER."

Now that we've outlined all the steps in the process of composing communications, we need to remind you once more that composing is a recursive process. Just because you have completed all the steps doesn't mean that your work is finished. In fact, many writers will argue that a work is never finished—there is always room for additions, deletions, changes, and new information. Therefore, we offer our last piece of advice for the communication process—NEVER throw away or delete anything! That scrap of paper you wrote a note on while listening to the radio just might be the inspiration for your next paper or speech. That speech you gave for class last year might just contain the ideas or bibliography that you could expand into a research project for your senior thesis. Or, as we do in our program, perhaps with a little more work, your exceptionally written paper might be accepted for the campus writing journal. Your professors will tell you that an article they wrote for publication five years ago can often be updated and expanded into a new article with a different approach or different audience, and as long as they credit the previous work, this practice is perfectly acceptable.

Of course, if you do save all those scraps of paper, old essays, once-used speech outlines, and promising bibliographies on paper, your room will begin to look like the Himalayas during a period of heavy snowfall. This is why, for students, the computer is once again your best friend. Save everything on your computer, then you will be able to access it whenever you want. But, just like your professors who submit a revised article, you need to be sure that you are actually reworking the piece, and not just submitting the same paper for a different course. This is called plagiarism and will be discussed in chapter 7.

If you follow this process we have outlined, we do not guarantee A's on your papers and speeches, but we do guarantee that *you*—and not the deadline, the computer, or the professor—will be in control of your own writing and speaking; you will be the master or mistress of your communication universe.

◆ EXERCISES

1. Older models of the communication process were developed before the era of computers, the internet, and cellular phones. Design your own communication model that accurately depicts the communication processes of email and instant messaging. This is an excellent opportunity to use color and creativity. (Hint: there is no "right" answer.)

2. With a small group, think about inventing a language. Where would you begin? How would you distinguish between naming

words, action words, and relationship words? How would you decide on meaning? If time permits, see if you can use your invented language to carry on a short conversation (of one minute or less).

3. Several years ago the following puzzle made its way around the internet. The original source is unknown. After reading the message, create a scrambled-letters version of a passage from another text. Trade your version with others and see if they can figure out the message. If not, consider what modifications you could make. How does this affect your approach to proofreading your writing? If the passage is correct in its assertions about comprehension, why should we bother with correct spelling?

> "Aoccdrnig to a rscheearch at Cmabrigde Uinervtisy, it deosn't mttaer in what order the ltteers in a word are, the only iprmoetnt thing is that the frist and lsat ltteer be at the rghit pclae. The rset can be a total mses and you can still raed it wouthit a porbelm. This is bcuseae the human mind deos not raed ervey lteter by istlef, but the word as a wlohe."

4. If grammar, spelling and punctuation are important, why do we consider them lower-order concerns?

WORKS CITED

Bitzer, Lloyd. "The Rhetorical Situation." *Philosophy and Rhetoric* 1.1 (1968): 1-14.

Burke, Kenneth. *Language as Symbolic Action.* Berkeley, CA: U of California P, 1966. 16.

Burgoon, Michael, Frank G. Hunsaker, and Edwin J. Dawson. *Human Communication*, 3rd ed. Thousand Oaks, CA: Sage, 1994. 26.

Dillon, S. "Harvard Chief Defends His Talk on Women." *New York Times* 18 Jan. 2005 late ed.: A16.

Goldberg, Natalie. *Writing Down the Bones.* Boston: Shambhala, 1986. 26.

Kurtz, Howard. "Ad Attacks Kerry Vote on Iraq Funds; Senator Calls Bush Campaign Spot a 'Distortion' of His Record." *Washington Post* 17 Mar. 2004: A7.

Shannon, Claude and Warren Weaver. *The Mathematical Theory of Communication*. Urbana, IL: U of Illinois P, 1949.

Sharber, Elisabeth. "Writing 'A' Papers: Low, Middle and High Concerns." *Suite 101.* 19 March 2009.Web. <http://elisabeth-sharber.suite101.com/writing-a-papers-a103282>.

Swift, Jonathan. *Gulliver's Travels.* (Orig. publication in 1727). *Project Gutenberg.* 1 Aug. 2007. Web. <http://www.gutenberg.org/etext/829>.

CHAPTER **4**

Communication Anxiety

*And then I rose to reply, and Heaven knows how
anxious I was, how uneasy, how apprehensive!
Personally, I am always very nervous when I begin to
speak. Every time I make a speech I feel I am
submitting to judgment, not only my ability but even
my character and honour, and am afraid of seeming
either to promise more than I can perform, which
suggests shamelessness, or to perform less than I
can, which suggests bad faith and indifference.*
— Cicero, from *Pro Cluentio*

IF YOU, like Cicero and millions of others, have ever suffered from trembling hands when you speak or "writer's block" in composing an essay, then you are probably familiar with the usual advice you get from friends who are trying to be helpful.

"Don't worry—even great actors get stage fright." (Yes, you think, but I am *not* a great actor—I should *really* be worried!)

"Don't worry about writer's block—just write through it." (If I have writer's block, how am I supposed to write through it?)

"You'll get over it—all you need to do is practice." (Fine—but practicing is a lot different than standing up before a whole crowd of people I barely know!)

"Just imagine the audience is all in their underwear." (Oh great—now I'm speaking to a *nearly naked* crowd of people I barely know. That's sure to give me the giggles.)

The problem with this advice and, sadly, the advice given in most textbooks is that it dismisses the real and often deep-seated fear that some people experience simply as a momentary, easily-remedied pseudocrisis, and places the fault firmly with the rhetor. The result is that the rhetor becomes less, not more, confident in his or her ability to perform because the underlying causes of the anxiety are seen as unimportant.

It reminds us of a very old, and very corny, joke. A man is on his hands and knees, crawling around a sidewalk underneath a streetlight, obviously searching for something. A friend approaches.

"What's the matter?" he asks. "Did you lose something?"

"Yes, I lost my bus token, and I need it to catch the last bus home."

"I'll help you look," says the friend.

After joining him on the sidewalk and searching fruitlessly for several minutes, the friend asks, "Where, exactly, did you lose the token?"

"Oh, about halfway down the block."

"Shouldn't we be searching down there then?"

"Yes, but the light's better here."

All the practice and tricks in the world will not help your communication anxiety if you do not look for its causes in the right places. Therefore, much of this chapter will be devoted to helping you understand why nearly everybody occasionally suffers from some sort of anxiety. After we discuss the causes for anxiety, we will look at how anxiety becomes manifest, and we will offer some measures you can take to deal with the problem. Please note that, from the outset, we make no claim about *curing* anxiety; there is no "magic elixir." There are, however, directions you can take to minimize and cope with the anxiety you may feel. That is all we can promise.

CAUSES OF COMMUNICATION ANXIETY

We argue that there are four primary causes of communication anxiety: cultural, emotional, experiential, and mental. The first of these, *cultural factors*, is often ignored by our society. Many Americans fail to understand that there are some cultures in which speaking out, especially in public, is discouraged, particularly among women and young people. Such behavior is considered inappropriate. Some cultures consider it rude to ask a teacher questions.

In the United States, however, questioning is valued, and even expected. In some cultures, women are not encouraged to challenge the opinions expressed by men. In other cultures, a great deal of respect is to be shown to elders. Still others encourage open displays of emotion among men—an action considered highly suspect by many in this country.

If you are from such a culture, you can't simply "turn off" cultural norms, and you should not be expected to, because cultural norms are an important component of who you are as a person. On the other hand, here you are in a situation where, whether you like it or not, it seems you are expected to violate some of those norms. We suggest that you seize this opportunity to explain your culture to your audience. If, for example, in your culture young people are not supposed to argue with their elders, perhaps you might prepare a speech about how elders are honored in your society and why young people do not contradict them. This approach accomplishes two purposes: First, it provides you with an unusual and highly personal speech topic. Second, it allows your instructor and your classmates to understand why you might seem reluctant to construct an argument that challenges the authority or knowledge of someone older than you.

If you have grown up in the American cultural milieu, it may be difficult to understand and appreciate cultural differences. Students from other cultures or countries tend to have anxieties related to communicating in English. Most ESL students are in American classrooms to learn and achieve. In this respect, students should work together and accommodate difference in order to come to common points of understanding about communication. No matter how difficult, however, making an effort to accommodate each other is essential to creating a productive learning environment for everyone.

Another very important cause of anxiety is *emotional*. When we speak of emotions, we are talking about feelings, particularly feelings about oneself. In terms of communication anxiety, there are two distinct but related concepts that we need to address: self-image and self-esteem.

Self-image is external; it is how you think you look, especially to others. Almost everyone has self-image issues. We think we are too fat, too thin, too short, too tall; we have straight hair, curly hair, thin hair, frizzy hair; our teeth are crooked, our lips are thin, our eyes are large, our noses are big. This is the kind of self-questioning that keeps plastic surgeons in business. Let's face it—and we mean this—no one is perfect. In fact, no one really agrees on what is perfect, and you will often find that features you see as blemishes or flaws may go completely unnoticed by someone else, or may even be seen by some as attractive. We also understand, however, that you've probably heard this a hundred times, generally from your parents, and you will probably dismiss it, so we are not going to discount your feelings by trying to convince you otherwise.

What we can do is suggest that your audience will pay much less attention to external appearances if the message you bring is well-constructed and meaningful. We can also suggest that trying to cover up a flaw generally only draws attention to it. For example, if you wake up in the morning with frizzy hair and decide to wear a hat all day, people will focus on the hat, and instead of listening to your speech, they will wonder why you are wearing a knit cap when the temperature outside is eighty-five degrees.

Self-esteem is more complex because it deals with internal, rather than external, issues. High self-esteem is associated with confidence and comfort, particularly when dealing with new situations and new people. That is why self-esteem is a central factor in the amount of communication anxiety a writer or speaker may experience. To understand this, let us examine two examples, based on students we have actually had in our classes, of how low self-esteem manifests itself in communication situations.

The first example is that of a student in a college composition class. The student was older than average and had been out of school for several years before starting college. Although she seemed to be very bright, knew the material, worked very hard, and did all the in-class assignments, she was failing the class because she had not turned in either of the first two assigned essays, though she reported spending many hours on drafting, revising, and editing. When confronted with the problem, she replied that she enjoyed the class and the assignments, but felt her work "wasn't good enough" to turn in. She admitted to spending over forty hours developing the first three-page essay. She produced her first draft; in fact, the work was really quite good. Her subsequent attempts to make the paper "sound better" resulted in diminishing quality. She was trying so hard to "get it right" that she had negative results. She had become so convinced that she could not write well that she was no longer able to see the few minor problems that needed correcting.

The second example is of a student in a speech class who was convinced he had nothing to say that would be of any interest to his classmates. His first speech was on the juvenile justice system. He was visibly shaking and spoke in such a soft tone that no one, especially the teacher at the back of the room, could hear him. He spoke for about thirty seconds (it was a three-to-five minute speech) then sat down. In conversation with the teacher after class, he revealed that he had been in a juvenile facility and had some very strong opinions about the system. This is a topic, and a perspective, that would have been of great interest to the class. Perhaps the student should have avoided self-disclosing at this early stage, but the point we make is that his perception was that he had nothing else of interest to talk about.

Happily, both of these examples had successful conclusions, but it took an entire semester—and more—to overcome the obstacles that low self-esteem presented.

A related issue is the anxiety caused by some sort of physical or learning disability. One case might be a speech impediment—a lisp, a stutter, an inability to pronounce certain sounds. Sometimes it almost seems cruel to make students with this problem take a class in public speaking. However, this is once again usually a case of the speaker being more sensitive and aware of the difficulty than the audience. Most audiences will be very patient and understanding if a speaker is having difficulty. We could annoy you by listing all the great speakers, from Demosthenes to Barbara Walters, who stutter or lisp, but we won't; we know that doesn't help you a bit. What we will do is suggest that you try to relax and remember that your audience is on your side.

There are disabilities that affect writing as well; foremost among these is dyslexia, which takes many forms, one of which is a tendency to reverse letters. This creates a spelling problem that is often interpreted as an inability to spell correctly. Many students who have dyslexia have had the experience of receiving a poor grade because of apparent spelling errors. (Once again, thank goodness for word processors with spell checkers.)

The good news is that there is help available at nearly every college for students with these and similar problems. If you feel you have a physical or learning disability, contact your disability services office; they can help make accommodations for you and can often provide tutorial assistance or technology that will assist you in performing well in all your classes. And please, tell your teachers! They will undoubtedly be willing to provide support and accommodation for you; in fact, the Americans with Disabilities Act requires that they do so, as long as you have given them evidence of a documented disability.

Experiential causes of anxiety remind us of a scene from the film *A Christmas Story* in which young Ralphie works very hard on an essay about a Red Ryder BB gun he wants for Christmas and dreams of the great acclaim he will receive from his teacher and classmates for such an outstanding effort. He imagines a very large A+++ marked on the paper. Instead, he is devastated when the paper is returned with a giant red C+ scrawled on the page; the teacher's only comment is, "You'll shoot your eye out." Poor Ralphie's dreams and ego are crushed at the same time.

When we were in school, every teacher was equipped with a red pen or pencil. Unless we were very careful, our papers looked like they had been graded by Dracula. During the past few years, many teachers got the message that it was not a good idea to use red ink when correcting papers; they often traded in their red pens for green, or purple, or brown. The effect is the same. Dismissive criticism and low grades with little or no explanation can convince young people that they are not capable of doing good work. It's much like the child who is told by a parent or other adult, "You're stupid," or "You're clumsy," or "You're no good." If children hear that message often enough, they will believe that it is true, and they will act in accordance with the message.

We should not leave this topic without discussing the issue of expectations, because much of the anxiety students suffer today is directly related to that in some way. Sometimes students set overly high expectations for themselves—they want to be the best, to be the valedictorian, to be the starting quarterback. Sometimes parents set high expectations; they want their children to attend prestigious universities, or win a soccer scholarship, or become a doctor or lawyer. In both cases, students often feel undue pressure, which creates anxiety. We have had students come to us and say, "I have to have an A in this class" or there will be a consequence, ranging from cutting off tuition funding to not getting into graduate school. We have had students who will argue endlessly because they got a B instead of a B+ and their arguments are based not on whether their work was of sufficient quality for the higher grade, but on their imagined need to make the Dean's list or get into graduate school.

There are other pressures as well. More and more states are adopting exit examinations; even though students have done all the coursework and have passing grades, they must pass the exit exam to graduate. The natural consequence, of course, is teaching to the exam; the result is that many students will graduate as experts in exam-taking, but not in much else. Think for a moment about the college entrance process you went through. Almost every school requires you take a standardized test such as the SAT or ACT. These tests were originally designed to test knowledge and aptitude as one measure for predicting college success. However, as the number of college applicants increased, admissions offices began using test scores and high school grades as the primary deciding factors in their decision-making. Suddenly the pressure was on, and students reacted. Large test preparation corporations sprang up across the nation and pressure was put on teachers to give high grades, leading to grade inflation. Now there are even very expensive "college prep summer camps" that not only offer test preparation, but help in writing admissions essays, and counseling about what high school courses to take in order to enhance a student's chances for admission to a prestigious school. The college entrance pressure has gotten completely out of hand, and the result is that we create even more anxiety in our students.

Furthermore, we seem powerless to do anything about this. Which will be the first university to say, "We will no longer consider inflated grades and 'bought' test scores for admission"? Which teacher will be the first to say, "C is an average grade, and that's what most of my students will receive; only the absolutely outstanding students will get A's"? And which student will be brave enough to say, "The grade is not important as long as I feel I've really learned something"? No matter what we say in this book, we understand that we will not convince you that the pressure does not exist; that would be foolish. What we can do, later in this chapter, is suggest ways to manage the pressure and feel less anxious when writing or speaking.

The final cause of communication anxiety is, for lack of a better term, *mental anxiety*. Whether you call this *writer's block, brain freeze,* or *spacing out,* it is that awful feeling that you have no idea what to say or write next. The thoughts have flown from your head, the words dry up on your lips—you are standing mentally naked before the world. The good news is that, of the four causes of anxiety, this is the easiest to diagnose and to remedy. Mental anxiety is nearly always caused by lack of preparation, and lack of preparation is nearly always caused by failing to allow enough time to go through all the steps of the communication process that we outlined in chapter 3. So, if you're suffering from mental anxiety, go back over those steps—and make sure you leave enough time to complete the process.

Neither an essay nor a speech will be outstanding if it is left to the last minute; time management is, therefore, the critical skill in overcoming this problem. One habit that will help you manage time is a reverse calendar, a simple technique but one that most students ignore. Here's the trick: When you get an assignment, be sure to record the due date as you always do (we hope), but then make a work plan backwards. How long before the due date do you need to set up a practice session or peer review; how long before that must you, therefore, have your draft or notes done; how long before that should you start your research, prepare your visual aid, or whatever is required; and how long before that should you settle on a topic and begin to get your thoughts on paper? Put these dates in your planner, too—then you'll have a series of benchmarks to judge your progress. Just writing them in the planner, of course, doesn't guarantee success; you have to meet the benchmarks, too. Then, when you do, you can give yourself a little reward—

watch a movie, order a pizza, take a walk, or whatever—and feel a sense of accomplishment, not panic.

MANIFESTATIONS OF ANXIETY: PRIVATE (INTERNAL) AND PUBLIC (EXTERNAL)

Even if you analyze and understand the cause or causes of your anxiety, you may not understand why that anxiety triggers certain behaviors, ranging from sweaty palms and trembling knees to nearly paralytic fright. In this section, we will examine some of those manifestations and, after each, give you some suggestions to minimize and cope with it.

One way to look at anxiety is to divide it between private anxiety, the fear you feel within yourself, and public anxiety, the fear you feel when addressing others. Private anxiety has to do with those internal feelings of doubt and inadequacy that interfere with your self-confidence and lead to a sense that you are not in control of the situation. Private anxiety manifests itself in questions such as "What should I write/speak about?" or "What if I don't have anything important or significant to say/write?"

Try rephrasing those questions. Why not ask, instead, "What do I know or want to know that's interesting to me and that I'd like to share with other people?" We all know more than we think we do, and that knowledge can provide the raw material for some terrific speeches or papers. However, you also need to think about rephrasing the second question. Instead of asking "What if it's not important?" ask "How can I make it important?" Asking this question will help you discover the exigence that we discussed in chapter 3. The point here is that the first questions put you in a weak position, where your subject matter controls you; the second, rephrased questions put you in control of your subject matter.

Even if you feel you have control of the subject matter, you may still have concerns about how your audience will respond to you and to your message; that is, you may experience public anxiety. You may ask yourself questions such as "What if I don't say it right?" or "What if they don't understand what I'm trying to say?" or "What will they think of me?" These are three entirely different questions, and each requires some thought.

The question "What if I don't say it right?" implies that there is a "right" way to write or speak. However, the art of rhetoric is looking at all the possible ways of making an argument, then selecting the most effective based on context. This suggests that there can be many "right" ways, and that your task is to select the best, not the only, arguments and presentational methods based on the rhetorical situation.

If you are concerned with the question, "What if they don't understand what I'm trying to say?" a question ESL students often ask related to their accents and pronunciation of certain words. Native English speakers ask this question when dealing with more abstract or complicated points. Here is a very simple and quick answer—rehearse your speech in front of someone else, or have another person read your paper—a mini-audience, so to speak. If they understand, chances are your larger audience will, too. If they are confused by your arguments or language, you have an opportunity to revise your work before presenting it. And remember—most audiences want you to succeed. A good audience will make an effort to follow your argument, but that doesn't mean you should take their effort for granted. You should attempt to make it as easy for them as possible; the audience will appreciate your concern.

OVERCOMING SIGNS OF PUBLIC ANXIETY

While most speakers can fairly easily disguise their inner private anxieties, the public anxiety that most of us feel is less easily hidden. Remember, actors call it "stage fright" not because they are afraid of the stage, but because they are afraid of the audience. When you are in front of an audience, do your knees knock? Do you sway from side to side? Do your hands get cold and clammy? Do you clench your fists or stuff your hands resolutely in your pockets? Do you play with the one strand of hair that seems always to fall in your eyes? These habits your audience will notice, so we need to discuss two simple ways to avoid, or at least minimize, the problem.

First let us declare that neither of these will solve the problem of anxiety; they are simply ways to cover it up so it is not as noticeable to the audience. The first remedy is your stance: Try standing with your feet about 10-12 inches apart; now put your right foot (left foot if you are left-handed) forward about 6-8 inches and at a slight angle, keeping the back foot pointing straight ahead. This approach should minimize both swaying and knee-knocking; it also conveys an air of confidence and helps you address your audience.

To relax your hands, think about holding a pineapple. If you hold a pineapple tightly, the scales on the outside will hurt your hands. If you hold it loosely, however, you will be quite comfortable. Practice this bit of silliness first with a pineapple, if you can get one, then without. Remember that if you shove your hands in your pockets, you will drop the pineapple. Although we think this is a clever device, we cannot take claim for originating it; one of us learned this trick from her college debate coach. It actually works!

One other issue in public anxiety is the presence of a video or audio recording device or, if you are speaking to a large group, a microphone. Even the calmest among us seem to turn to gelatin when the camera or microphone is pointed in our direction. Worse, the most common advice is "Just forget it's there," which is not only impossible, but seems to make us even more aware of its presence.

The best plan is to practice well ahead of time with whatever device you will be using, and make sure that all the bugs are out of the system before you begin. We are reminded of a speech by President Clinton during which the teleprompter malfunctioned, yet he was able to go right on speaking, appearing to "ad lib" a good part of the text. Had he not practiced the speech thoroughly, it might have been a disaster.

Nervous speakers looking for shelter from their anxieties often seek the refuge of the lectern. The lectern often provides some psychological comfort because it helps conceal the physical manifestations of fear. In this respect, using the lectern can be helpful in delivering your first speech. However, because the lectern is a barrier that prevents the audience from seeing most of the speaker, teachers will want their students to move away from the lectern at some point to develop a better relationship with the audience. Remember: a speech is not just an oral performance; it is a visual one as well, one that involves speakers using non-verbals to add another dimension of support for their words.

In this respect, communicate with your teacher about the etiquette involved with using the lectern. There are general principles (don't grip the lectern and rock it while speaking, etc.), but as a matter of growth, discuss how to better involve using supportive non-verbals to add another dimension of persuasion to your speech. Moving away from the lectern may better enable using supportive non-verbals that allow the speaker to use other ways to support the speech.

EVALUATION ANXIETY

It may seem that one feature of a class in public speaking or composition that differs radically from speaking or writing in the "real world" is that you are being graded on your speech or paper. There at the back of the room or at the desk sits the teacher, poring over every word. We have already noted the effects that prior bad experiences with the "red pen" syndrome can have on your anxiety, and now it all comes back. The good news is that teachers want you to improve; they will make constructive comments that, if taken to heart, will help you do a better job on the next assignment. The bad news is that this is not solely an academic phenomenon; in the "real world," whatever that is, you are, in a sense, being graded on your written or oral performance as well, but often that entails more than just a red pen.

As teachers, we realize that students are often mystified by the grading process: you hand in your papers, the teacher secludes herself, and in one or two weeks, your paper reappears with a grade on it. What happened during this time? Though we champion the process of learning as the primary goal of instruction, we realize that, in grading, the stakes are high—compliance with financial aid requirements, athletic eligibility, and the obvious—continued enrollment at the university itself—is contingent upon grades.

As teachers, we also realize that if we are being honest we must admit that grading is ultimately a subjective process in which your *ethos* will play an important role. Even the most fundamental of objective tests—the true/false quiz—has elements of subjectivity: Why were certain ideas included and others omitted? Is a statement *always* true or *always* false? Can the phrasing of the question be interpreted in another way? Imagine, then,

The Power of Praise

When the ancient Greek, Demosthenes, considered the father of oratory, "first addressed himself to the people, he met with great discouragements, and was derided for his strange and uncouth style, which was cumbered with long sentences and tortured with formal arguments to a most harsh and disagreeable excess. Besides, he had, it seems, a weakness in his voice, a perplexed and indistinct utterance and a shortness of breath, which, by breaking and disjointing his sentences, much obscured the sense and meaning of what he spoke. So that in the end being quite disheartened, he forsook the assembly; and as he was walking carelessly and sauntering about the Piraeus, Eunomus, the Thriasian, then a very old man, seeing him, upbraided him, saying that his diction was very much like that of Pericles, and that he was wanting to himself through cowardice and meanness of spirit, neither bearing up with courage against popular outcry, nor fitting his body for action, but suffering it to languish through mere sloth and negligence."

—Plutarch, translated by John Dryden

the vast opportunities for subjectivity in grading such items as style, logic, or concern for audience in a paper or speech. This may not seem fair, but it is the reality that both teachers and students encounter in grading.

Our advice is: once you've delivered your speech or turned in your paper, you generally have a sense of relief. Allow this sense of relief to grow into a good mood. This good mood will affect your self-attention. Quite often, we pay more attention to other people (teachers, roommates, parents, fraternity brothers, etc.) than we do to our own feelings. Good moods increase the attention we pay to ourselves and our studies. Even if you believe you made mistakes or forgot some minor points, allow yourself to feel some sense of accomplishment for completing your assignment.

These good moods will be extended if your teacher rewards your speech or paper with a good grade. Students understand that classroom anxiety ebbs and flows when performances are evaluated. There is a certain amount of anticipation and anxiety when your teacher is walking down the aisles and handing back graded essays or speech evaluation sheets. Of course, your mood for a brief time is affected by the grade. It is quite normal to grit your teeth upon seeing a C or exude joy when you have earned an A. Good grades typically evoke good feelings; bad grades invoke feelings of disappointment. Above all, remember this: the grade is an evaluation of the particular assignment you have completed; it is not a judgment of you as a person. If you fail an assignment, it does not mean that you are a failure; it only means that there are some flaws in your work that need to be revised. If you will concentrate on the work itself, and not take it personally, you will feel better about the process and you will profit more from the instructor's comments.

What do you do when you earn a grade that was lower than what you expected? Most teachers give written explanations to justify their grades. Read these comments carefully in order to understand your teacher's perspective. Because most teachers have open door policies for their students, you should visit your instructor during office hours or make appointments to discuss the reasons for the grade. Focus on the reasons given for the grade and not the grade itself. Use the meeting as a starting point to improve your communication skills as a writer or as a speaker. More often than not, teachers will elaborate on their grades by giving you more information. Normally, teachers are happy to expand on their brief margin notes or their extended summaries if you do not think what they wrote down is clear enough.

Finally, rather than angrily rushing up to the front of the room, try meeting with your teacher well after you receive a disappointing grade. For good reasons, many teachers have a 24-48 hour "cooling off" policy before they will discuss grades. This period often creates some distance between you, your paper, and your teacher's comments.

Myths about Grading

Many teachers hand out grading rubrics at the beginning of the semester or hand out grading criteria related to each assignment. Quite often, teachers go to great lengths to explain carefully the grading policies of the course and elaborate on how students will be evaluated as writers and speakers. Often, teachers will show models of success in the name of good teaching practices: good or exceptional speeches are discussed and model essays are analyzed and critiqued. Teachers use positive modeling as a teaching tool to help their students understand what good communicative methods are.

In this spirit, we hope that the chart on the following pages will dispel some myths about grading, myths that often create unnecessary anxiety for students.

Myth	Truth
1. Teachers want to see you fail.	1. Quite the opposite. Most teachers have a vested interest in seeing you succeed. Believe us: there is no joy in failing students. But there is great joy in seeing students excel.
2. There is a quota on the number of A's a teacher can give. If a teacher is giving out too many high grades, the Dean gets upset about grade inflation.	2. False. Dean-mandated grade quotas are part of the campus folklore. Though we have known teachers who impose their own quotas on grades, rare is the case of a Dean "dressing down" a teacher for giving out too many As.
3. If a teacher dislikes my political stance, my grade will suffer.	3. Overall, most teachers will reward good research and good arguments with good grades—regardless of political ideology. If you truly feel your grade is based on bias, talk to your teacher **after** a cooling off period.

Myth	Truth
4. If a teacher dislikes me, my grade will suffer. Conversely, if a teacher likes me, my grades will improve.	4. Neither assumption holds much weight. As a rule, teachers do not grade based on the personality of the student; teachers grade a student's performance as a communicator. Teachers realize good students will write good papers but might make mistakes in their speeches. Accordingly, teachers will give honest grades to these performances.
5. A is for effort.	5. Effort alone will not achieve the grade you desire. A grade has to be, in some sense, a measure of quality; otherwise, we encourage mediocrity. On the other hand, a lack of effort is a sure way to fail. Just showing up is not enough.

We discuss these myths not just to allay certain anxieties about grading, but to encourage teachers and students to discuss this process as openly as possible. We've touched upon only the most popular myths about grading. Can you think of others? If so, discuss these issues with your teacher.

THE LAST WORD

We began this chapter by quoting Cicero, and it is only fitting that we end with him, as well. Cicero believed that all orators should take classes in acting because everything we do as writers and speakers is an act; we are playing a role that is described by our audience, ourselves, and our circumstances.

◆ QUESTIONS FOR FURTHER THOUGHT AND STUDY

1. Watch some speakers on television—news programs and C-SPAN are good resources—and try to determine what coping and/or minimizing strategies they are using to overcome their nervousness. Watch for hints such as holding the podium, taking a drink of water, glancing at a particular spot, making predictable gestures.

2. Now try making the same analysis of your own habits. Watch a videotape of yourself speaking. Look for signs of nervousness that might be apparent to others, such as pulling on a strand of hair, and see if you use any minimizing and coping strategies of which you might not be aware.

3. Look up quotations from famous authors about "writer's block." What do their words tell you about this phenomenon? Why do you suppose the authors of this text assert that "writer's block" is a myth? Can you argue against that position?

4. To what extent is the audience responsible for a speaker's nervousness? What actions can the audience take that will put a speaker more at ease?

WORKS CITED

Plutarch. "Demosthenes." Trans. John Dryden. *MIT Internet Classics Archive.* 2007. Web. <http://classics.mit.edu/Plutarch/demosthe. html>

SECTION TWO

Rhetoric and Your Audience

CHAPTER 5

Audience

The play was a great success, but the audience was a disaster.
—Oscar Wilde

The audience is never wrong.
—Billy Wilder

THE TWO FUNDAMENTAL CONSIDERATIONS of rhetoric are audience and purpose. You must think about to whom you are writing or speaking and what your purpose is for the rhetorical undertaking. In other words, you must know the "who" and "why," and of these, the first consideration is "who." Of course identifying an audience seems fairly simple—in the classroom setting your audience is most often your teacher or your classmates. You have been a part of this setting for some fifteen years, and you know the scene pretty well. Teachers, as much as those of us who teach would like to disagree, are fairly predictable, at least with respect to levels of education and their interest in students. Students, most of whom are about your own age, are fairly similar, too, and after all, you've been sitting in class with them this semester and have gotten to know many of them. There is, of course, diversity even within these two groups in terms of such important factors as cultural background, outside interests, socioeconomic status, and political leanings. What makes the two groups similar is their function. The teachers are there to help you, to critique your work, and ultimately to assign a grade. You are there to learn, to participate in the construction of knowledge, and, let's be honest, to get a grade. Everything that happens revolves around some aspect of the education process.

Our goal, though, is not to write and speak only within the narrow confines of the classroom, because we live our lives beyond the classroom and venture into the public sphere. In this sphere, your audiences will no longer be so easily definable. There may be few, if any, unifying factors such as age, function, or common interests. Further, you may have to speak or write to an audience in situations that you have never before encountered and of which you have no prior knowledge. This chapter is directed primarily toward that audience. You will learn some common factors in audience analysis, and learn to understand the members of your audience and how to best communicate with them. Let us begin, then, with the fundamentals.

Ethos, Logos, Pathos

Throughout the previous chapters, we have mentioned the terms *ethos, logos,* and *pathos,* but have not defined them or discussed their application. Understanding these terms is essential for an understanding of audience, and also for an understanding of argumentation, for they are used in two separate senses. The first sense, especially in composition texts, is that they are appeals to the audience; the second sense, more often found in communication texts, is that they are proofs offered for an argument. The latter understanding is closer to the sense in which Aristotle uses the terms, but both are absolutely essential for a complete understanding of rhetorical communication.

In book I, chapter 2 of *The Rhetoric,* Aristotle posits two kinds of rhetorical proof, or pisteis: artistic proof relies on the skill of the rhetor; nonartistic proof is that which exists outside the composing act of the rhetor, such as, examples, testimony, and observed data. Nonartistic proof will be discussed in the chapters on argumentation and evidence; in this chapter we are concerned with the artistic proofs—*ethos, logos,* and *pathos.*

ETHOS

Ethos derives from the credibility of the rhetor. Quintilian had *ethos* in mind when he described rhetorical success as "a good man speaking well." Aristotle highlights three signs of a speaker's credibility, the first of which is fair-mindedness. That is, the audience must perceive that the speaker is treating the subject matter and the audience fairly, giving thoughtful consideration to opposing arguments and points of view, rather than dismissing them out of hand or distorting them. The second sign is a sense of good will toward the audience; that is, the audience must feel that the speaker intends to do no harm by trickery or deceit, or by moving the audience toward unjust or unwise action. In this respect, the sincerity of the rhetor is important. The third sign is expertise; the rhetor must demonstrate an advanced knowledge, skill and experience related to subject matter. This kind of expertise is often demonstrated by education, credential, training, and profession. But what makes this rhetor a credible expert is a demonstration of reliability, one who consistently retains a reliable authority by a consensus of peers.

Aristotle points out that the controlling factor in a persuasive process is the demonstrated character of the rhetor. He states that the audience is more likely to believe a speaker's arguments if they trust the speaker's character. However, if the audience feels they have been betrayed in any way once the rhetor demonstrates that he or she is not of good character, convincing them otherwise is nearly impossible. If you've watched many television shows or films about trials, you are undoubtedly familiar with the attorneys' attempts to impeach the credibility of the witnesses for the other side. The standard accusation is, "You lied once before; why should the jury believe you now?" If a witness has lied in the past it is difficult, if not impossible, for that witness's credibility to survive such a challenge.

LOGOS

Understanding why the term *ethos* is the root of ethics is hardly difficult. Similarly, *logos*, derived from the Greek word for *word*, is the root of our system of logic and reasoning. Because the generally accepted translation of *logos* is "word," *logos* is interpreted by some to mean the words we use to express ourselves, but that is a misconception. The language itself is contained in discussions of style. *Logos* refers to the reasoning used by the rhetor to persuade the audience; *logos* is the primary subject matter of the chapter on argumentation. In particular, the audience wants to understand how certain conclusions are reached. They also must be able to determine that the rhetor uses logic that is not flawed. For this reason, we study logical fallacies so that we can avoid them in our own discourse and detect them in the discourse of others. Flawed reasoning will diminish your *ethos* in the same way that deception will; if you make an error in reasoning, your audience may anticipate that other parts of the argument are flawed as well.

Beyond simply avoiding flawed logic, the connection between *logos* and audience is most explicit in the use of a rhetorical strategy called the enthymeme. In the chapter on argumentation you will discover that the enthymeme is technically defined as a truncated syllogism, or a syllogism missing a premise, but for the purposes of understanding audience we think of the enthymeme as a sort of "fill in the blank" argument. That is, the rhetor makes an argument for which the audience fills in part of the reasoning or evidence from their experience or knowledge. For example, if we argue that in order to conserve energy and become less reliant on foreign oil, we should reduce highway speed limits to 55 mph, we assume the audience knows and can supply the information that speeds over 55 mph use a proportionally higher rate of gasoline.

The use of the enthymeme can be both valuable and dangerous. The value lies in its ability to draw the audience into the argument; the danger lies in the possibility of misinterpretation. Because the audience has to supply the missing information, they become involved in the presentation. They have an investment in the process; they not only take ownership of the subject matter, but also—because they are now helping you—begin to identify with you. The danger of using enthymematic argument is that you must trust that the audience will supply the information you desire. If they do not have the information, then the point of your argument will be lost. If they have the wrong information, the point of the argument will be misconstrued. Therefore, a key factor in constructing an enthymeme is being fairly certain of the level of knowledge or experience and the particular biases of your audience.

PATHOS

Just as *ethos* and *logos* are related to common words that provide clues to their meaning, so *pathos* is related to two words that suggest the dimensions of this term: sympathy and empathy. However, like *logos*, the derived terms can be misleading. *Pathos* is defined by Aristotle as persuading the audience through emotions, which can be invoked in an audience by relying on their values and beliefs. To know the values and beliefs of our audience, we must analyze the audience; we must see if there are any clues that might let us discover more about the people to whom our message is targeted. For example, what is the cultural background of the audience? What is their disposition toward religion or family? Do they share a common interest for or against, say, gun control? The problem is, of course, that knowing this information is not always possible. Politicians and interest groups spend enormous sums to conduct polls and focus groups to ferret out exactly this sort of information about potential voters and contributors. Most of us, on the other hand, do not have those resources, nor are we likely to be speaking to a group that would make such analysis possible.

Here is the important point: if you do not know where your audience's sympathies lie, do not presume that you do. For example, if you are opposed to capital punishment, do not assume that your audience agrees with you. Instead, treat them as a hostile audience. In the chapter on organization, we will deal in depth with how to lay out a case for exactly this situation. For now, however, let us simply say that you must find some way of establishing common ground with your audience. That is, find something that you all share in common. In your class, the most obvious common ground is that you are all college students. Beyond that, however, you must determine if there are other commonalities. You may all be approximately the same age, or not; you may all be computer science majors, or not; you may all commute to campus, or not; and you may all be residents of the state, or not. When you can determine the commonalities, these can be used to advantage in your speech or essay, but guard against the temptation to assume commonalities that do not exist.

One more cautionary note: Just as in the use of the enthymeme, the use of *pathos* can also be dangerous. Emotions can easily outweigh sound reasoning. Perhaps the most visible and dramatic example of over-reliance on *pathos* occurs during a trial when a sympathetic victim demands the conviction of a less sympathetic defendant, and the jury convicts in spite of negligible evidence. However, this is far from the only example. Think for a moment about a political campaign in which the candidate appeals to patriotism rather than discussing the issues, or a charity that uses in its advertising a picture of an emaciated child to cover up the fact that most of the collected funds go to administration.

The Importance of Audience

AN AUDIENCE OF ONE

One of the popular old philosophical questions asks, "If a tree falls deep in the forest where no one can hear it, does it make a sound?" That is, is the sound real if it is not heard?

By the same token, does a speech exist if it is not heard, or writing exist if it is not read? Even apart from the physical artifacts—notes or a manuscript—we believe that it does, for you yourself are the first and most crucial audience for your work. You must be satisfied with the message you are conveying and you must be convinced that the message is expressed in the most effective manner. Beyond the self, though, the audience expands in ever-widening circles, much like the ripples created when a stone is tossed into a pond. If we think of the ripples as layers of audience, we begin to see there is an ever-increasing circle of those whom we wish to influence with our message. This chapter addresses the questions of who constitutes an audience and how the rhetor can most effectively address the identified audience.

WHO IS THE AUDIENCE?

Before the advent of modern media this was a much easier question to answer. If you wrote, only a few people were likely to read your words; in fact, only a few people could read. If you gave a speech, the only way others outside the immediate group of listeners might hear your message was if someone told a friend. Newspapers, radio, television, and the internet have changed that intimacy forever. Now an important speech can be heard by audiences around the world at the very moment it is being given; an important written communication can be delivered and printed out almost instantaneously. Immediacy changes some of our preconceptions about audience, but it does not alter the fundamental factors each rhetor must consider in analyzing his or her audience.

GENERAL AND SPECIALIZED AUDIENCES

The first question we must answer about our audience is whether the audience is general or a specialized group. Is the audience unified by common interests or beliefs, or is it an assorted group of people whose interests and beliefs we may not know?

A general audience is the one most writers encounter because once a piece is published, the author generally has no way of knowing who might read it in the public sphere. That is a function of the distance between the author and the audience. One might think that speakers, on the other hand, would be at less of a distance from their audience because they are generally physically present (with the exception, of course, of broadcast speeches), but that is not necessarily true. Quite often speakers, though they are physically present, know little more about their audiences than a writer would. If you are speaking to a group of people about whom you know little, or who may have varying interests, information, and beliefs, we can call that a general audience. As strange as it might seem, this also includes your classmates and instructors. While there are some things you share in common, they are probably not the unifying factor in their coming together as an audience, and you probably do not know how much prior information they have about your subject, what their interests are, or their beliefs. There are some exceptions, of course: you might expect that both students and instructors would be interested in issues affecting the university such as bookstore or library hours, tuition increases, or the grading system. If you are giving a speech on one of these topics, your audience would then be considered a specialized audience.

A specialized audience is one about which you know some specific information that would allow you to tailor your topic to its needs. Most often, you know that the people in the audience have either a common purpose or a common knowledge base. The audience might be a group of people who are protesting the development of wetlands, in which case there is a common purpose. Or it could be a group of geology majors to whom you are speaking about the rock formations under the San Andreas Fault; you can reasonably assume that they have some knowledge of rock formations and fault lines since they are geology majors.

SPHERES AND FIELDS

One way to think about the differences between general and specialized audiences is to think about the places of argument, as expressed by Thomas Goodnight. Goodnight suggests there are three spheres in which argument occurs: the *personal*, the *technical*, and the *public*. He defines a sphere as "the grounds upon which arguments are built and the authorities to which arguers appeal" (216). To make the concept of spheres of argument more clear and concrete, let us think about the following three scenarios:

1. Two friends are trying to decide which movie to see. One says, "Anna saw it last week and said it was great!" They decide to choose that movie over another that they had heard nothing about.

2. Two newspaper movie reviewers have viewed the same film. One says it is too long, is poorly acted, and lacks a sensible plot. The other says the film is exciting, historically accurate, and beautifully costumed. Both reviews are presented in the newspaper.

3. Two professors of cinema studies at a major university are discussing a film. One says it is reminiscent of early Sergei Eisenstein; the other disagrees, saying it is an attempt to caricature the worst of film noir. They decide to research and write an article for a scholarly journal discussing their views.

In the first scenario, two friends are willing to accept a third friend's recommendation without any further evidence. Their decision really affects no one but themselves. They do not expect anyone else to see the movie based on Anna's testimony. This decision affects the personal spheres of the two friends and no one else.

In the second example, the two critics do have some criteria for their opinions, but their criteria and critical evaluations are expressed in language that must, necessarily, be accessible to whoever happens to pick up the paper and read their reviews. Although they may have considerable expertise—more than they reveal in their reviews—they must keep their general audience in mind. Formulating an argument intended for wider public dissemination is the earmark of the public sphere.

Finally, in the third scenario, we have an example of a conversation in the technical sphere. The two professors can assume that each understands the specialized vocabulary used by the other. At the same time, they do not need to define, nor in their article will they need to explain, who Sergei Eisenstein is or what the term *film noir* means. Because the article will appear in a scholarly publication designed to be read by other cinema studies experts, they can assume this level of knowledge by their audience.

In each of these scenarios, *ethos* plays a central role, but in each case you will notice that the standard by which *ethos* is measured is dictated by the sphere. In the first scenario, credibility is established on the basis of the personal relationship the students have with their friend and with each other. They trust the friend's recommendation based solely on their knowledge of her. On the other hand, in the second scenario the two movie critics in the public sphere may or may not have a personal relationship with each other; it is unlikely that their readers have a personal relationship with either of them. Instead, their credibility with their reading public is established by their body of work and their reputation. Readers who have read their work in the past will know which critic's ideas and criteria are most similar to theirs, and will form their judgment based on that. The body of work is also important in the third scenario, but in the technical sphere, an additional element is required. To establish credibility in this sphere, one is generally required to have some sort of credential—a law degree, an engineer's or architect's license, for example. In the academy that credential is generally an advanced college degree—the doctorate—as well as a body of work. Before we can assess the credibility of someone in academia, we must know not only whether someone has a doctorate, but frequently where he or she received the degree, who that person's mentor was, and the quality of journals in which his or her body of work has been published.

FIELDS

In the third scenario above, we presented two experts—professors of cinema studies—in a conversation about cinema. Suppose for a moment that they had been discussing not cinema, but agriculture. Would you still consider them experts? No, probably not—at least not without additional information. Within each of the spheres we can determine fields of expertise. The authors of this text have at least some expertise in rhetoric, composition, and public speaking. We are able, we hope, to write authoritatively in the technical sphere about those fields. On other topics, however, such as physics, anthropology, or sociology, we would be considered part of a general audience. Our knowledge of those subjects is no greater, and may be less, than that of the general public. Fields often have a field-specific vocabulary, often called jargon, that can only be thoroughly understood by others in that field. The most common sites for specialized fields are, of course, the professions—law, medicine, business, engineering, and the sciences, among others—but any enterprise which demands a vocabulary in which words have particular meanings unique to that specialty could be described as a field. For example, law enforcement officers, basketball players, movie crews, or fashion photographers might all have specific, and very different, meanings for the word *shoot* that would generally be understood only by others in that field.

Although jargon is correctly used to describe the specialized language in any field, when most people hear the term *jargon,* they think immediately of what we generally call *bureaucratese.* Every so often a public official will rail against the complex language of government regulations, the tax code, or a specific piece of particularly dense legislative language. However, government officials are far from the only miscreants. Among the worst offenders, at least in the public's view, are academics, ironically often professors of composition and communication. Consider the following passage from a past issue of the *Journal of Advanced Composition*: "Because student subjectivities are complex, divided and open to reformulation in group settings, classroom structures should provide ample spaces to develop critical self-awareness" (331). Or this, from *Communication Research Reports*: "In summary, the current study provides support for a uses and gratifications framework in that variations in channel use are associated with the gratification of relational maintenance in long-distance relationships" (127). A blogger commented on such discourse, noting, tongue-in-cheek, that "the tendency to value overly abstract polysyllabic diction and seemingly interminable and convoluted syntax along with increasingly abstract theoretical concepts is to be bemoaned."

While such sentences may seem like dense, almost incomprehensible prose to a general audience, both these passages would be easily understood by the intended audience—other professionals in the field. The reason that such thick prose is acceptable in some cases, but is roundly criticized in many government documents, is that governmental discourse should be accessible to those for whom it is intended, and that is frequently a general audience. Tax instructions, small business loan applications, and environmental impact reports affecting where a plant can be built all need to be accessible to those who have to read them for guidance. It is when jargon interferes with understanding that it becomes a problem. Therefore, since most of your speaking and writing will be done for a general audience, it is best to keep your own discourse simple, clear, and direct. In other words, eschew obfuscation.

RHETORIC AND THE ACADEMY: A SPECIFIC AUDIENCE

As we suggested earlier in this chapter, the academic audience should be considered in the technical sphere, but within that sphere each academic discipline has its own standards of language and evidence. Writers in the field of psychology, for example, use the style manual of American Psychological Association (APA) when composing papers and books, while literature professors use the manual of the Modern Language Association (MLA). In psychology, one almost never uses the first person pronoun ("I") in writing; such use is becoming increasingly common in literary criticism. In psychology, opinion rarely counts as evidence; clinical research and observation are the types of evidence most often cited and used to support arguments. In literature, on the other hand, there is less empirical research. Instead, writers rely heavily on the opinions and historical research of others. There are also differences in how one assesses the credibility of an expert and how the fields expect arguments to be organized and constructed.

The problem with this, of course, is that you are probably taking courses in several academic fields—communication, history, literature, biology, sociology, or perhaps astronomy, psychology, or philosophy—at the same time, at least until you begin doing extensive work in your major. What is the poor, confused student to do?

If the professor does not specify a style manual and structural expectations, always ask. It will undoubtedly impress your professor that you actually know that there's a difference. It will also be a great service to your classmates, who are probably as confused as you are but are afraid to inquire.

MULTIPLE AUDIENCES

Finally, when you assess your audience, you must consider the issue of multiple audiences—perhaps even unintended audiences. Before the creation of the printing press—and much later, radio, television, and computers—considering the content of your audience was rarely a difficult issue. Politicians showed up at town halls expecting to speak to their constituents. They could control the process of communication by establishing an interpersonal relationship with their specific audience. However, the advent of mass communication has created a more complex situation in which a communicator often has more than one audience for a speech or essay. Whereas before you would have been speaking only to those within earshot, or writing for the relatively small number of people who were literate, now an argument can be heard by those in the room, by those listening on radio or television, by those following on the internet; speeches can also lose their original acoustical intent by becoming objects to be read. In this sense, speeches can be reprinted in other media and the direct and personal connection with the speechmaker is almost completely lost.

Likewise, an essay might be published in a specific journal and initially read by one group, such as a specific political group or a highly trained group of doctors. But this essay can be reprinted and read by other groups and excerpted in magazines or anthologized in textbooks and read still by others. In many ways, mass communication has decontextualized communication by emphasizing sound bites and video clips. Similarly, speeches and writing often are decontextualized when these texts are taken from the original or local contexts and disseminated throughout the world to new audiences, perhaps even global audiences.

If you have ever listened to the floor debate in the House of Representatives, you may have heard speaker after speaker ask for "permission to revise and extend" their remarks. The reason for this is that all speeches, which are generally delivered extemporaneously, are reprinted in the *Congressional Record*. If the speaker's remarks were reprinted verbatim, it is likely there would be grammatical errors, omissions, or perhaps even errors of fact. In addition, there may be letters from constituents, tables and graphs, and other materials that the speaker cannot or chooses not to recite while speaking. Therefore, the speaker asks for a chance to revise and add to the oral transcript before it is published. This allows for the best possible presentation before it is read by the public. Similarly, if an essay is written for a class paper, then for publication in a professional journal, then reprinted in a trade magazine, the author generally revises the language each time so that it is appropriate for each intended audience.

While a broader audience may give attention to a worthy point of view or may have a broader understanding of a specific or local problem, a decontextualized argument may create problems by shedding light on values not shared by the larger community. You may recall the example from chapter 3, "The Communication Process," in which Lawrence Summers, the former President of Harvard University, made comments about women to a group of faculty members—comments that, once they were made public, resulted in widespread public criticism and forced him to retract his statements.

Since the advent of radio and television, it is no longer possible for any public figure to assume that he or she will be speaking directly and exclusively to the audience present. In a sense, then, all truly public speeches have a multiple audience. Sometimes, however, speakers are not only aware of their wider audience, but use the multiple audiences as a rhetorical strategy. This has become common in recent political campaigns and Presidential addresses. Typically, the speaker will ensure that the entire audience, or at least those who are visible on camera, supports his or her positions. In this way, the enthusiasm and *ethos* of the audience itself can become a persuasive part of the message. For example, if a candidate wishes to convince the wider audience that more support is needed for the military, the audience may be composed entirely of former or uniformed military personnel who, of course, support the idea. But it is not necessary to convince them; the real goal is to convince the wider audience. The military personnel in this situation function as visual aid than audience. In addition, like Cicero who paid citizens to show up and applaud for certain speakers, including himself, in hopes of gaining the favor of the audience—the enthusiastic applause that the military personnel creates something called a "band-wagon" effect. The larger, multiple audience might assume that there is widespread approval of both the message and the messenger and, therefore, "get on board the bandwagon."

This strategy becomes more problematic when the bias of the audience is less obvious. In the example above, most viewers would assume that the military would, of course, be in favor of more support, just as teachers would be in favor of safer classrooms and smaller class sizes, union members would be in favor of higher wages and better working conditions, and college students would be in favor of lower tuition and better cafeteria food. What happens, though, when a hand-picked group of citizens is gathered to lend support to an otherwise unpopular idea? To promote President Bush's plan to reform Social Security, according to Jonathan Weisman, the Republican strategists carefully hand-picked a group of supporters who agreed with the President's plan to allow individuals to invest part of their Social Security taxes in private accounts, although polls showed this idea was widely opposed by a majority of Americans. These supporters were invited to hear the President speak about Social Security at a "town hall" meeting which was televised to a much wider audience. The immediate audience all appeared to be in favor of the President's plan, and the impression was that the plan was far more popular than it actually was. Spokesmen then claimed that the response of those in the immediate audience demonstrated how popular the plan was.

FACTORS IN AUDIENCE ANALYSIS

Now that you have a general understanding of the dimensions of audience, you can consider three important elements in audience analysis: determining shared values and beliefs, choosing the appropriate level or levels of discourse, and fulfilling audience expectations.

DETERMINING SHARED VALUES AND BELIEFS

We've given hints earlier in the book about how to go about determining your audience's values and beliefs, but we should review those points and perhaps add a few notes about this important topic. This task is relatively easy if you are speaking to or writing for an audience that you know fairly well, for example family, friends, or classmates. You probably know enough about them to treat carefully those "hot button" issues that often set off arguments. You also know what will be most persuasive to your audience, and you can generally count on a high degree of *ethos* with that audience. Furthermore, you, literally as well as figuratively, speak their language.

Remember, however, that even though these people are your friends, they may not agree with you on every issue, so it is important to show them you have considered possible arguments they might make against your position.

It is very difficult, if you have an audience that is largely unknown to you, to determine values and beliefs of its members. You can, of course, get some clues from what you do know about them. What are their commonalities? Age? Income level? Religion? Political affiliation? Geographical location? Professions? Hobbies and interests? This information can often be determined by simply observing the audience, as in the case of age; other factors may be more difficult. But presumably they are gathered together for a reason, and that is where you should start. Give some serious thought to why the audience is there. To use some relatively obvious examples, if you have been invited to speak at a meeting of the National Rifle Association, or the Coalition Against Homelessness, or the Eastborough Garden Club, you have a pretty good idea in each case of at least one thing your audience is interested in. That, of course, is where you should begin. And if you have been invited by them to speak about Second Amendment rights, the need for more shelters, or the dangers of the potato bug, that may be all you need to know.

Suppose, however, that you are presenting a business proposal to a group of potential clients, or you are speaking to your city zoning commission about plans for a new factory in your community. Here the problem is more difficult. You want to make the most persuasive possible argument and you know that in order to do that you must find some common ground. You cannot assume that your potential clients have the same interests that you do; to do so might lose you the sale. Nor can you assume that the zoning commission shares your concerns about the environment or about the economic climate of the community. Their primary concern may be political.

In such cases, the first thing you should do is research; find out as much about both the body itself and the individual persons to whom you will be speaking. Try to discover which arguments will be most persuasive to them. If possible, look back at records of previous meetings, or of successful sales. Determine what worked and what didn't, and plan your presentation accordingly. If the zoning commission is composed of environmental activists, focus on the environmental advantages or disadvantages first, depending on whether you are for or against the project.

Many times, such helpful clues are not available. In these situations, it is always best to assume your audience disagrees with you, and plan your presentation accordingly. This scenario is called addressing the hostile audience. The strategies to use with hostile audiences will be discussed in the chapter on argumentation.

◆ OPPORTUNITIES FOR CRITICAL THINKING

1. Because *pathos* is tied so closely to the audience's values, it is worth identifying and understanding what these values are. There are any number of organizations that list and define what is uniquely called American values. Some values are expressed by traditional organizations, such as the Boy Scouts, but these values are also identified and framed by organizations that work to educate foreign visitors and immigrants. Conduct some research on the internet; locate and list these values. What are these values? Do any of these values seem contradictory? If so, why?

2. In every election cycle it seems that someone in Congress proposes a Constitutional amendment to make desecration of the United States flag a federal crime. Thousands of Americans send letters and emails or make phone calls in support of such an amendment. Flag-burning legislation becomes a rallying cry for certain groups and, by invoking the value of patriotism, becomes an issue difficult to oppose. Yet, can any of you recall an instance where you witnessed a flag being burned in this country? Probably not; there appears to be no evidence of a widespread problem with flag-burning. In fact, this harkens back to the anti-war protests of the 1960s and 70s. The flag desecration argument does, however, invoke patriotic values and recalls the culture clashes of the Vietnam era. In other words, its only justification is *pathos*. The proponents know that it will appeal to a certain group of voters and will solidify their base. It is relatively easy to invent a logical argument in opposition to such an amendment, but can you invent an argument *against* a flag desecration amendment that appeals to *pathos* as much as the arguments *for* does?

WORKS CITED

Aristotle. *On Rhetoric: A Theory of Civic Discourse.* Trans. G. Kennedy. New York: Oxford UP, 1991.

CJO, response to "No Field, No Future." *Inside Higher Ed* 7 Dec. 2005. Web. <http://www.insidehighered.com/views/2005/12/06/soltan>.

Dainton, M. and B. Aylor "Patterns of Communication Channel Use in the Maintenance of Long-Distance Relationships." *Communication Research Reports.* 19.2 (2002): 118-129.

Foster, D. "Community and Cohesion in the Writing/Reading Classroom *JAC: A Journal of Composition Theory.* 17.3 (1997): 325-341.

Goodnight, G. Thomas. "The Personal, Technical and Public Spheres of Argument: A Speculative Inquiry into the Art of Public Deliberation." *Journal of the American Forensic Association.* 18 (1982): 214-27.

Weisman, Jonathan. "Bush Social Security Plan Proves Tough Sell Among Working Poor: Investment Choice Has Limited Appeal." *Washington Post.* 18 April 2005: A01.

Purpose

The secret of success is constancy of purpose.
—Benjamin Disraeli

JUST AS Disraeli argues it is unwise to wander through life, so it is unwise to wander through a speech or essay without knowing why. You must have a purpose, a reason for communicating. Certainly, the paper and speech prompt will give you the shape and scope of your assignment. Usually, teachers want their students to demonstrate mastery over content, so they will assign different kinds of assignments for different purposes, such as rhetorical acts that explain or inform, convey personal ethics or feelings, or argue and persuade. Understanding your teacher's intent will help clarify your focus and determine which rhetorical strategies will be most effective. There are several ways to think about purpose.

In *The Rhetoric*, Aristotle identifies three rhetorical purposes: forensic, deliberative, and epideictic. The purpose of a forensic speech or essay is to determine the truth of a situation—to delineate the facts. Forensic rhetoric is most closely identified with legal proceedings. The purpose of a trial is to determine the relevant facts of a case—generally leading to guilt or innocence. Deliberative rhetoric aims at decision-making, balancing two opposing viewpoints, and forming a policy. This rhetoric is related to legislative bodies—city councils, university faculty committees, and the US Senate and House of Representatives, to name but a few. Any time a policy or plan is being discussed, there is deliberative rhetoric occurring. Finally, epideictic rhetoric is often defined as ceremonial rhetoric, the kind of rhetoric that reflects community values by celebrating or commemorating a person or event. The traditional Fourth of July speech, the eulogy, and the retirement speech are examples of epideictic rhetoric.

In many communication and composition texts, purpose is also divided into three categories: to inform, to persuade, and to entertain or delight. These are often called general purposes. The informative speech, or expository essay, is designed to present information. In this sense, it is similar to Aristotle's conception of forensic rhetoric. The persuasive speech or essay is designed, obviously, to persuade, and is generally deliberative in nature. The speech or essay to entertain is exactly that—a piece that one might read for enjoyment, which may or may not have a more serious intention.

It is our contention that none of these classification schemes is sufficient to explain the possibilities of purpose. First, such schemes seem not to allow for the possibility that a single rhetorical act might, in fact, have several purposes intermixed. We are convinced that it is probable—and often desirable—to have an informative speech that is also entertaining, just as we hope that you will find this textbook informative, occasionally persuasive, and, at times, even mildly amusing.

Second, such schemes do not account for all the varieties of written and oral discourse that fall within the field of rhetoric. How should we, for example, classify a sermon? A diatribe or polemic? A motivational speech? As we discuss each category, we will present a rather wider variety of purposes and explain some considerations of each.

A cautionary note: Be careful not to confuse the terms *purpose* and *genre*. They are related in some ways, but very distinct in others. Genre, as we have noted before, refers to the type of communication: a personal essay, a political campaign speech, a wedding toast, a letter to the editor. Genres have certain expectations as to form, style, and content. But an essay can have several different purposes, as can the letter to the editor, or even the toast, even as it fulfills the expectations of the genre. In Pericles' famous funeral oration, for example, he eulogizes the dead Athenian soldiers, but then issues a patriotic call to arms as a way to prepare for more war. The genre is the eulogy, but the purpose, ultimately, is to commemorate the dead and spur the Athenians on to victory. With that distinction in mind, let us look at the varieties of rhetorical presentations and examine the characteristics of each.

THE ARGUMENT TO INFORM

The central argument of informational discourse is that the facts stated in support of the thesis are probably true. It is most closely related to Aristotle's forensic purpose; that is, the purpose is to discover the truth of the matter. There are some who would argue that merely giving information is not rhetorical because it does not contain an element of persuasion. We disagree. At the very least, you must persuade your audience that the information you are giving is credible. In that respect, *ethos* is a critical factor in the speech to inform. Your audience must not only believe that what you are telling them is honest, but that the evidence you use is accurate and credible.

Perhaps the most common public application of the basic argument to inform is the report. Whether it is the fifth grader's report on the agricultural practices of the Maya or the corporate executive's annual report to the stockholders, the purpose of the report is to give the facts.

But if all you are doing is presenting the facts, why do we call this an "argument" to inform? Because, with the exception of empirical facts such as the fact that my desk is exactly 60 inches long, which can be verified by accepted measurement standards, most facts are, in a sense, filtered by your *interpretation* of the facts. Some say, for example, that the death penalty is a deterrent to crime. Is this a fact? Would all experts in the field agree with this? No. If you are reporting on the use of the death penalty and say it is a deterrent, you must support that with both reasoning and evidence. Is global warming a fact? What do the experts say? In other words, when you make an informative argument, you are essentially asking your audience to believe that your information is correct. That is why *ethos* is incredibly important. In order to establish your own credibility, you better know what you are talking about, or better do necessary research, before attempting to present your audience with the speech or essay to inform and, unless you are yourself an expert on the particular subject, you had better find some other experts to support your point of view.

THE ARGUMENT TO PERSUADE

Whether you are trying to convince your parents to loan you the car, convince your teacher to give you a better grade, convince someone to elect you to the student senate, or convince Congress to pass a law, you are engaging in a deliberative process. You are trying to convince them they should adopt a certain policy or follow a particular course of action. You are engaged in what most believe to be the essential activity of rhetoric—persuasion. Persuasion is the core of all personal and civic deliberation. It should not surprise you, then, to know that hundreds, perhaps thousands, of books have been written on the subject—Aristotle was not even the first. They have been written by rhetoricians, communications scholars, psychologists, political scientists, lawyers, and even comedians. Both undergraduate and graduate curricula feature courses in persuasion. Persuasion is frequently the subject of in-service training in fields from sales to education.

Clearly, it is not possible for us to give you, in this short text, even two percent of the knowledge about persuasion that has been accumulated over the centuries. We can, however, give you a few things to keep in mind when your purpose is to persuade:

> *Consider the audience.* (You've heard this before, right?) Don't alienate them. Before plunging into the purpose of your speech, establish common ground so that you can then move them to the place you want them to be. If you are certain that the entire audience shares your values and beliefs, then get right to the action you want them to take. If, as will be true in 99% of the audiences you speak to, you really don't know what everyone believes or what their values are, err on the side of caution. Carefully lay a groundwork of inductive reasoning before asking them to trust your argument.

> *Pull out all the stops.* This is the time to carefully consider exactly what will be most persuasive to your audience. Use reason, of course, and establish your credibility—especially that part about having the good of the audience at heart—but beyond that, employ *pathos.* Think about how you can appeal to their values and beliefs. Even symbolism counts here. Why do you suppose that all members of Congress appear on television wearing little American flag pins? Tell a story that tugs at their heartstrings, makes them feel proud, or creates a hero. But here's a caution— when you're using this approach, nothing is worse than insincerity. If you tell a story, it should be true (or you should tell the audience it's hypothetical). Nothing will make them turn on you faster than playing with their emotions and lying to them.

> *Ask for their help.* Tell your audience specifically what you want them to do, or think. Do you want them to join a march, send a letter, vote for a candidate, find your client innocent, or start recycling? Tell them. And tell them how to do it. Make it easy.

Organize your speech or essay. One of the most effective means of organizing a persuasive speech is to follow what is known as Monroe's Motivated Sequence (Ehninger et al. 92-3). It is comprised of five steps that move the audience toward accepting your specific purpose:

- *The attention step:* Gets the attention of the audience and involves them in the discussion.

- *The need step:* Shows the audience that a problem exists, that there is a need for a change.

- *The satisfaction step:* Tells the audience how the problem can be corrected.

- *The visualization step:* Tells the audience how their world will be better if the solution is adopted.

- *The action step:* Tells the audience specifically what you want them to do to accomplish the proposed solution.

The advantages of this approach are fairly obvious. Remember that your purpose is to persuade an audience to do something, and by using the Motivated Sequence, you involve the audience from the very beginning. Let's look at an example of a bare-bones outline based on the Motivated Sequence:

Purpose: To persuade audience to take action in support of bill to protect homeless children

I. Attention step: Anecdote about a child living in a homeless shelter
II. Need step:
      A. Statistics on number of children in homeless shelters.
      B. Statistics on effects of homelessness on children.
      C. Impact of homeless children on society, education, health care system.
III. Satisfaction step:
      A. Government program to provide clean, adequate private shelters for all homeless families with children.

          B. Paid for by raising property taxes on second homes.

    IV. Visualization step: If there were no homeless children, children would be happier, healthier, better-educated, and grow into more capable adults.

    V. Action step:
          A. Attend the hearings of the state legislature that will be held on this issue in two weeks to support this bill.
          B. Write to the speaker and ask to be put on the agenda to speak for the bill.
          C. Here are the names and addresses you'll need to contact: (handouts or postcards available at end of speech)

From this example, you can see that this format is relatively easy to follow. It follows a logical order, it seamlessly moves the listener through the persuasive appeal, it is sufficiently flexible to apply to a great variety of topics, and above all, it is clear and simple.

This format is not the only one, however. One model, the problem-solution argument, calls for establishing a need for some change in the status quo, showing that the problem created by the needed change is significant (that is, it causes great harm), that the current system is incapable of solving the problem. A solution is then proposed and the proponent must show that the solution will, in fact, solve the problem. This format, too, requires a call to action at the end. You will observe this is very closely related to the Motivated Sequence.

A third possibility is what we call the comparative advantage approach, in which you argue that although things aren't bad right now, they could be much better if we would only do X. You might, for example, argue that health care would be better if we concentrated more on prevention than on cures, or that the university would be better if we had more variety in the cafeteria. Neither one of these proposals involves a radical change; they both just tweak the system a little without seriously altering it. This is often a good organizational approach for persuasive arguments about values, for reasons that will be explained in the chapter on argumentation.

THE ARGUMENT TO ENTERTAIN

There are occasions that call for entertaining the audience, and should you ever find yourself being called upon to speak at or write for one of these occasions—watch out! It is, in our opinion, the most difficult of all speaking or writing assignments. Most people are not naturally funny, as you may have observed after listening to dozens of people on television who try. The annual dinner of the Washington Press Club is a good example.

There are, however, a few things you can do (short of hiring a professional comedian or gag writer) to better your chances of actually being mildly amusing. These are lessons learned both from our experience in writing speeches for other people and from our own often failed attempts to liven up our classes.

First, immerse yourself in models. Whether it is one of the more successful speeches from an event such as the Press Club dinners, which are usually available on the web, or a humorous column of a writer such as Dave Barry, read or listen to see where you laugh and where the audience laughs, and analyze what the speaker or writer did to evoke that response. Then practice following that model in your own work.

Second, have a serious point. Humor just for humor's sake is best left to the stand-up comedians. Use your humor to accomplish a specific purpose; otherwise the audience will feel they have gained nothing from the speech and will leave slightly disappointed. For example, you could write a humorous essay about global warming in which you hold up some of our habits—idling the car in the drive-thru lane, mowing a small patch of grass with a gas-powered mower—to gentle ridicule and perhaps make the audience more aware of how we contribute to the problem. Be careful, though, not to insult the audience or make them uncomfortable.

Be sure to practice with an audience, even an audience of one. Some of the lines you think are funniest may not seem at all funny to someone else. Should you be tempted to think that your larger audience will react differently, please remember Billy Wilder's warning at the beginning of chapter 5.

Finally, remember that timing is everything. If you rush through the funny parts, no one will get them. On the other hand, if you pause expectantly wherever you *think* you're being funny, you may soon discover your audience has other ideas. Remember the goal is to have the audience laugh *with* you, not *at* you. The best advice is to be prepared to pause wherever the audience laughs, but don't assume any "laugh breaks" or applause lines.

Now, here are some very important *don'ts* to remember:

1. Don't confuse telling jokes with being humorous. They are seldom related.
2. Don't use language that is offensive and don't make fun of race, ethnicity, religion, or the disabled. Never. Not ever. It is patently *not* funny, and will immediately alienate your audience.
3. In spite of what some may say, we feel it is best *not* to start a speech with a joke. It often sets up audience expectations that you will not meet. In most cases, you should leave "A funny thing happened to me on the way here" to a handful of tired, outdated comedians unless it can be very specifically related to your topic.
4. Don't read from a manuscript—especially the funny parts. Humor should at least appear to be extemporaneous.

Other General Purposes for Discourse

To inspire and/or convert. We generally credit St. Augustine, the third century Bishop of Hippo (a town in what is now Turkey), with realizing that Aristotle's art of rhetoric could be put to good use in converting people to the relatively new Christian religion. By explicating the beliefs of the church, and by informing congregants of the consequences if they did not accept those beliefs, Augustine began the tradition of preaching that we generally call *homiletics*. Thus rhetoric became an instrument of the church as well as of the assembly and the court.

As a rule, the chief characteristic of this kind of argument is that it is an argument from authority. In some cases, the authority is scripture; in others, authority may be invested in God or a religious leader. In the case of religious testimonials, the authority is the faith experience, usually a conversion or healing, of the speaker who is testifying. Except for true conversions, a common factor is that, in general, the audience is favorably disposed to the authority. It is unlikely, for example, that persons who do not accept the authority of God, the Bible, and the priest or minister would regularly attend a church service where a sermon is the central feature. Unlike a persuasive speech in which you do not know the values and beliefs of your audience, if you are called upon to speak in church you can safely assume your audience shares certain common values and beliefs.

Given that, you have two choices: exegesis or inspiration. *Exegesis* means explanation; it involves explaining or interpreting the meaning of a particular passage, generally from scripture. Inspirational speaking, including the testimonial, requires using the common authority, values, and beliefs—often through narrative—to make your audience become more faithful, more dedicated, or more active in applying those principles to their lives.

Motivational speeches. These speeches are closely related to the testimonial. Every year certain "motivational" speakers earn hundreds of thousands of dollars running around the country telling people how to make their lives better, how to become rich, how to have more friends, how to be more influential, or how to succeed at a particular endeavor—sports, business, marriage, or life. Generally the speakers are big names in sports or business, but there are a few whose only claim to fame is that they can give a gripping motivational speech. Perhaps now you're asking yourself, "They *pay* people to do that? How can I get in on this game?"

Well, we can't promise to make you millionaires on the basis of your speaking skills, but we can tell you how to deliver a first-rate motivational speech. First, be passionate. Second, be dramatic—tell stories. Third, mix humor with the drama. Finally—and this is really the key—go back and reread the Motivated Sequence. You'll notice that this is exactly the pattern all those motivational speakers follow, and you can follow it, too. Good luck on your future career!

To blame and inflame (polemic). The polemic is essentially an aggressive argument designed to attack a person, group, or idea. These attacks are often characterized by generalizations, a lack of credible evidence, name-calling and labeling, and an assumption that the world is divided into black and white, us and them, good and evil. There are popular uses for the polemic, particularly for television shows that employ political pundits who use the polemic to aggressively confront and attack people. In many ways, such contexts can be entertaining, if you accept them for which they were intended—as conflictive arguments meant to illustrate stark differences. Beyond looking at the gaps between different positions, there are edifying reasons for the polemic, too.

Controversial or subversive arguments meant to challenge civic leaders and social policies are legitimate uses of the polemic. For instance, civil rights advocates such as Martin Luther King, Jr., praised an egalitarian vision of America and argued that vicious racists were dividing the country. Quite often, social activism is based on sobering and effective epideictic arguments that legitimately attack someone or a group of people for causing social problems. These days, one often sees the polemic appear in the form of *op-eds* (opposite-the-editorial) where the rhetor has a finite space to make arguments, so claims are made quickly and are often supported more by opinion rather than a carefully developed argument based on research and sources.

To apologize *(apologia).* When you do something wrong, you should apologize. We all know that. The question, if you are a corporation or small business, or maybe a politician, is how to apologize without making yourself look bad. Come to think of it, that's probably a handy trick even if you're not in the public eye. To accomplish this, you need to be familiar with the art of the argument of apology, known as *apologia.* From tainted pet food to an arctic oil spill to the excesses of Enron, companies and individuals are often required to make a public statement about a dangerous or damaging situation.

Just like the auto insurance agents who tell you that if you are involved in an accident you should never admit fault, many corporations take steps to re-establish their image without admitting they were at fault.

It is important to recognize this "non-apology apology" when it occurs in the public sphere, but we shouldn't be too quick to place blame on business and government. We often adopt the same tactics on a personal basis. Suppose you have just broken your mom's favorite lamp while tossing the Frisbee™ in the living room. Do you say, "Mom, I broke your lamp!" or "Mom, the lamp fell off the table and broke!"? You probably say the latter, then follow with something like, "I'm sorry your lamp broke. Let me help pick up the pieces and I'll try to glue them back together." You have tried (successfully, you hope) to move her from focusing on the problem to focusing on the solution. Maybe it won't even occur to her to ask *why* the lamp fell.

The basic elements of *apologia* are apparent here. First, focus on the problem and not on who or what caused it. The ever-popular use of passive voice in constructions such as "mistakes were made" acknowledges the problem but does not define who is responsible. Next, express your sympathy, again without pointing to your guilt. "I'm sorry your lamp broke," not "I'm sorry I broke your lamp." And finally, focus attention on the resolution of the problem rather than the problem itself. This simple stratagem works on everything from broken lamps to broken oil tankers, but as we will discuss in the chapter on ethics, what you gain in momentary resolution may be lost in long-term credibility, because sooner or later, Mom is going to ask why, in a perfectly calm living room, with no earthquakes, breezes, or other people, the lamp suddenly fell off the table.

SPECIAL OCCASION SPEECHES

Some messages are controlled by the occasion for which they are composed. We often encounter three specific situations: the eulogy, the toast, and the speech or essay of praise.

A *eulogy* is generally given at a funeral or memorial service. The speech consists of words of praise for the decedent, some personal shared memories, and words of comfort for the family and friends. The tone should be somber but warm, and the language should be more formal and, often, ornate. Above all the message must absolutely be sincere. There are many examples of eulogies we can study; one of the most famous is Pericles' *Funeral Oration,* but there are many, many more, including Lincoln's *Gettysburg Address,* Robert F. Kennedy's eulogy for Dr. Martin Luther King, Jr., and President Ronald Reagan's speech in memory of the *Challenger* astronauts. These last two are still among the most inspirational speeches of our time.

A *toast* is a ritual speech designed to briefly honor someone before a dinner or other festivity, most often a wedding reception, where it falls to the best man to give the first toast. If you are called upon to give a toast, we have three words of advice: "Keep it short!" The purpose of a toast is to extend wishes for health and happiness, not to give a rambling dissertation on the life and habits of the honoree. No one will be listening anyway; they all want to get on with the party. Therefore, we suggest you use the following format: "Here's to George and Martha," and then a one-sentence wish that in some way captures the sentiment of Mr. Spock's famous line from *Star Trek,* "May you live long and prosper."

An *encomium* is a speech or essay of praise. There are a number of occasions when such a message is required, including award ceremonies, retirement dinners, and recognition ceremonies. If you are called upon to speak at one of these occasions, there are two cardinal rules to remember: first, keep it short; second, it's about the honoree, not about you! It is often a good idea to introduce a bit of humor into this type of speech or essay, but it should never belittle or make fun of the recipient—or of anyone else, for that matter! The "celebrity roasts" that occasionally appear on television are very bad models of an appropriate *encomium.* Depending on the occasion and on how well you know the recipient, a personal anecdote may be used, and you may quote from other friends of the honoree. Again, though, this is an occasion to celebrate the contributions of the recipient—in a sense, it's a eulogy for the living.

There are many fine examples of *encomia*. One of the most interesting comes to us from classical rhetoric, Gorgias' *Encomium of Helen*, about the legendary Helen of Troy, in which he defends Helen against her critics by making an argument about the power of language.

SPECIFIC PURPOSES

In addition to the general purposes shown above, each speech has a specific purpose—you want your audience to do, think, believe, or feel something in particular.

Here are some examples:

- Topic: sharks
- General purpose: to inform
- Specific purpose: to inform my audience of college students about the dangers posed by sharks along the California coastline.

- Topic: global warming
- General purpose: to persuade
- Specific purpose: to persuade my audience of college-age drivers that they should never let the car idle for more than one minute in a drive-thru lane.

Notice that, in addition to the general purpose, the specific purpose includes a statement about who your audience will be and spells out quite narrowly exactly what you want that audience to do or think. Every time you write an essay or prepare a speech you should first have the specific purpose in mind. It will help focus your work and prevent you from going off topic. In fact, we think it a helpful idea to write out your specific purpose at the top of your rough draft so that you may refer back to it as a self-check as you complete your speech or paper.

HOW OTHER FACTORS MAY INFLUENCE PURPOSE: A CASE STUDY

One of the major media events every January (except in the first term of a new President) is the State of the Union address. We have come to think of this as a political speech, a persuasive speech, but it did not start out that way. In fact, this is the mandate as written in our Constitution:

> "The President shall from time to time give to Congress information of the State of the Union and recommend to their

Consideration such measures as he shall judge necessary and expedient."
—*Article II, Sec. 3, US Constitution*

Although George Washington did deliver his report to Congress in person, beginning with Thomas Jefferson the message was written and simply delivered to the members.

It was generally a detailing of where the nation stood—regarding income, expenditures, land, treaties, and trade—and a recommendation of measures Congress should consider for the welfare of the country. Key passages may have been reprinted in a few newspapers of the time, but for the most part it remained a message for one audience—Congress.

The tradition of the written message continued until the early twentieth century, when President Woodrow Wilson reinstituted the practice of delivering the State of the Union in a speech to Congress. With the advent of mass media—first newspapers, then radio, and now television and the internet—the audience gradually shifted from Congress to the American public, then to the world. And as the audience shifted, so did the purpose. What was formerly a rather dry cataloging of American progress became instead an opportunity to persuade the people, who would then hopefully persuade Congress, to carry out the President's programs and priorities. Because the speech has become primarily persuasive, rather than informative, the media now offer the opposition party the opportunity to respond to the message. If the speech were "just the facts," this would hardly be necessary.

As a result of the media's influence, we have the State of the Union spectacle we see today. Members of Congress arrive hours early just to get the coveted aisle seats so that they can be seen shaking hands with, hugging, or even kissing the President as he makes his way down the aisle to a standing ovation. Members of the Cabinet and Supreme Court are arrayed in their most ceremonial robes, uniforms, tuxedos, and elegant suits. The President evokes *pathos* by telling a story about a war hero, or a severely disabled person, or a teacher, or a foreign dignitary as a symbol of the good his administration has done; the aforementioned person stands, and is also greeted with a standing ovation. The cameras pan the audience to see who is applauding and (Oh, the embarrassment!) who is nodding off. There is almost nothing left of the informative report to Congress about the state of our nation.

✦ AN OPPORTUNITY FOR FURTHER RESEARCH AND WRITING

1. Try to find copies of the State of the Union speeches from the time period between the presidencies of Thomas Jefferson and Woodrow Wilson. Compare them to the transcripts of speeches given by presidents in the media age—from Johnson to Obama. Are there noteworthy differences in style, purpose, and evidence of audience awareness? What evidence supports your comparative analysis?

2. College students have used Monroe's Motivated Sequence to analyze advertising commercials. Many of their analyses are available online. Consider watching these videos. Then, relate Monroe's sequence to "Trouble in River City" from the musical, *The Music Man*, also available online, to see the extent to which Monroe's Motivated Sequence is used in this number.

WORKS CITED

Aristotle. *On Rhetoric: A Theory of Civic Discourse.* Trans. G. Kennedy. New York: Oxford UP, 1991.

Ehninger, Douglas, Bruce Gronbeck, Ray E. McKerrow, and Alan H. Monroe. *Principles and Types of Speech Communication.* Glenview, IL: Scott Foresman, 1986. 153.

CHAPTER 7

Ethical Communication

Reading about ethics is about as likely to improve one's behavior as reading about sports is to make one into an athlete.

—Mason Cooley

WITH THE NIGHTLY NEWS endlessly bringing us stories about corporate and political corruption, negative political campaigns, widespread cheating on standardized tests, and various other misdeeds of American life, some would argue that devoting a chapter to Ethics is much like rowing against the current. In spite of such cynicism, we remain optimists. We believe that students want to act ethically and want others to do so as well. We believe that if you know what defines ethical behavior, you will be guided by it, understand its benefits, and be a better communicator, a better audience member, and a better person. Quintilian and Cicero agreed that a true rhetor was, above all, a model of *vir bonum*, which we translate loosely as "a good person speaking and writing well."

This ethical guide is based on Aristotle, who notes three important aspects of credibility: *phronēsis* (practical wisdom), *aretē* (virtue), and *eunoia* (good will) (Aristotle II.1.8). The connections between each of these and the three Aristotelian proofs you read about earlier is evident.

Phronēsis is the realm of *logos*, or reasoning. Arguments must make sense to the audience. They must meet the test of practical wisdom—in other words, common sense. If the audience senses that your reasoning is out of touch with their knowledge and their experience, they will soon distrust your argument and, therefore, distrust you. If, for example, you argue that UFOs are a principal source of air pollution, people will think about the cars and factories that emit pollutants and the somewhat questionable theories about extraterrestrial travelers, and are likely to conclude that you are perhaps not the brightest bulb on the Christmas tree. It is generally good to remember the principle known as Occam's razor: The simplest explanation is usually the best. (An aside to rhetorical scholars: At this point, you may be screaming, "But you can't do this—rhetorical theory is more sophisticated than that!" Yes, we know. We hope that students will later take a course in Classical Rhetoric, the Rhetorical Tradition, or Rhetorical Theory and Criticism, where they will discover the intricacies and subtleties that make our field so rich. For now, though, as we have done throughout the book, we ourselves are following Occam in order to give our students a basic understanding of principles. If you would like to elaborate on any of our ideas, we encourage you to do so.)

Aretē is an important factor in *ethos*, or credibility. Virtue is what Cicero meant by a good person. Does this mean that only those who have never sinned can get an A in public speaking or composition? We certainly hope not! But what does virtue mean? Virtue is trying to do the right thing, to act consistently with your values. We also think, however, that the demand for virtue is not an open invitation for people to snoop into your personal life to determine whether you should be allowed to speak on public issues. Living a virtuous life means avoiding hypocrisy, saying one thing but doing another. If, for example, you are a member of the local committee to encourage recycling, but dump all your trash without sorting it, that is definitely not virtuous.

Eunoia, good will, is a fundamental principle in appealing to the values, beliefs, and emotions of your audience—*pathos*. The audience must believe you have their best interests at heart. You should not "toy" with their emotions; you should not urge them to take illegal or unwise actions; you should not distort the truth; you should not be dismissive of their points of view; you should not give false choices; you not should promise that which you cannot deliver. In other words, treat your audience as you would like to be treated.

Abiding by these standards is a tall order—one that we will all occasionally fail to meet. However, what counts is your *intention* toward the audience, so as a first step in preparing to write or speak you should examine your intentions. Ask yourself, "Why am I doing this?" and "Am I doing this for me or for them?" If, for example, you are giving a speech filled with big words and ornate phrases (grand style, see chapter 13) simply to show the audience how smart you are, the intention might be suspect.

It may build up your own ego, but will probably not help your audience understand your topic.

A common phenomenon is the rhetor with the hidden agenda. Hidden agendas are dishonest, and as a speaker or writer you have an obligation to avoid them. As an audience member, you need to have your radar on to detect these attempts at unethical persuasion. A hidden agenda means that there is some sort of ulterior motive or purpose that is intentionally obscured from the audience. For example, during the Civil Rights movement of the 1960s, some Southern legislators made a passionate argument for preserving the US Constitution's guarantee of States' Rights. Who could argue against the Constitution, right? However, what many of them were really arguing for—their hidden agenda—was preserving the system of segregation that had permeated the South since reconstruction.

A second question that must be answered as you think about your intentions is, "Is my purpose worthwhile?" Is your speech or essay going to be worthy of your effort and considerate of the time and effort of your audience? For example, suppose your topic is homelessness. Simply persuading people to smile a cheery smile at the next homeless person they see does nothing to solve the problem and is therefore wasted time and effort. Yet another example is persuading people to annoy businesses by sending spam emails; spamming is not worthwhile because it is not honorable.

The third question you should ask is, "Is this topic significant?" This is the "So what" question. Ask yourself, "Who cares, or should care, about this topic?" If you can't answer that, find another topic. Just because people are *interested* in something doesn't necessarily mean the topic is suitable, though. The key word is *care*—that is, will hearing about or reading about your topic make a difference in their lives? If not, why are you wasting their time?

SOME ETHICAL PROBLEMS

Even if you have made every effort to ensure the good will of your audience, pitfalls await the unwary. Once again, you must not only guard against using them yourself, but must be able to detect these ethical lapses in others.

These are primarily problems with the message; however, the first group of ethical problems has to do with the intention of the speaker or writer in forming the message. These include bias, narrow-mindedness, and knowingly giving false information. Bias occurs when only one side of an argument is presented without acknowledging the existence, to say nothing of the legitimacy, of other opinions. Over the past few years there has been a good deal of discussion about bias in the media. Some conservatives charge that the media has a liberal bias because, according to their figures, many journalists tend to vote Democratic. Others contend that talk radio, for example, has a conservative bias because many of the commentators support Republican candidates. Some news networks claim that their programming is "fair and balanced" when, in fact, it is often neither. We must cut through these claims and determine whether bias really does exist. The issue is not whom the journalists or broadcasters vote for or whether they *claim* to be balanced, but whether they accurately present multiple sides of an argument. If that is the case, then they should not be accused of bias unless they distort the facts or present one side as clearly wrong.

You may have heard or been told that we should always be objective; however, we think you need to know that absolute objectivity doesn't exist. None of us can ever be truly objective because we are not automatons or robots. Everything we say, write or do has an emotional or intellectual connection, even when we think otherwise. *Star Trek's* Mr. Spock, who was supposed to exemplify the Vulcan trait of objectivity, was angry, afraid, or loyal at times because he was half human, and those emotions occasionally led to less-than-completely-objective decisions. Journalists are supposed to be objective when writing their stories, but a subtle connotation of one word can indicate that they are more, or less, sympathetic or hostile to their subject. For example, suppose you were reading two articles about a particular political leader: one author describes him as "rotund," the other as "fat." You can easily figure out which author likes the man and which one does not, can't you? This is why we must be careful about connotations in choosing our words.

If your audience detects that you are biased despite your claim to be objective, they will doubt your motives and your words. The best thing to do, if you have a bias, is admit it up front by stating your position in the thesis (most of us call this taking a stance, position, or standpoint). You must also make sure you give your audience an honest summary of both sides of the argument. Here are two examples of thesis statements on the same topic in which opposite biases are stated:

1. Although homelessness is a serious problem in our cities, federal tax dollars should not be used to alleviate the problem.

2. Because homeless is a serious problem in our cities, federal tax dollars should be used to alleviate the problem.

The common ground in these two statements is the recognition that homelessness is a serious problem in our cities. The issue is whether or not federal tax dollars should be used to alleviate the problem. In writing or speaking on either thesis, you would need to acknowledge that homelessness is a problem—there is no argument about that, so you don't need to present two sides—then consider arguments on *both* sides of the issue of using federal money before persuading your audience to adopt your position.

Of course, just because you consider both sides of an argument, that doesn't mean you must *accept* both sides. We all function from a certain worldview, a product of our cultures, values, and beliefs that determines how we feel about particular issues. This accounts for the differences in political parties. In general, those who are strong capitalists and favor a weak central government tend to be Republicans, and those who favor a more important role for a central government tend to be Democrats. This forms the partisan argument over many issues such as tax cuts, social security, and health care. There is nothing wrong with partisanship—to be partisan simply means you are acting on your values and beliefs, and therefore see issues in a particular way. Partisanship only becomes a problem when it descends into factionalism—a blind adherence to a party or cause that no longer permits reasonable discourse. There is nothing new about this issue—if you are interested, you can read about it in one of the earliest United States documents, *The Federalist Papers*. In "Federalist 10," James Madison describes faction in a way that sounds eerily familiar today.

Many people use the terms *bias* and *prejudice* interchangeably, but there is a difference. Prejudice means "pre-judgment"—that is, deciding before all the facts are in. Colloquially we say, "My mind's made up; don't confuse me with the facts." Closely related to this is narrow-mindedness—not admitting the validity of other points of view. The term *prejudice* is frequently applied in situations where, for example, a potential jury member decides before the trial that the defendant is guilty or a member of a particular ethnic or racial community may have been unfairly accused of a crime. The question we must look at is whether such accusations are true examples of prejudice, or whether there is validity to the accusation. This issue occurs frequently in the news. For example, if a white policeman tickets a young African-American male driver for speeding through an upper-class, mostly white neighborhood, is it a case of "racial profiling"? Not necessarily. It depends on whether the driver was, in fact, speeding. If he was, then there are two other questions that need to be answered: First, would he have been ticketed for the same offense in a primarily African-American neighborhood? Second, would a white driver have been stopped for the same offense? If both questions can be answered affirmatively, then prejudice is not a factor. If, on the other hand, the answer to either or both questions is "No," then the ticketing officer may legitimately be accused of prejudice because he apparently pre-judged the driver's guilt based on race. The point is, we can't know whether someone is guilty of prejudice before all the facts are known. When we accuse someone without knowing all the evidence, we are ourselves guilty of prejudice. The dictum that a person is innocent until proven guilty is not only a staple of television crime shows—it is a fundamental human right in our democratic society.

In many respects, giving false information—lying—is an even more egregious ethical violation than bias or prejudice because, rather than simply making a decision without evidence, in this case the evidence is patently false. That is why bias and prejudice, though reprehensible, are not illegal, whereas, at least in courts of law, false testimony, known as perjury, is a punishable offense. If you don't know, for example, how many persons were killed by drunk drivers last year, then admit you don't know and tell your audience you will find out; don't simply invent a number that sounds about right. As soon as you do that, there will be someone from the National Transportation Safety Board, or Mothers Against Drunk Driving, or simply somebody who happens to have read an article about accident rates last week, who will pop up and say, "I don't know where you got that number, but your information is wrong." There you are, with egg on your face, caught red-handed in a lie. Your credibility on the topic is blown, you have committed an ethical violation, and your audience will not trust your information in the future.

Worse, if you have lied or knowingly used incorrect information about a person or organization, you can be sued for libel (written or recorded) or slander (spoken) if your intent was to harm the subject. You can even get in trouble for libeling food—just ask Oprah Winfrey! Several years ago, after interviewing someone about food safety and other issues in the cattle industry, she made an off-the-cuff remark that she would never eat beef again. The beef industry sued her for libel. The case dragged on for months—with the attendant hundreds of thousands of dollars in lawyers' fees—was appealed, and was finally dismissed nearly four years after the suit had first been filed, because there was no evidence of malicious intent.

In this respect, doing diligent research, fact-checking, and finding credible, supportive evidence are essential for the rhetor to providing an ethical context for making arguments.

THE ETHICAL RESPONSIBILITY OF THE AUDIENCE

In an age where everything can be put into the media without the traditional filters, the audience must filter out unethical communications and shine the light on them. Shining the light of truth is not easy. If you, as an audience member, don't put in time doing research and asking questions, you will be as guilty of ethical violations as the person delivering the message. The most important task is checking facts, and fortunately there are resources that can help. Perhaps the most reliable and effective of these is FactCheck.org, sponsored by the Annenberg School of Communication at the University of Pennsylvania. The least reliable and effective are websites that post information without adequate verification. Each of us must take the responsibility for separating fact from opinion, from rumor from blatantly false information, and for insisting on high standards of accuracy in media as well as in our own speeches and essays. When we do not do this, we fall prey to distortion and we enable politicians and others to get away with half-truths, and we encourage the perpetuation of slander and negative advertising.

Every election cycle, the public decries the use of negative advertising such as the "swift boat veterans" ads directed against John Kerry in 2004 that have become part of our discourse. So why do they persist? There have been a number of studies that reinforce the conclusions of a 1995 study of California elections: negative ads depress voter turnout, weaken confidence in the government, and manipulate voters, but we have to put up with them election after election because they work (Ansolabehere and Iyengar). Look at the low voter turnout in most elections. This low turnout is partly due to the depressing effect of negative ads. Until we refuse to be swayed by these ads, until we show that we will not allow them to dissuade us from voting, they will continue to assault our ears and our reason.

PLAGIARISM

All evidence to the contrary, we and your teachers continue to be optimistic that if students will only understand what plagiarism is and why it is wrong, they won't plagiarize. Therefore we will valiantly try once again to make a case for the ethical issues involved in plagiarism. First, plagiarism is cheating, pure and simple. Plagiarism is just as harmful to our ethics as manipulating corporate books to make stock more valuable than it actually is, thereby cheating hundreds of employees out of their entire life savings. Plagiarism is the same as using illegal substances to win a home run record that will be forever marred by an asterisk in the record books. In other words, plagiarism is a despicable act that takes advantage of others for self-aggrandizement. Plagiarism also ruins your *ethos*. If you plagiarize, you will feel smarmy, and your teachers are likely never to completely trust you again. You may even fail a course or be expelled from the university.

Etymology:
The word *plagiarism* is derived from the Latin "*plagiarius*," an abductor, and "*plagiare*," to steal.

Plagiarism is defined as:

• Intentionally or unintentionally representing the words, images, or ideas of another person as your own

• Failure to cite references properly

• Making up references

• Working with another person when individual work is required

• Submission of the same paper or speech in more than one course without the specific permission of each instructor

• Submitting (in whole or in part) a paper or speech written by another person or obtained from the internet.

The first area we want to address is what we might call *collaborative plagiarism*; that is, plagiarism that involves another individual or group. Questions of collaborative plagiarism, such as working together on an individual project, double-submitting a paper, or borrowing or purchasing someone else's work, arise frequently in coursework. There are some simple and logical rules you should follow in doing work for any of your classes. First, unless your instructor says you may work on something with a friend or in a group, you should always assume the instructor intends for you to work alone. To avoid being accused of a misdeed, don't cheat on tests, don't work together on homework, and don't "group write" a paper. However, in some cases, your instructor will permit you to work together but does not say so directly, or simply forgets to mention that. Therefore, and you will hear this phrase frequently in this section: "When in doubt, ask!" If you think it is possible that this should be a collaborative project, simply raise your hand and say something like, "May we work in pairs?" or "Is this a group project?"

Second, the area of multiple submissions: submitting a paper or giving a speech in more than one class without the specific and express permission of both instructors is considered plagiarism. This includes papers you wrote in high school! (You should also know that if, later on, you decide to submit something you've written for publication, you should not send your submission out to more than one publisher at a time unless you have permission from both publishers.)

The logical question many students ask is, "How can I be cheating if I did the work?" When you double-submit a paper, you are stealing from other students who put in the time and effort to create an original assignment and you are stealing from the instructor, who expects that you will apply the concepts taught in the class and demonstrate your learning, but most of all, you are cheating yourself because by simply re-submitting or double-submitting a paper, you have learned nothing new from the experience of researching and writing the paper or giving the speech. Again we say, when in doubt, ask! Some instructors have no problems with double submissions, but you need to know before you take the risk. Think you won't get caught? Strange things happen. Several years ago one of us was taking a graduate class that had both high school and community college teachers from the local area enrolled. (You can see where this is going, can't you?) For one class we were all supposed to bring in samples of good student writing. Yep! Two teachers brought in their samples—one from a high school AP class, the other from a community college first-year composition class. Sure enough— same paper, same student. Oh yes, and don't loan your papers to a friend, either; that has a way of coming back to bite you as well, especially if your friend forgets to take your name off the header on each page. (That really has happened—more than once!)

Third, you must not use something someone else wrote for you. Period. Do not help support the paper mills and speech mills—or your friends and neighbors—by paying them to do your work for you, and don't go to some obscure speech website and pull off an entire speech that you then read to the class as your own. The issue of paper mills—web merchants who write papers "to order"—is not solely a concern about your honesty and credibility; it is an issue of fairness and social justice. Those who can afford to pay large (or even small) sums of money to someone else to write a paper or speech are reaping the results of wealth—in a sense they are trying to buy success and respect. There are many students who cannot afford that kind of "help," and that is patently unfair to those students, including you, who work hard, study hard, and follow the rules.

The second category of plagiarism is *individual* plagiarism, that is, dishonest acts that you perform without the assistance of others:

- Intentionally or unintentionally representing the words, images, or ideas of another person as your own

- Failure to properly cite references

- Manufacturing references

First, we need to explore the difference between *intentional* and *unintentional* plagiarism. Intentional plagiarism means that you acted affirmatively to cheat. That is, you intended to copy someone else's work or intentionally did not give credit to an author. Unintentional plagiarism means that you acted out of ignorance or carelessness—not understanding what sources must be cited or accidentally omitting the source of a quotation, for example. This is what you must understand—plagiarism is plagiarism, intentional or not. You can be held responsible not only for what you know about proper citation and documentation, but also for what you *ought* to know. In other words, ignorance is no excuse. In the next chapter, "Evidence," we will explain how to incorporate, cite, and document evidence. For now, however, we wish to concentrate on *what* must be cited.

The rule of thumb for citing sources is that you must cite your source for any information that is not common knowledge. (In this context we use "information" broadly to include words, ideas, images, and other intellectual property.) Let us examine some examples of materials you might use in speeches and papers, or even in your personal work, that need sourcing.

- A quotation from a former president that you use at the beginning of your paper.

- A brief summary of a speech by Rachel Carson on the environment.

- A photo that you use in a newsletter.

- A graph showing temperature increases over the past century.

- An idea that you got from reading a book.

- The words of a song you quote in a speech.

- A favorite line of poetry.

- A fact that you got from a newspaper.

- Something a friend said.

We could go on and on; the point is that anything that you didn't know when you started the paper or speech, anything you know that the audience doesn't, or anything you know because you read or heard it somewhere should be documented. This may be easier to understand if we look at some examples of things that do *not* need to be documented:

- A song, poem, or picture that you created yourself (unless it has been published somewhere else).

- Common knowledge—for example, George Washington was our first President; 2+2=4; the earth revolves around the sun.

- Peer knowledge—for example, if you are speaking to an audience entirely composed of business majors, you probably don't have to cite a source for the definitions of macro- and microeconomics unless your definitions diverge from those that are commonly accepted in the field.

- Your own ideas (unless they've been published elsewhere).

A final word: Always err on the side of caution. Criticism for documenting texts unnecessarily, which is a simple thing to fix, is better than being penalized for failing to document, which is plagiarism. When in doubt, ask your instructor or a campus librarian.

The next instance of plagiarism is failure to cite properly, which will be discussed thoroughly in the chapter on evidence. The general rule is to give as much information in the in-text citations or footnotes as necessary for the reader to locate your exact source. In the bibliography, you should include author, title, date (periodical), volume and issue (journal), publisher (book), page number, and, in the case of web sources, URL and date of access. Most instructors won't accuse you of plagiarism if, for example, you have the date in the wrong place, or forget to put a period after the author's name, but they may lower the grade, or at least ask you to correct your errors. Improper citation includes using the wrong source or including an in-text citation but forgetting to include the work in your reference pages. The easiest way to avoid such errors is by inserting an abbreviated source reference as you draft the paper or outline, then immediately putting that source on your reference list. We recommend composing a reference page for all drafts—do not wait for the final paper to create your reference page. Many students have forgotten the origin of their quoted material because they put off creating a source page.

Finally, don't manufacture sources. If you want to argue that seeing the color blue causes leg cramps, but can't find any expert who agrees with you (for obvious reasons), don't make one up, because sure enough, your instructor is going to check that source to see what kind of quack scientist would say that. And don't put words in the mouths of legitimate sources, either. If you can't find someone who agrees with you, admit that. You can claim that your idea is so fresh, so original that no one has thought of it before. Or you can argue that your topic is an area that clearly needs more research. Or you can decide that you will study further to become an expert yourself, and then other people will quote *you*.

INTELLECTUAL AND CREATIVE PROPERTY RIGHTS: COPYRIGHTS, DOWNLOADING, AND PIRACY

The theft of intellectual and creative property is an increasingly important issue that affects many college students. In essence, this is plagiarism for profit. You are using the words, ideas, and images of others without compensating them for their creative work. Suppose you, in your ceramics studio, created a cookie jar. You want to sell your creation in order to pay for the rent on the studio, the cost of the kiln, the clay and glazes, and other overhead. Instead, someone steals the cookie jar. Now you are stuck with all the bills and no income. Worse, someone else may claim to have made your cookie jar, and if you try to reproduce it, you will be accused of theft. Is this fair? Certainly not! But this is exactly what happens when you copy or sell someone else's work. You are stealing their creative work and passing it off as your own, or sharing it with others, thus denying them the profit of their labor. (And yes, thinking and writing are labor—we can attest to that.)

Fortunately, there are some guidelines for fair use of copyrighted material. You are entitled to make a one-time copy of something for your own personal use, but you may not reproduce or share that with others unless you have specific written permission from the copyright owner. For example, you can record a TV show to watch later, but you cannot then take that recording to school and show it to your friends. You can listen to a song on the web once, but unless you have written permission (such as a registration agreement) you cannot download it to your iPod without paying a small fee. You can make a single copy of a journal article to use in your own research, but you cannot then make copies of the article for your whole class. Intellectual property law is a complex field, but if you will just remember this simple rule, you can avoid most problems: one time, one use, one person. For additional information on copyrights, we suggest you refer to *Q&A: Questions & Answers on Copyright for the Campus Community,* Association of American Publishers, 2006.

ETHICAL FALLACIES

As you will discover in chapter 8, thinking critically is an important element of arguing, and it is important that you think clearly as well as critically. Fallacious reasoning is an act that impairs your prose, arrests your thinking, and confuses and annoys your audience. When you use fallacious reasoning on purpose, however, it becomes more than annoying and confusing; it becomes a serious ethical violation. In fact, ethical fallacies are frequently classified as propaganda devices.

Labeling or Stereotyping. One of us used to admit to being politically liberal, but opponents have succeeded in making *liberal* a pejorative word. Now all opponents have to do is label a candidate *liberal* or *socialist* to imply a whole raft of political attitudes and beliefs that may or may not accurately reflect those of the candidate. As a defense, some liberals have taken to calling themselves *progressives* instead and have abandoned, or at least renamed, the traditional tenets of liberalism.

This little political spat may seem unimportant, but there is an important lesson here about labeling and stereotyping. When stereotypes are used—when certain ethnic groups are portrayed as lazy, or dirty, or dishonest, or a threat to national security—audiences are no longer allowed to see individual members of that group as equal human beings who have just as much right to their beliefs, opinions, and actions as you have to yours. The problem with labeling is that people who use labels have to create new ones, for the repeated use of a label tends to diminish its power, so the labels and the stereotypes get more extreme and vicious.

Straw Person. The straw person fallacy is usually used to distract the audience from an obvious flaw in your own argument by incorrectly attributing an argument, a "straw person," to your opponent, then refuting it. A frequent election issue is the Social Security system. Many candidates want to reform the system. However, it is not uncommon to hear a candidate claim that his opponent wants to "do away with" Social Security, then proceed to tell us why keeping Social Security is important. The candidate has falsely accused the opponent of holding a particular view, then he told us why that view is wrong. In fact, the opponent might not, and never did, hold that view.

Red Herring. This fallacy is similar to "straw person" but in this case, an irrelevant but inflammatory issue is used to divert attention from another issue. In the last few years, one of the hot button political issues has been immigration reform. In 2001, President Bush proposed a Guest Worker Program. This bill would have provided for a temporary worker program and allowed undocumented immigrants to become citizens after learning English, paying a significant fine, and then returning to their country of origin—a process that would take 8–12 years. Opponents falsely accused proponents of providing amnesty for law breakers; amnesty, in this case, was a red herring that distracted people from the actual provisions of the bill.

Bandwagon. This is a version of the *ad populum* fallacy. It is often expressed in the phrase, "Everybody's doing it." The implication is that if it's popular, it's good. This is a line of reasoning frequently used in advertising. Just because Smilealot is the most popular brand of toothpaste does not mean that you need to rush out and buy it. Similarly, in politics one often hears candidates argue that we should contribute money or vote for them not because we agree with their positions on the issues, but because they are leading in the polls.

Personal attacks. The old adage, "Sticks and stones can break my bones but words will never hurt me" is wrong, wrong, wrong. Words can hurt, and one of the most hurtful uses of words is attacking the person rather than the idea. We have become so desensitized to the harm that name-calling can do that we hear it now routinely on our airwaves and in our schools. In some cases, name-calling descends into hate speech. In other cases, a personal attack obscures the legitimate argument of opponents. A candidate's hairstyle tells the audience nothing about where the candidate stands on the issues. A student's clothing tells us nothing about his or her intellect.

Personal attacks can even be dangerous. Though school violence statistics show that campus-based youth violence has gone down, recent school shooting incidents have been attributed in part to the fact that the shooters were tired of being personally attacked—"bullied"—by other students. Children who are called names such as "stupid" or "retard" begin to believe that they are, in fact, less capable of succeeding. Recent news stories have described terrible stories about young people who took their own lives because they had been bullied. These personal attacks are examples of verbal abuse, which is an increasingly serious problem in our society—just look at the incidences of battered women, road rage, and hate crimes, and you will understand why personal attacks are harmful.

Though there are any number of programs related to preventing bullying at school, the one way we know how to stop this problem is for adults to stop using these kinds of attacks and to stop others from using them. It is up to every one of us to stand up against those who persist in personally attacking others. When attacks lead to violence, injury, and even death, it is no longer an issue of free speech.

♦ OPPORTUNITIES FOR CRITICAL THINKING

In this chapter, we discuss the terms prejudice and lying. However, how does the notion of bias relate itself to these ideas? What is bias? In what sense is bias a positive attribute? Negative? Give some examples.

WORKS CITED

Ansolabehere, Stephen and Shanto Iyengar. *Going Negative: How Political Advertisements Shrink and Polarize the Electorate*. New York: Free Press, 1995.

Cooley, Mason. *City Aphorisms*, Fifth Selection. New York: 1988.

The Federalist Papers. Ed. Clinton Rossiter. New York: Mentor (New American Library), 1961.

Q&A: Questions & Answers on Copyright for the Campus Community. New York: Association of American Publishers, 2006.

SECTION THREE

Discovering and Developing Your Ideas

CHAPTER 8

The Art of Argumentation

Histories make men wise; poets, witty; the mathematics, subtle; natural philosophy, deep; moral, grave; logic and rhetoric, able to contend.
— Sir Francis Bacon

S IR FRANCIS BACON'S argument that a liberal arts education can mold young minds in responsible, well-rounded ways ends emphatically with a comment on rhetoric. Rhetoric, he argues, gives people—regardless of their circumstances—the ability to defend themselves. A rhetorical education is one in which people can turn their persuasive instincts into a reliable skill that will make them trusted and credible advocates. Notice that Bacon did not write that knowledge of "persuasion" allows us to contend. Rather, he wrote "logic and rhetoric," for he understood that the discipline of rhetoric is quite different than knowing how to be persuasive. So what's the difference?

PERSUASION AND RHETORIC

Most of us know how to be persuasive. Without formal training, we talk, plead and argue about the things that are important to us. In our day-to-day lives, we persuade our friends about what to do, where to go, what to eat, or what movies to see, and even when we are not active agents in this process, we are the recipients of persuasion. We intuitively understand that our "ordinary speech" is involved with communicative action—that our speech initiates action among our peers, friends, and family. We call this natural instinct or knack to argue *persuasion*.

Because our relationships with people are often formed through the use of language, we understand—without much formal training—how reason (and the tools of reason) help shape our relationships. Most of us make honest attempts to be reasonable and fair when we converse within our different social groups. Within these social networks, we communicate in different ways. Whether using small talk, gossip, argument, or passing and receiving information, we dip into our rhetorical registers to be credible when we communicate because irrational statements and fallacious reasoning tend to get dismissed fairly quickly in most group situations.

Although the term *persuasion* helps define our inherent or natural instincts to argue, the term *rhetoric* means something more. Unfortunately, general knowledge of rhetoric is miniscule, and the popular use of rhetoric often leads people to misunderstand this term. Rhetoric is a system of instruments and tools that help people create arguments and communicate their arguments to an audience. Like all disciplines, rhetoric has terminology and multiple theories relating argument to varying social contexts and historical situations. Since antiquity, rhetoric has been a varied discipline that gives us processes of inquiry and methods for creative self-expression. Studying and understanding this system can help students gain a better understanding of arguing in cogent, coherent ways.

WHAT IS AN ARGUMENT?

When most people hear the word "argument" they immediately think of verbal sparring, but argumentation (the act of arguing) does not imply hostility. Rather, argumentation, in the rhetorical sense, is a way of discovering probability by weighing two or more sides of a question to determine which claim is more valid, or at least which is more in agreement with common beliefs and values. What, then, is an argument? Traditionally speaking, an argument is a claim (or a chain of claims) supported by evidence and reasoning, with which you want someone to agree.

Let us examine each of the parts:

An argument is a claim . . .

To make an argument, you have to state a position, a claim, a thesis. The thesis limits the subject matter and focuses the argument. For example: "Friday the Thirteenth is unlucky." In this claim, the audience understands that you will be arguing about Friday the Thirteenth, about luck, and superstition. You will not be arguing about the oddities of the Gregorian calendar or how your Great Aunt Matilda died.

... supported by evidence and reasoning...

To make an argument, you must present evidence and/or reasoning; in other words, you have to prove your point. An argument without evidence is simply an opinion or assertion by an individual, and its entire credibility depends on the expertise of the person offering the opinion. It is not enough to say, "You're wrong, I'm right, and that's that," for such schoolyard antics won't always pass muster in academic contexts.

... with which you want someone to agree.

Arguments are both intentional and persuasive. There's no point in making an argument if you don't care whether someone agrees with you. For example, we could argue that our offices are decorated nicely. The only persons we need to satisfy are ourselves, so there is no need to pile up evidence from interior designers to convince us that we like our offices. On the other hand, if we argued that our offices were unsafe and therefore needed remodeling or repairing, we would have to convince the administration to take action, so we would need evidence and reasoning to support our argument.

The purpose of having rational discussions is to decide what action to take or what to believe—whether we are evaluating someone else's or our own beliefs. Applying logic—a process by which we "think" rationally—allows us to distinguish valid from invalid claims and to distinguish good from faulty proposals. By this process, then, logic is a social norm because we must agree on the value of this process.

Now that we have defined arguments and examined briefly why we use them, we can proceed to learning how to construct them. But first, a caveat: there are dozens, perhaps hundreds, of textbooks and even several scholarly journals devoted entirely to argumentation, each of which takes a slightly different approach. In this brief chapter, we cannot possibly begin to cover everything about the complexities of argument. Our goal is to give you enough information to help you form valid arguments and use them in your papers and speeches. If the subject interests you, as it does us, we recommend that you take an additional course in argumentation. Most colleges and universities offer these courses; some deal with theory, some with application, and some with analysis, but all are invaluable for increasing your ability to present effective arguments, a particularly important skill if you're thinking about a career in politics or law.

ARISTOTELIAN (CLASSICAL, FORMAL) LOGIC

You may recall from our discussion of the history of rhetoric that the sophists, Plato, and Aristotle held three different views regarding the nature of truth, which—if the goal of argument is to discover the truth—is a rather important distinction. While Plato, the idealist, held that absolute truth was revealed (to philosophers, of course) and the sophists—the skeptics or relativists—believed that there was no such thing as absolute truth, Aristotle, whom we can consider to be an empiricist, held that truth was a matter of determining probability through weighing the validity of various arguments. It follows then that there must be a method of evaluating those arguments and judging which of the two or more arguments is the most probable.

The Aristotelian method of argument is based on the *syllogism*, a logical construct that has three parts: a major premise (a statement of the general principle); a minor premise (a statement of the specific case); and the conclusion (the logical product of the major and minor premise). This movement from the general to the specific is called deductive reasoning. Here is a classical example of the syllogism:

> Major premise: All men are mortal.
> Minor premise: Socrates is a man.
> Conclusion: Socrates is mortal.

This sequence relies on the arguer to relate the premises together in order to form a clear conclusion, a conclusion that is irrefutable.

Alternatively, the syllogism is expressed by the following formula:

> All A are B.
> C is an A.
> Therefore, C is a B.

This sequence is called a categorical syllogism or categorical proposition. There are a multitude of variations on this, each of which has a name. You will study all the variations if you take a course in formal logic. Here are two variations. The hypothetical syllogism:

> If A exists, then B exists.
> A exists.
> Therefore, B exists.

The disjunctive syllogism:

> Either A or B exists.
> A exists.
> Therefore, B cannot exist.

You will notice that each of these begins with premises and ends with a conclusion.

One way to attack someone's logic is to examine the premises and conclusions. If you find fault in either of the premises, you can easily refute the argument. If you find fault with the conclusion, you can, again, easily refute the argument. For example, in the categorical syllogism, notice what happens if the order of items in the minor premise is changed.

> Correct: All dogs eat meat.
>   Blazer is a dog.
>   Therefore, Blazer eats meat.
>
> Faulty: All dogs eat meat.
>   Blazer eats meat.
>   Therefore, Blazer is a dog.

What's the problem here? Clearly, since other animals also eat meat, Blazer could just as easily be a cat or a hyena. This logical error is called the *undistributed middle.*

Another problem is the faulty major premise. Suppose we said, "All dogs are vegetarians." That would not be true, so the entire syllogism would be faulty. Or perhaps, "All dogs like Smiley brand dog food." We don't know if that's true or not; if there is even one dog that doesn't like Smiley, the entire premise is false.

You will recall that in chapter 5, we discussed the difference between friendly and hostile audiences. Deductive reasoning can be used when addressing a friendly audience because they will agree with the general principle, or major premise, you are arguing for and don't therefore need much convincing. However, a hostile or adversarial audience will not necessarily accept the major premise—even if you sincerely believe it to be true. For example, suppose you are arguing that a particular political candidate is unethical using the following syllogism:

> All politicians are unethical.
> Candidate X is a politician.
> Therefore, candidate X is unethical.

You can see the problem. If your audience does not agree that *all* politicians are unethical (and we hope that they don't), then they have no reason to be persuaded by your argument. Such statements of value are always debatable; however, there are statements of fact which can be refuted as well.

> All birds have feathers.
> Penguins are birds.
> Penguins have feathers.

The validity of the statement rests on the major premise. Do all birds have feathers? Even penguins? Yes. All birds do. How about this syllogism:

> All birds can fly.
> A penguin is a bird.
> Therefore, a penguin can fly.

Can all birds fly? No. You can easily attack this syllogism because the facts contradict the major premise. Not only cannot penguins fly, but ostriches, emus, and cassowaries can't fly either.

There is little doubt that syllogisms are useful in our quest to figure out what is valid and invalid. But most of us rarely employ the syllogism when we argue. Imagine speaking in syllogisms all day long. The social consequences would be severe: impatient co-workers and lost friendships.

Alternatively and more interestingly, one of the most important facets of Aristotelian argument is the enthymeme. George Kennedy translates *enthymeme* is as "something in the mind" (Aristotle 34). That is, something (an assumption, an expectation, or such) that you understand without being told. Another more technical definition is "a truncated [cut off] syllogism"—a syllogism in which one of the premises is missing.

The enthymeme is an argument that assumes the truth of a premise that is often concealed or unstated. The reason this assumption often remains hidden is because of the commonly accepted nature of the assumption. For Aristotle, the enthymeme is the cornerstone of deductive logic because we use enthymemes more in our daily lives than we use syllogisms. For instance, enthymematic arguments are often based on common assumptions. Here's a frequently heard expression on campus:

> Gloria failed her audition because she didn't rehearse.

In order to discover what the hidden assumption is, ask yourself this question: what does a person have to believe in order to make this statement? The answer is simple. You must believe that practicing and rehearsing can improve the chances of success, right? However, this assumption will rarely be stated because it is commonly assumed to be true. Consequently, such an assumption will stay concealed from the argument. Here is another common expression around campus:

> Sparky failed his exams because he didn't study.

To make this statement, you have to believe that studying can improve your chances of success. This assumption, in addition to the relationship between rehearsing and auditioning, seems to make sense.

Why is the enthymeme useful? Because we have to make decisions based on probability. Even though the enthymeme is not absolute, this form of deduction works because the enthymeme relies on what we generally believe to be true (the hidden assumption). We employ enthymemes regularly because using syllogisms all of the time would be, to some extent, too ponderous.

◆ EXERCISES

Given the statements below, deduce the hidden or unstated assumption that must exist in order for someone to make these arguments. Read the first sentence to understand how to "puzzle out" the hidden assumption.

1. "My university refuses to provide toilet seat covers. Obviously, the administration doesn't care much for our health."

2. A student's comment about stealing from the cafeteria: "I don't feel like I'm doing anything wrong. It's our school cafeteria, and we pay a lot of money to go to this university, so we deserve something for free."

3. "I am a faithful husband, a great father, and an experienced civil servant. Come November, I deserve your vote."

SYLOGISMS, ENTHYMEMES AND THESIS STATEMENTS

An enthymeme asks the audience to supplement the premises with information of their own. Remember the "Socrates" syllogism? Is it necessary to tell the audience that Socrates is a man? Certainly it would not be necessary to tell that to anyone who knew him—it would be obvious. You could also assume that you audience knows that all men are mortal. Therefore, why state the obvious? You could simply say, "Socrates is mortal."

As we learned in chapter 5, the advantage is that not only is your argument less wordy, but more importantly, the enthymeme draws the audience into the argument. Now they are participants, not merely bystanders. Because audiences are supplying part of the reasoning (either consciously or subconsciously), they are invested in the argument, a circumstance that makes them more likely to be persuaded.

The enthymeme in writing and speaking is most commonly expressed as a thesis.

Here is a syllogism you might use:

> *Major premise:* All air pollution is harmful.
> *Minor premise:* Burning fossil fuels increases air pollution.
> *Conclusion:* Burning fossil fuels is harmful.

You might then write a thesis statement:

> Burning fossil fuels is harmful because it increases air pollution and air pollution is harmful.

However, you don't really need that last clause, do you? The thesis will be stronger if you omit it and say:

> Burning fossil fuels is harmful because it increases air pollution.

Congratulations! You have created an *enthymematic* thesis.

This version of your thesis statement is not very elegantly phrased, and it's not sufficiently complex, but you can tinker with it until it sounds better.

This embryonic stage is the starting point for crafting a good argument. Remember, though, you need to be sure your audience has the information you want to supply; they must have it "in the mind" and they must think of it in a way that is consistent with your argument. If, for some unimaginable reason, your readers think air pollution is not harmful, your argument is in jeopardy because they will not be able to supply the missing premise.

Notice, in the syllogism above, we can omit the major premise or the conclusion and it would still be a reasonable argument. However, if you omit the minor premise you end up with a case of circular reasoning:

> Burning fossil fuels is harmful because air pollution is harmful.

And if we omit both the major and minor premises, all we are left with is an opinion:

> Burning fossil fuels is harmful.

As interesting and useful as the classical argument using the syllogism is, it has one major shortcoming—it is not very flexible. Either a claim is probably true or it is not. Nevertheless this was the only system of argument that was used from the time of Aristotle until the late 1950s—nearly twenty-five centuries. But in 1958, two separate books appeared that rewrote rhetoric and logic for the modern age. The first was *The New Rhetoric* by Chaim Perelman with Mme. Lucie Olbrechts–Tyteca; it reinterpreted Aristotelian rhetoric for the twentieth century. The second was a slim volume by philosopher Stephen Toulmin that proposed a new system of logic that would allow for flexibility and uncertainty.

INFORMAL LOGIC (THE TOULMIN MODEL)

While Aristotelian argument is based on a deductive (general to specific) pattern of reasoning, the Toulmin model is based on induction—specific to general. In this model, you collect specific instances—called *data* or *grounds*—then draw a *claim* based on that data. The argument is supported by reasoning, or *warrant*. In addition, Toulmin allows for *qualifiers* on the claim, *rebuttal*, and *backing* for the warrant. On the following page you'll find a model of the Toulmin argument:

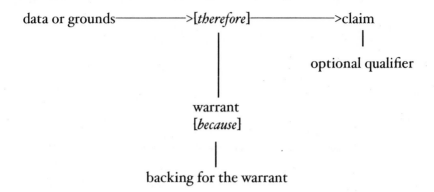

To see how this rather unwieldy model actually works, let us first review the syllogism we looked at above:

Major premise: All air pollution is harmful.
Minor premise: Burning fossil fuels increases air pollution.
Conclusion: Burning fossil fuels is harmful.

In the Toulmin system it might look like this:

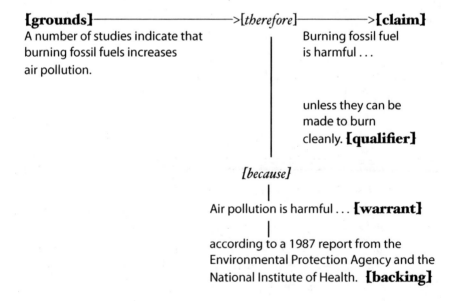

Look at all the additional information you have to use here when you form your working thesis. Now you can construct a more clear, more elaborate, and more informative thesis:

> Because a number of studies indicate that burning fossil fuels increases air pollution, we can conclude that fossil fuels are harmful unless they can be made to burn cleanly.

You will notice that the warrant is missing. In informal logic, we say that the warrant is *implied;* this is the equivalent of the classical enthymeme. The other feature of this example is that some people might indeed question the validity of the warrant; therefore we have offered some backing for the warrant. Nevertheless, one still might argue with the recency or validity of the particular study, or with the conclusions we draw from it. The warrant "Air pollution is harmful" could in itself be another claim, which we could then set about to prove. If we were to do that, we would have an *argument chain* in which the warrant of one argument becomes the claim of the next argument.

This is precisely what you do when you write a paper or give a speech. You have the main claim, or thesis, which is followed by a series of subclaims. You set about to prove each subclaim, and when all the subclaims are proved, the totality of those specifics then prove your main claim.

The other feature of the Toulmin model is that it allows for rebuttal. We need to define two terms here: refutation and rebuttal. *Refutation* means challenging the claims, evidence, or warrant of your opponent. *Rebuttal* means rebuilding your own arguments in response to those challenges. If, in the above example, your opponent challenges your statistics or makes a counter-argument in response to one of your arguments, that is refutation. If, after that challenge, you provide additional evidence showing your evidence is valid, or if you show the counter-argument to be unreasonable, that is rebuttal.

ROGERIAN ARGUMENT: RESOLVING CONFLICT

The humanist and psychotherapist Carl Rogers argued for an alternative approach to arguing. He conceded that even the most fair-minded audiences are emotionally invested in their beliefs. Consequently, if a person were confronted with views that were opposed to her own, this person would spend the majority of her intellectual energy evaluating, judging and even rebutting those statements rather than trying to understand them. As a result, arguments tend to end in an impasse or stalemate rather than be resolved.

Rogers's view of argument is one based on enticement rather than deduction, of developing partnerships by improving relations between disputants. In Rogerian rhetoric, the rhetor's goal is to bring about cumulative change (rather than immediate persuasion) by developing an empathic understanding of his audience's arguments, beliefs, assumptions, and fears. The Rogerian model accounts for the "other side's" arguments as integral to the one you are advancing.

In this respect, if you are developing a pro/con paper, you must research and present the "other side's" argument in a substantive, substantial and fair way as a basis for presenting your own views, for summarizing, paraphrasing and quoting from your opponent's arguments allows the audience to see how much you understand the opposing position. In this process, finding common values or common ground between the sides and using concessions are essential to developing your argument.

For Rogers, the key to creating partners out of disputants was based on understanding mutual goal-sharing. This process required negotiation, and using negotiation as a context for advocacy is often how conflict resolution specialists work to bring disputants together. There are separate text books and entire classes dedicated to teaching conflict resolution ideas and techniques.

For more information on how to develop and arrange the Rogerian argument, please see the section on Rogerian Argument in chapter 10 and the student paper in the appendix.

INVITATIONAL ARGUMENT/CONSENSUS MAKING

In the 1960s, the feminist movement became prominent and eventually struggled with issues of how to argue in a less competitive manner—a manner that many feminists viewed as patriarchal. Some, of course, suggested that women should learn to "argue like men;" others thought women shouldn't speak out in the public sphere at all. In 1995, Sonja Foss and Cindy Griffin proposed a new form of persuasion that they titled *invitational rhetoric*. In their scheme, argument is "grounded in the feminist principles of equality, immanent value, and self-determination" (2). The chief goal of argument is not winning, but consensus-building and understanding, both of self and of others.

STASIS

No matter which style of argument you choose, the first decision you'll need to make is exactly what you are arguing about. That is, you must decide where the disagreement between two sides or points of view lies. The point at which an argument can occur is called *stasis*.

For example, if you are writing about education, there are certain areas that we can all agree on; these areas are called the common ground—matters not in dispute. We can agree that education is important. We can agree that not all children can read and write as well as they should. We can agree, because we can see the numbers, that average test scores for certain groups are lower than for others. However, there are several points on which we might not agree: teachers need merit-based pay; schools should run year-round, and the government should pay tuition for private schools. If we choose to argue one of these points, we can arrive at stasis by identifying the opposing positions and stating them as opposites. The way to start is with a question arising from the disagreement: Should teachers be paid according to merit? By forming our answers—yes, merit pay is a good idea; no, merit pay is a bad idea—we can identify the main issue and we have reached stasis—the starting point of the argument. If we say "Teachers should get merit pay" and you say "Teachers are overpaid" we have not reached stasis—there is no argument because we're talking about two different issues.

CATEGORIES OF ARGUMENTS

From Aristotle's idea that there are three categories of argument—forensic, epideictic, and deliberative—comes our modern classification of arguments of *fact*, *value*, and *policy*.

Arguments of *fact* declare that something was, is, or will be true. That is, there are arguments of past fact, present fact, and future fact. We suspect you are wondering, at this point, how one argues about a "fact," and that's a good point, but there are certain facts that are, indeed, arguable. Look at these examples:

Past fact:　　Slavery was the main cause of the Civil War.
　　　　　　　　(Some historians argue that slavery had very little to do with causing the war; that instead, the causes were economic and political.)

Present fact: The present economy is strong.
(Some economists argue that in spite of record growth, the economy is verging on a recession or worse.)

Future fact: The Republicans will win the election.
(The Democrats no doubt have a different argument here. There's no way to prove it with certainty until the election is actually held.)

Note that arguments of past fact contain a past tense verb, often a form of *be*; arguments of present fact contain a present tense verb, often *is*; and future fact arguments nearly always contain a future tense verb formed with *will*.

Arguments of *value* debate the relative value of two ideas or policies or things. They must contain an *evaluative term*. For example:

The pen is *mightier* than the sword.

It is *better* to raise taxes then to cut Social Security.

Our schools are *more important* than our prisons.

Arguments of *policy* are deliberative, and they always contain (or imply) the verb *should*. In order to construct a policy argument, you must identify a problem, show that the problem is significant, and propose a solution (and who should take the action) that will actually solve the problem. Example:

Because medical expenses are very expensive for individual workers to afford, employers *should* help cover the cost of paying for health care.

OTHER TYPES OF ARGUMENTS

Arguments of Definition: An argument of definition defines a term about which there is some controversy—a *contested* term. If you can simply look up a word in the dictionary—for example, *magazine*—and agree on the definition, there is no need for an argument. However, if the term means different things to different audiences, then sometimes before even beginning a longer argument, you must argue for your definition of the term. For example, during the Iraq War there was much debate about whether or not the United States can achieve "victory." But what is the meaning of *victory?* Some say victory means eliminating the terrorists;

others say it means setting up a stable, democratic government. Unless the disagreement over the definition of "victory" can be resolved, it is not possible to argue the basic question of whether it can be achieved.

Cause/Effect Arguments: In this argument, you argue that X is a cause, or that Y is an effect, of a particular action, policy, or phenomenon. For example, you might argue that burning fossil fuels causes global warming and/or that the effect of global warming is the melting of the polar ice caps. Be careful here: it is seldom the case that any event has just a single cause, or that it is the only cause of an effect. You may want to limit your statement with phrases such as "one of the causes/effects" or "a major cause/effect," because if you simply state X is *the* cause or Y is *the* effect, you have committed to proving that there are no other possible causes or effects.

THE LAST WORD

Argument is a way of seeking probable truth, not a means for shattering an opponent. It is the soundness of your argument—not the loudness of your voice—that will persuade others. Many people see argument as a way to make distinctions and mark differences, to recognize and acknowledge that Republicans stand over there and Democrats stand over here. No doubt, this frame of reference is a powerful means of understanding people and their ideas. Just as important, however, is the idea that argument is about inclusion. That people—from all walks of life—who live and work together should share in the greater responsibility of voicing their arguments in the debates that shape all of our lives.

We believe that people who are persuasive can achieve great personal success. But we also believe that people who study, understand, and practice rhetoric often have a distinct advantage in the marketplace of ideas, for within this public sphere is a fascinating kinetic competition of energy, intellect, wealth, and reason. And, as Sir Francis Bacon remarked, knowledge of rhetoric allows the student of rhetoric to compete in this great sphere against those who have other distinct cultural advantages. But always, as Cicero noted, remember your ethos: always treat opposing ideas gently, always treat opponents with respect, and honor the principle of *vir bonum dicendum partibus*.

✦ IDEAS FOR FURTHER EXPLORATION

1. Watch a tape of a candidates' debate from one of the recent elections. Is it really a debate? Do the candidates reach stasis? What can you identify as common ground? What kinds of arguments do the candidates make?

2. Arguments of Definition: What is the definition of life? No doubt, the stasis of the abortion debate relies on defining this important term. Can you think of other arguments in which different or opposing sides argue not just about cause and effect arguments but make arguments about definitions?

WORKS CITED

Aristotle. *On Rhetoric: A Theory of Civic Discourse.* 2nd ed. Trans. George A. Kennedy. New York: Oxford UP, 2007.

Foss, Sonja K. and Cindy L. Griffin. "Beyond Persuasion: A Proposal for an Invitational Rhetoric." *Communication Monographs* 62 (March 1995): 2-18.

Perelman, Chaim and Lucie Olbrechts-Tyteca. *The New Rhetoric: A Treatise on Argumentation.* Trans. John Wilkinson and Purcell Weaver. Notre Dame, IN: U of Notre Dame P, 1969.

Rieke, Richard D. and Malcom O. Sillers. *Argumentation and Critical Decision Making.* 5th ed. New York: Longman.

Rogers, Carl R. *On Becoming a Person.* Boston: Houghton Mifflin, 1961.

Toulmin, Stephen. *The Uses of Argument.* Cambridge: Cambridge UP, 1958.

Evidence

Facts speak louder than eloquence.
—Chinese proverb

If you have the facts on your side, pound the facts. If you have the law on your side, pound the law. If you have neither on your side, pound the table.

—old legal aphorism, source unknown

IMAGINE TRYING to put up a tent without tent poles. When you set up a tent, you must have support or the tent will just lie on the ground in a muddle of limp canvas. Likewise, when you make an assertion or claim, the assertion remains an opinion until it is supported by proof. Earlier in this text we introduced Aristotle's concept of dividing proof into two categories: *artistic* and *inartistic*. The artistic proofs—*logos, ethos, and pathos*—are those created by the rhetor. Inartistic proof, on the other hand, exists independently of the rhetor; although the rhetor may show skill in using inartistic proof, it is not created by him or her. Just as there are three kinds of artistic proof, there are three categories of inartistic proofs: "facts," examples, and testimony.

Some scholars would argue with our category labeled "facts," but we are using the term in the sense that even facts can be in dispute and open to interpretation. In this category we place observations and statistics. By observation, we mean those things that can be observed or measured, for example, the weather, the temperature of water, the presence or absence of an object or sound, or those things which have been experienced. We know not to touch a hot stove with a bare hand because when we did that before, we got burned. In academic argument, observation is frequently used in scientific papers; you have undoubtedly written lab reports in biology, chemistry, or physics that record your observations of physical phenomena.

Observation is also the instrument of qualitative research. A typical psychology research project, for example, might involve observing and recording the interactions among a group of children. Recording the practices of a group or culture is a form of qualitative research called ethnography, a very common form of investigation in communication and the social sciences. These studies are often very interesting to read and can be quite revealing. We should note, however, that one observer may differ from another in her observations and especially in the interpretation of those observations.

The realm of statistics, on the other hand, is known as quantitative research. Statistics condense observations to numbers. They are so common we sometimes fail to see them as research, but behind every poll, graph, survey, or economic indicator we see, someone has had to do a great deal of research on both the method and the data itself. Unless the underlying method and data are valid and made known to the reader, the statistics themselves may be highly misleading.

Validity: The ability to generalize from a study. For example, if watering one plant in your garden produces faster growth, does that mean that if you water all your plants, they will all grow faster?

Reliability: The ability to repeat an experiment under all the same conditions and get the same results. If you water a plant and it grows, the plant should grow some more the next time you water it (if all other conditions are the same).

As an example, suppose you read two election polls: one has a certain candidate ahead with 43% of the vote; the other has the same candidate second with 36%. What explains the difference? There are many possibilities. One poll might have been taken among all eligible voters, the other among only those who actually were likely to vote. The survey questions might have been asked differently in each poll. One poll might have had a larger or more demographically representative number of respondents. The point is that statistics are not facts in the way we normally think of them; they, too, are subject to bias and interpretation. That's why polls should always have a note somewhere about the margin of error.

Another example of statistical proof is the array of economic reports that the government publishes every month that show the growth in our gross national product (GNP), unemployment, consumer confidence, and trade deficit. Here again, the figures are open to interpretation and error. Before we can rely on statistics, we need to assess their validity and reliability. There are statistical measures that perform this function, but they require some training to understand. That is why many colleges encourage or often require their students to take a course in statistics even if they are not majoring in fields such as business, economics, or the social sciences that rely heavily on statistical information.

Examples, and their longer version, illustrations, point to real-life or hypothetical situations that clarify or illuminate a point or that serves as an analog. The distinction between example and illustration is somewhat fuzzy, but we like to think of the difference in this way: An illustration spells out the situation in some detail—probably more detail than is necessary or desirable in a short speech or paper. On the other hand, an example points to the longer illustration. The example must, however, be something that is known to the audience or else they won't get the point. Throughout this text you have no doubt noticed many instances of the use of illustrations and examples; studying how several of them function will help you understand how important examples can be to making your argument clear and meaningful.

We need to pay special attention to the hypothetical—an imagined example or illustration. These can be especially handy when you wish to avoid identifying a particular person or situation. Hypotheticals can often be quite useful, but they have several danger points.

First, a hypothetical should not be too far-fetched; the example must have some basis in reality. You shouldn't say, for example, "Suppose for a moment that you have been abducted in a UFO." An audience that could really relate to that is hard to imagine. Nor should the hypothetical be contrary to fact: "Suppose President Gore (or President Kerry or President Dukakis) were a Republican." That fails the test on two counts: first, none of those men is president and none are Republicans. A hypothetical based on future predictions should not be used as evidence, either; there are just too many unknowns. The unknowns are the reason that political candidates will often, rightly in our opinion, refuse to respond to questions based on hypothetical examples or situations. You should not construct a hypothetical merely to cover up a lack of more reliable evidence. Finally, when you do use a hypothetical, you must always identify it as such; neglecting to do so is an ethical breach.

Testimony is the category of evidence that is used most often in academic writing, but it is useful in other areas as well. There are three kinds of testimony: *eyewitness, reluctant*, and *expert*. Eyewitness testimony, based on observation, is most useful in reconstructing the details of what happened in a situation—but unfortunately eyewitnesses are often unreliable. You might describe to your audience what you observed when a rock fell on the highway. However, although that indeed describes the event—where and when the rock fell, whether or not it damaged any property—there are many details that you could not have seen. What caused the rock to fall? How fast was it going? Later you may discover that you don't even remember the color of the rock. In ancient times, eyewitness testimony was considered the least reliable form of evidence; since then, we have relied more and more on eyewitness testimony, sometimes with devastating results. The recent work of the Innocence Project has found a number of prisoners on death row who were convicted on eyewitness testimony and later exonerated by other evidence.

Many people believe that reluctant testimony is the most valuable and most convincing evidence because the witnesses are essentially giving testimony against their self-interest. If someone is accused of a crime, who is the jury most likely to believe, a casual acquaintance who says he is innocent, or his mother, who says he is guilty? The same is true for a scientist who says, "I don't care how much other research has been done that disproves my theory; I know I'm right," or the one who says, "I held this theory for years, but now I see where I was mistaken." Are you more likely to listen to an anti-war argument from a pacifist or a general who formerly supported the war?

By far the kind of evidence that you will use most during your academic career is expert testimony. When you do library research this is primarily what you are looking for, so let's spend a little time discussing this very important idea. Expert testimony means that you are using the words or ideas of someone who is an expert in the field about which you are writing or speaking—a molecular biologist writing about DNA, a literary scholar specializing in the English Renaissance writing about Shakespeare, or a clinical psychologist speaking about personality disorders. There are several steps you should take to ensure that your testamentary evidence is valid and reliable.

1. Try to use primary sources whenever possible. First, though, you need to understand the difference between primary and secondary sources. Primary sources are the words as written or spoken by the actual author, for example, Martin Luther King, Jr.'s *Letter from a Birmingham Jail*. Secondary sources are those which repeat, reprint, or republish the author's words. The account of the *Letter* in a newspaper would be a secondary source. You can see that if you're quoting King, using his own words would be best, not his words as reprinted elsewhere, because the reporter, the printer or the editor might have made an error, or put in some sort of commentary that wasn't in the original. If you're using material from an article that quotes someone else's article, see if you can find that original article by checking the bibliography.

2. Make sure the person you're quoting really is an expert in the particular subject. First, check his or her credentials. Academic articles generally have that information either at the beginning or end of the articles, or in the back or front of the journal. If the article is in a peer-reviewed journal, you can be fairly sure the author knows what he or she is talking about. However, you can't be sure of that if the source is from a periodical, a website, or a newspaper, so you may have to consult a source such as Google to discover what else this author has written and what his or her credentials are. Would a popular author or radio "psychologist" who uses the title "doctor" be as qualified to give psychological advice as a practicing clinical psychologist? Perhaps—but what if you discovered the doctorate was in English or history and not psychology? What would you say then about her qualifications?

3. Ask yourself whether or not this expert is generally recognized by others in the field: Is this opinion held by more than one person? How many disagree with it? What are their comparative credentials?

What Counts as Evidence:
Field and Sphere Differences

Earlier we learned that communication can generally be divided into three spheres: personal or private, public, and professional or technical. Within these spheres the requirements for sound evidence vary. Your word is generally good enough for private communication, but public and technical spheres require more. In the public sphere, writing a letter to the newspaper or making a statement to the city council requires proof. In this case, proof is often public opinion surveys, opinions of other citizens, local examples, and material from newspapers and periodicals. In the technical sphere (the sphere of academic writing), however, more is required. In addition to expert testimony, the technical sphere often demands proof consistent with research findings, generally presented in peer-reviewed professional journals. It often discounts sources such as popular opinion or general circulation magazines.

To further complicate the issue, within the technical sphere there are many different fields, each of which has its own criteria for what is or is not a reputable source. In the field of law, for example, there are strict rules of evidence, but these may vary from state to state; you may be familiar with some of them from watching courtroom dramas on television. For example, hearsay evidence cannot be considered unless special circumstances—such as an excited utterance or a deathbed declaration—are present. Items seized or confessions obtained illegally cannot be used as evidence.

The same principle is true in academic writing. There are certain disciplinary rules as to what constitutes evidence. In most of the humanities, including rhetoric, there is an emphasis on textual evidence. In the sciences and engineering, there is an expectation that primary emphasis will be based on original quantitative research findings. In social sciences, communication, and composition we often find reliance on experimental and qualitative research. In law, precedent plays a very important role. In religious studies the role of scriptural authority is important in varying degrees. The point is that evidence does not fall into the "one size fits all" category. To have your arguments considered seriously by your peers, you must follow the rules of evidence of your own discipline, or, because you are a student who may take classes in a variety of disciplines as well as your major, you need to learn what the requirements are for the field which you are studying. Unfortunately, in most cases these rules are not written; those in the field are simply expected to know them. How, you ask? There are two ways. First, read articles written by those in the field and notice the style, types of arguments, and what counts as evidence—are there quotations from a text, lots of charts and graphs, or details of an experiment?

Second, ask! Ask your instructor or ask others in the field. Most instructors would be absolutely thrilled to have an earnest young student show up during office hours to discuss field-appropriate evidence.

DISCOVERING EVIDENCE

There are two pieces of advice we'd like to give you before we even begin this section: first, librarians are your best friends; second, purchase a good handbook or style manual. If you are not familiar with your campus library or media center, you need to become so—quickly. Most college libraries have a series of tours, orientation sessions, and skills courses that can help you become a real expert at using all the resources a library has to offer, including library databases. You also need to figure out who's who in the library: Who can give you information about resources? Who can answer questions about documentation, fair use, and copyright laws? Who can help you use the equipment? Try to establish personal contact with as many librarians as possible—especially those who are responsible for resources in your particular field of study. The help librarians offer is invaluable and you should take advantage of their expertise.

Second, in this book we are not going to duplicate information that you can easily get elsewhere, so you need a good handbook or style manual that shows you how to document sources, preferably one that shows several different styles of documentation, such as APA, MLA, and Chicago. (We'll explain what those stand for a little later.) There are literally dozens of such handbooks; you may have purchased one for this class. If not, there are several online sources for this information. The one we like best is the Purdue University Online Writing Lab (OWL) at http://owl.english.purdue.edu.

THE RESEARCH PROCESS

For the purposes of this book, we are assuming that most of the research you will be doing during your college career is text-based research. Some of you may be involved in doing original empirical research—for example, surveys, laboratory experiments, or clinical trials—at some point, especially as upper division students in your major. However, those opportunities will be accompanied by discipline-specific instructions from your professor. Here we are most concerned about equipping you to successfully complete the average college writing or speaking assignment that requires some amount of textual support for arguments.

Let us make very clear from the beginning that research is not a matter of just finding a few quotations that sound good and agree with you. There is much more involved. First you must find a topic area. We suggest you spend a good deal of time thinking about what might sustain your interest through the several weeks, sometimes months, you will probably spend working on this paper. The topic area should allow for considerable exploration. For this reason, we suggest you steer clear of topics that are overdone or that are so narrowly limited that you will have trouble finding resources. Often the topic area will be defined by your course or assigned by your instructor; that is, if you're assigned to write paper for a class in Asian history, you can reasonably assume that your topic area should be Asian history.

Next, you will need to come up with a specific topic by narrowing the topic area. If the paper is for a class in rhetoric, you need to decide whether you want to write about Classical rhetoric, American rhetoric, the rhetoric of a world leader, or any number of other possibilities. Again, some of this may be determined by your instructor.

At this point, having narrowed the topic, you should locate articles, books, and websites that relate to the topic. Do some preliminary reading (or skimming) to see what others have written about the topic, how much material is available (too much may lead to further narrowing), and what sources seem to be most interesting. Keep rough notes as you read so you'll know which sources you may want to use.

The next task is to think of some research questions that might arise from the reading you've done. For example, suppose you've decided to write about the rhetoric of former president John F. Kennedy. After reading, you might come up with the following questions:

1. Did he write his speeches himself?

2. If not, who did write his speeches?

3. Did Kennedy ever study rhetoric?

4. What are the main themes he speaks about?

5. What is the rhetorical situation in X speech?

6. Why were his speeches so popular?

7. Did his delivery enhance or detract from his speeches?

Some of these are better research questions than others. Any question that can be answered yes/no is not going to be productive. On that basis, we can eliminate questions 1 and 3. The rest of the questions, though, can all be used for a research paper—all you need to do is decide which one you are most interested in, for example, "What was the rhetorical situation in Kennedy's speech to the Houston Ministerial Association?"

Now that you've selected your research question, you need to form a hypothesis. Based on what you already know, and what you've learned in your preliminary reading, answer the research question in one sentence: "In his speech to the Houston Ministerial Association, Kennedy was trying to overcome criticism of his Catholic faith by explaining his views to Protestant clergy." The elements are all there—audience, purpose, constraints = the rhetorical situation.

That one-sentence answer is now your working thesis, the argument that you will make in your paper. Of course, you must also consider other interpretations. Please remember that as you do more research you can modify the working thesis before you come up with a final thesis statement for the paper or speech. As you work, you also need to include a preview of the subpoints you will make.

We're going to modify the hypothesis now, because it has become a statement of fact, and there needs to be more room for expansion, so try this: "Although some critics believe that Kennedy's speech to the Houston Ministerial Association was simply a defense of his Catholic faith, Kennedy's purpose was to explain and interpret his views on the relationship between government and religion to an audience of skeptics." Now you have some real meat to your argument. Note that you have modified your hypothesis from a general argument about the rhetorical situation to a specific thesis about one aspect—purpose. You have a thesis, an antithesis (opposing view), and a preview of the main argument. All you need now are some subpoints, which can be added in a second sentence: "The language he chooses, his references to the Constitution, and his appeals to the patriotism of the audience all make his purpose clear." Now you have the plan for your entire paper laid out in front of you. The time to begin the research has almost arrived.

Before you start the formal research process, however, there's one very important step that most students never take. We hope that you will, because this step is one of the best ways to avoid accusations of plagiarism. Before you do anything else, we suggest you sit down with just your thesis in front of you—without your notes or references, without an outline— and write down what you think **you** want to say about the topic. Present your own arguments, based only on your own knowledge before you did any reading on the topic. Some people call this version a free-write, some call it a "zero draft," others call it a context statement; the name makes no difference. What does make a difference is that the draft will later help you distinguish what does or does not need to be documented. To prod your thinking, you might want to start some of your sentences with "I believe" or "I think." Be sure, though, to remove such phrases before the next draft so you won't include them in your paper. As you progress, you may find that some of these ideas are wrong; you may find that others are shared by experts; you may even find that some of your ideas are the centerpiece of a controversy. The point is that you can document that these are your original ideas, not those you borrowed from someone else. Once that's done, it's time to begin your research.

First, look for primary sources. Get a copy of Kennedy's speech. Then consider your secondary sources. These might include a biography of Kennedy that covers the campaign, newspaper articles from the day after the speech was delivered, critical analyses of the speech in professional journals, or political assessments of the speech's impact. These materials could come from the library, from print or electronic periodicals and journals, or from websites.

Be sure to assess the credibility of the source. Is the source generally accepted as credible? For example, some newspapers are considered newspapers of record—for example, *The New York Times* or *Washington Post* (for political matters), but not the *North Farmville Gazette* or *The Enquirer*. Do periodicals have a bias, as with *Mother Jones* or *The Weekly Standard*, or are they generally more balanced—like *Time, Newsweek,* and *U.S. News and World Report?* If you are using books, look up the authors to see what their credentials are and what else they have written.

As you read, take notes. We used to have to keep notes on 3"x5" notecards—a time-consuming and labor-intensive process—but now you can print out or photocopy almost anything (except books, and you can copy individual pages of those) and simply use your highlighter to mark relevant passages or make notes in the margins. (Of course, we hope that you will **not** highlight or make notes in library books!) Be sure you have all of the relevant information about the source—title, author, dates, name of article and publication in which the material appeared (including volume and issue), book publisher, website URL, and especially page numbers. Give each separate piece of source material a letter—an article might be letter A, another article B, a website C, and so forth. You'll see why in just a bit.

Once you have finished the note-taking process, make an outline of the course of your argument. You do not need a formal outline unless your instructor requires one, and it doesn't need to be a full-sentence outline unless you find that helpful. But—and this is very important—as you do the outline, write down the source and page number of any evidence you want to include. This simple act will save you hours and hours of effort later. Once you've finished the outline, you are ready to begin your first draft.

USING AND INCORPORATING EVIDENCE

The most frequently neglected aspect of researched writing or speaking is actually using the evidence that has been collected. You are faced with a pile of notes and you have no idea how to incorporate them into your paper. First you must be selective. Don't just throw in everything you've got. Select the particular pieces of evidence that will most effectively support or advance you arguments. As you write your draft, think about the sources you have that relate to each point, then find specific passages or quotes that will help advance your argument. Here's another really valuable tip: Remember that you gave each source a letter? Now when you find a particular sentence or paragraph you want to use, number it. A quotation from that first article might be A3 or A7 or A42. Put that letter and number into your rough draft. That way you know exactly where the material came from, but you don't have to stop writing to worry about properly formatting the citation, looking up the page number, later forgetting where you got the information, or worst of all, risking plagiarism by not putting in the citation at all. The same applies if you are preparing a speech manuscript or outline—remembering where you got the material is always important.

The next problem you will encounter is exactly how the materials should be incorporated; should you use a quotation, a paraphrase, or a summary? Each has its special role to play. Looking at some examples from Lincoln's *Gettysburg Address* will make the distinction clear.

Quotations are, of course, the exact words of the speaker or writer. Example: Abraham Lincoln said, "We cannot dedicate, we cannot consecrate, we cannot hallow this ground." Use direct quotations when the words themselves are important. Here, the parallelism and word choice build to emphasize Lincoln's meaning. Quotations should be used exceedingly sparingly. Generally, summaries are the best way to present research material. This is especially true in the sciences and social sciences where the ideas are generally more important than the exact words. In the humanities, quotations from literary texts are used more often because the exact words do make a difference.

Paraphrases restate the author's words in order to clarify meaning. A note: Simply changing one or two words is not a paraphrase. If you use a quotation but change one or two words, you must put the material in quotation marks, and the changed words in brackets [ ]. Nor is it true that you don't have to cite the author if you change the words around. You must still cite the paraphrase properly.

A paraphrase of the opening words of the *Gettysburg Address,*

> "Four score and seven years ago our fathers brought forth on this continent a new nation . . ."

might read:

> Eighty-seven years ago today the founders initiated a new country in North America.

Notice that only three of the original words have been retained (*years, ago,* and *new*), and they are words that are common and not easily replaced. If some of the more distinctive words had been used in the paraphrase (*brought forth*, for example) they would need to be enclosed in quotation marks. Except in a few circumstances, we discourage using the paraphrase. As this example demonstrates, the paraphrase frequently ends up being awkward and prosaic and not nearly as good as the original.

There is one circumstance, however, in which paraphrases are extremely useful: when you are trying to present technical material that you understand, but chances are your audience won't, paraphrasing is often helpful to translate the technical jargon into more comprehensible prose. For example, in the chapter on ethics we present several logical fallacies, some of which have Latin names. Suppose you were talking to someone and said, "You have committed the *ad populum* and *ad vericundiam* fallacies." Chances are, all you would get in response was a blank stare. However, you could add a paraphrase: "In other words, you're appealing to popularity and tradition." The paraphrase is much easier to understand and will, therefore, get a much more positive response, and that is always a good thing.

Summaries are the lifeblood of academic research. A summary is a condensed version of a paragraph, article, or sometimes even a whole book that covers only the main points. Most students don't realize how often they use summaries.

A friend says, "I went to see a movie last night." You say, "Oh, what was it about?" and your friend gives you a one-minute version of the main points of the movie. That's a summary.

Your friend didn't go to class and asks you, "What did I miss?" In one minute or so, you cover the main points of the lecture. That's a summary.

During class, a friend asks you what your essay is about. In 30 seconds or so, you cover the main points—and that's a summary.

In research, summaries are used to present research findings made by others (usually called a review of literature), to compile information for an annotated bibliography, or to present the ideas of others. A summary placed before the beginning of a paper is called an abstract. Like quotations and paraphrases, all summaries must be documented.

INTRODUCING EVIDENCE INTO THE TEXT

One of the major complaints of college writing instructors (and other faculty as well) is that students just insert evidence without relating the evidence to the argument they're making. In fact, faculty often call this "helicopter evidence" or "parachute evidence," implying that their students "dropped" the evidence with only a vague prayer that perhaps the quotation would land in the right spot to bolster their papers or speeches. While we find the image of a little helicopter flying around the room with pieces of evidences plummeting to their final resting place somewhat entertaining, we believe that a better analogy is that pieces of evidence are small offshore islands, and that in order to get there you need to build bridges to them. (One could, of course, use a rowboat, but they're often leaky and unreliable.) There are three ways to build a sturdy bridge that connects your evidence to your argument: *introductions*, *transitions*, and *explications*.

When you use a piece of evidence, whether a quotation, a paraphrase, or a summary, you must somehow introduce the material. This is generally

A Short But Handy List of Rhetorically Accurate Verbs

acknowledges	agrees	argues	asserts
believes	cautions	challenges	claims
comments	confirms	contends	contradicts
concedes	denies	describes	disagrees
discusses	emphasizes	explains	highlights
illustrates	implies	maintains	notes (use this sparingly!)
observes	proposes	refutes	rejects
reports	responds	shows	suggests

done either through introducing the source or by the use of signal words, or some combination of those. For example: According to the *New York Times*, the number of people in college will increase dramatically this year [*summary*] or John Smith asserts that "The recent trend is for women to attend college in increasingly larger proportion than men" [*quotation*]. (These pieces of evidence would also need to have documentation, which we shall get to in a later section.) In the second example, please note that we used the word *asserts* rather than *says* or *states*. We would prefer that you not use either of those words. *Asserts,* on the other hand, is a rhetorically accurate verb; that is, the verb expresses precisely what the author is doing—he is making an assertion.

In addition to signal words, you should also be sure to transition in and out of the material gracefully by using transitions or, in speaking, signposts. For example, you say: "As Smith emphasizes in his article, women are becoming better educated [*signpost.*] Now what are the implications of this?" Or you write, "Although [*transition word*] Smith argues more women are attending college, he fails to assess the implications," then move on to your own argument.

When you use a direct quotation in your papers, you let the audience know where the material begins and ends by using quotation marks. When you speak you must also indicate where the quotation begins and ends. The best way to do this is by using a pause at the end of the quotation then signaling you've moved on. For example, you say: "Abraham Lincoln once mused that 'A nation divided cannot stand.' [*pause]* When Lincoln expressed this idea. . . ." You can accomplish this same purpose by verbally saying "quote," but we think that generally distracts from the message. For example, you say, "Abraham Lincoln once mused, quote 'A nation divided cannot stand' end quote." This is awkward—but even worse is making little quotation marks with your fingers. The gesture always ends up looking like little bunny ear shadow puppets.

When you insert a paraphrase, the most helpful introduction is something like "In other words . . . " or "The author essentially argues that . . ." This indicates that you are using source material but putting the author's ideas into your own words. This, too, will require documentation.

The problem of announcing the parameters of the source material is more complicated when you use a summary because the summary becomes part of your argument, so sometimes readers and listeners have difficulty in figuring out where the summary begins and ends. Thinking of your introductory and transitional material as a set of bookends will help. Begin with a phrase that says, "Ta-da—I'm now using someone else's idea," and end with a firm acknowledgement. In written work the ending will often, but not always, be the documentation (author and page). For example:

> [*introduction of summary*] Jones holds that women comprise a larger percent of the population and therefore the growth does not predict an increase in the proportion of educated women (22). [*citation*] (*Note that since you've already said Jones is the author you do not need to repeat his name in the citation; you only need to give the page number.*)

You can see that the introduction and citation act as bookends for the summary of Jones's argument. Another way to provide the bookend would be:

> [*introduction of summary*] Not everyone agrees with Smith, however. One researcher argues that women comprise a larger percent of the population and therefore the growth does not predict an increase in the proportion of educated women (Jones 22). [*citation*]

This becomes more complicated with longer summaries because the audience has difficulty figuring out where your argument ends and the summarized argument begins. In these cases, you need to be doubly sure that you have bookended accurately. Introducing summaries can also be a problem when speaking. You can, of course, use the introductory strategies above to begin the summary, but you don't want to abruptly say "page 22" or "Jones, page 22" at the end. Instead, we think the best course is to say something at the end of your summary like "This summary of Jones' argument captures the essence of the controversy," or "Now what Jones means in this passage is. . . ."

INTEGRATING EVIDENCE AND ANALYSIS TO STRENGTHEN ARGUMENT

Finding the methods of introducing and concluding bits of evidence is certainly important, but to avoid helicopter evidence you must thoroughly integrate your evidence with your argument. In other words, now is the time to build the bridges that connect the islands of evidence. We call this explication.

The key point to remember is that *your evidence is not your argument— evidence only supports your argument.* Therefore, you must explain how the evidence relates to the argument, how it supports the argument, and how it advances the argument—in other words, how the evidence fits into the bigger picture. There is not a formula or a set of handy phrases that will accomplish this kind of analysis for you. You need to figure out why you decided to use this piece of evidence, then tell your audience. Here's an example from an article that one of us wrote for the *Southern Communication Journal* in Spring 2002:

> To understand how wedge issues are effective rhetorically, we must look at theoretical assumptions. Aristotle tells us that rhetoric is "an ability, in each particular case, to see the available means of persuasion" (*Rhetoric* I.2.1). In his footnote to this definition, translator Kennedy notes that the Greek phrase that he has translated as "available" is "*endekhomenon pithanon*, 'what is inherently and potentially persuasive'" (37). This implies no value judgment. Therefore, the discussion of the persuasive techniques may be conducted without, initially at least, making any ethical judgments, because any technique may be used for good or evil. (Wiant 297)

The first sentence functions as a transition from the previous point (which was an explanation of what a wedge issue is), and at the same time advances the argument to the next point—rhetorical function. The reader can tell what came before and what is coming next. The last two sentences summarize the evidence ("implies no value judgment") and advance the argument to the next step, which is clearly going to be a discussion of how the lack of the ethical implications contributes to the rhetorical effectiveness of wedge issues.

You should be able to do this analysis with every piece of evidence you use. If you find you can't, that probably means the evidence is either unnecessary or irrelevant. In either case, you should omit it.

The point here is that summary begets analysis, and your teachers want to help you develop your analytical abilities to help you strengthen your arguments. If you are crafting a thesis-structured argument, then your analysis should work to support and prove the validity of your thesis. More on how to create analysis will be discussed in chapter 13.

CITING AND DOCUMENTING SOURCES: AVOIDING PLAGIARISM

You may recall that at the beginning of this chapter we said you need a good handbook or style manual (or an online source such as the Purdue OWL<http://owl.english.purdue.edu>) that shows you how to document sources. Rather than repeating information that is available elsewhere, we are concluding this chapter on the importance of citing sources. Remember, whenever you use the words, ideas, images, or sounds of someone else, you must properly cite your sources.

If you do not, you may be accused of academic dishonesty—plagiarism—and may suffer serious consequences. All that can be avoided if you remember to consult your handbook and your instructor and apply these principles. And, finally—if you have any questions related to citing sources, ask your teacher.

WORKS CITED

Chicago Manual of Style. 15th ed. Chicago: U of Chicago P, 2003.

MLA Handbook for Writers of Research Papers. 6th ed. Ed. Joseph Gibaldi. New York: The Modern Language Association of America, 2003.

Publication Manual of the American Psychological Association. 5th ed. Washington D.C.: American Psychological Association, 2001.

Scientific Style and Format: The CSE Manual for Authors, Editors, and Publishers. 7th ed. New York: Cambridge UP, 2006.

Arrangement:
The Dispositions of Argument

Neither can embellishments of language be found without arrangement and expression of thoughts, nor can thoughts be made to shine without the light of language.

—Cicero

Without skilled organization, the most elegant material would be nothing more than rubble.

—Quintilian

AS COMMUNICATORS, we understand that speeches and papers should be well organized. Usually, we start organizing our thoughts based on what we already know about our subject. Quite often, we refine and revise our thoughts after looking at research and developing some preliminary arguments. Because the invention process yields more information than we could possibly use, we tend to use the organizational process to trim and focus our arguments.

Aristotle defined arrangement as a means by which arguments are placed in an effective order. He explained that the disposition of an argument had an introduction, a statement of the issue, the argument, and a conclusion. Bright students will realize quickly that the five-paragraph essay, a staple of high school writing, seems to incorporate Aristotle's method, for the five-paragraph model has an introduction (with a thesis), three paragraphs that prove the validity of the thesis, and a summative conclusion. All of these parts must work together to make the argument coherent.

FIVE EASY STEPS TO SUCCESS?

Many composition and speech teachers criticize the five-paragraph model because of the narrowness of its perspective; however, we take a more encouraging but cautious approach to this model. Clearly, students will compose many papers and speeches that will exceed the limits of the five-paragraph model, but there are still many teachers who want a two-page response paper, and these papers will be graded. Therefore, if your history teacher wants a five-paragraph essay, give her an effective five-paragraph essay.

In chapter 8, we acknowledge that academic writing is primarily guided by thesis-support structures. A strong thesis typically (1) announces the subject, (2) provides a <u>claim</u> about the subject, and (3) gives at least one good <u>reason</u> to support this claim. Formulating a working thesis is one way to help organize your ideas. For example, below is a thesis that was created after some preliminary research:

WORKING THESIS:

[**Claim**] University sports programs should be reformed because [**Reason**] they have eroded into a corrupt spectacle antithetical to the academic mission of the university. Ernie Chambers, a state senator in Nebraska, argues that colleges and [**Solution**] universities should pay their athletes. The reasons for paying athletes are: (1) when students work for the university, they are paid, so athletes should be paid; (2) universities earn revenue off of television contracts and athletic apparel, so they should pass on these funds to the folks whose images and jerseys are sold; and, (3) most importantly, compensating athletes with a stipend could help take the graft out of university sports programs, many of which have been mired in charges of corruption for years.

Here, we use a thesis in the five-paragraph frame to help organize this argument:

Par. 1: *Introduction and thesis*: introduce your topic by giving some general and specific information that clarifies the importance of your topic. Discuss why university athletics are important, how athletes contribute to the welfare of the campus, and explain why your audience should care about your argument. Then, introduce your thesis that contains three major points and divide them into three successive paragraphs. As a matter of principle, you should list your three arguments in climactic order: from the most common (or basic) to the strongest. Use each of the three claims as the topic sentence for each paragraph.

Par. 2: This paragraph should present your most basic argument: "When students work for the university, they are paid, so athletes should be paid as well." This argument will not surprise anyone. Putting the most common argument first is meant to solicit quick agreement from your audience. This claim, however, must prove that athletes are, indeed, laborers and that their work is the same as those students who work on campus.

Par. 3: "Universities earn revenue off of television contracts and athletic apparel, so they should pass on these funds to the folks whose images and jerseys are sold" is a fundamental argument. But this paragraph must establish that universities do, indeed, generate revenue from their sports programs (from television contracts, stadium concessions, clothing sales, etc.), particularly men's football and basketball, but, as a matter of practice, do not pay their players because of their amateur status as college athletes. This paragraph is meant to show the lack of fairness in labor relations between the university and its athletes.

Par. 4: "Compensating athletes with a stipend could help take the graft out of university sports programs, many of which have been mired in charges of corruption for years." Because athletes are unpaid, some have received money in envelopes from members of the booster clubs, have taken jobs at car dealerships without ever showing up for work, and have accepted gifts they shouldn't have. Paying college athletes, then, could diminish some of the corruption from college sports.

Par. 5: *Conclusion*: restate your thesis and briefly summarize your main points. Predict what may happen if your proposal is not accepted (that student athletes will continue to be exploited) and what will happen if the solution is accepted (integrity will be further established in labor relations between administration and students).

The five-paragraph method is easy to memorize, and, if done properly, can help students achieve succinctness and clarity. Although the five-paragraph model imparts some fundamental strategies for organizing material, this structure is limiting. Because paying athletes is a controversial and complex subject with many arguments, most English and Communication teachers will require a more complex structure that compels you to extend your argument.

To broaden the dimensions of the argument, your teacher may want you to account for questions that go beyond your argument (How much would these athletes be paid? Would there be differences in pay between starters and non-starters?). You might also be asked to provide arguments against your thesis to avoid the fallacy of suppressing evidence. For instance, your teacher may question the very assumption that universities and college sports programs generate any profit. In fact, sports programs (outside of major universities with large television contracts) are notorious money losers because of expensive coaching contracts, high administrative costs and insurance premiums, and low attendance figures. In fact, most athletic programs fail to generate enough revenue to pay for the costs of running their individual programs. In a five-paragraph essay, how do you address these issues?

We concede that the five paragraph model is a good place to start in a student's learning process; however, we believe there are other models of organization that allow students to sustain more complex arguments. Part of the ethical charge for students is to take on the challenge of exploring, studying and understanding the complexities of arguments and responding to them in responsible, interesting ways.

Most teachers believe arguments become clearer when alternative arguments are explored and refuted, for confronting and refuting competing claims strengthens your position by making your argument more persuasive.

THE CICERONIAN MODEL: EXPANDING AND SUSTAINING YOUR ARGUMENT

Many years after Aristotle, the Roman orator and writer, Marcus Tullius Cicero, in *De Inventione* (*On Invention*) formulated a *schema* that had seven distinct divisions. These divisions or parts function in different ways, but they serve an overall purpose: to persuade an audience of the validity of an argument.

1. Introduction or *exordium: the rhetor prepares the audience for the subject.* Here, you set the table for your audience. The popularity or obscurity of your subject will determine how much time you spend here. If you are discussing an issue with long-standing history, such as euthanasia

(Greek for "good death"), you might have to give a historical account of this practice before illustrating Oregon's controversial Death with Dignity law. Your audience, as well, will help you determine the length of your introduction. For instance, if your class has studied the history of euthanasia and knows the legislation regarding Oregon's law, then you don't have to spend too much time introducing the subject for a speech. Rather, you may introduce the controversy and debate regarding this law as the focus of your subject. However, your teacher may want a thorough introduction of the history of euthanasia to determine your mastery of the subject. Once you have determined what kind of introduction best suits your audience, you are faced with many more choices. A common approach to introducing a subject is to move deductively. Many rhetors will begin with some general statements that introduce the subject and move to specific illustrations as a way of leading into the thesis. Another approach begins inductively with a specific incident or example that moves into broader examples to illustrate the gravity or importance of the subject. Regardless of your choice of approach, you must be clear about your subject and clear about the focus of your argument. For the most part, if your subject is a public issue, you can assume your audience knows something about the issue but could profit from more information—to what extent is up to you as the rhetor. If your subject is a personal issue, then you must assume (even expect) they know little about your circumstances, so you could contextualize your issue within a broader perspective that your audience can better understand.

2. Narration: *Here, the rhetor provides an account of what has happened and generally explains the nature of the subject.* Many students mistake "narration" for a personal narrative, but narration in the traditional sense means giving a factual account of something or telling a story. For instance, if you are arguing about euthanasia, you might consider describing and illustrating a sequence of events that led up to the controversy surrounding Oregon's law and how the medical establishment and the terminally ill view the "Death with Dignity Act." Here, you must give significance to describing the most important facts and circumstances related to your subject. Historical facts alone, however, may not make your narration a strong one. You might also factor in stories regarding people and

their circumstances. Certainly, you could evoke pathos by telling individual stories of terminally ill patients (their diagnoses and prognoses, their pain, their medications, the costs of their illness, etc.) as a way of illustrating why this law was created and explain why people try to use this law to end their lives. One way of creating a narrative that validates your thesis is to piece together your research in a linear fashion. You may choose to tell this story from a chronological perspective, a climactic perspective (with incidents arranged from least to most important), or from a logical perspective, but the narration should give an honest accounting regarding the circumstances of your subject.

3. Partition: *In this section, the rhetor outlines what will follow, in accordance with what's been stated, or focuses on a particular issue.* This section works well for lengthier speeches. Before an orator transitions from the narrative to the main body of the argument (confirmation), she should outline what has come and what will follow, especially if the speech will last more than 20 minutes. This kind of planned reflection will help a listening audience remember what's been stated in order to focus on what will come. For a reading audience, a partition can help the audience stay focused on a longer argument, particularly for research projects. For example, this section could help the rhetor focus on one aspect of his research to achieve clarity and depth. In a shorter speech we call this preview *signposting*.

4. Confirmation: *The main body of your argument.* Here, provide logical proofs to support your thesis. You must make some careful decisions regarding the strengths of your arguments. As you might suspect, not all arguments are equal, so decide which of your arguments are weakest and which are strongest, and arrange these arguments in a climactic order (weakest to strongest). However, if you think your arguments are equally important, then you might consider putting well-known or familiar arguments first as a way of leading into a lesser-known or more unique or unusual arguments to achieve a didactic emphasis. Overall, your task for this section is to confirm your argument with valid reasoning, so you should employ, for the most part, logical proofs and/or qualified expert opinions to support your points.

5. Refutation: *The rhetor answers the most important counterarguments to the thesis.* This section is predicated on understanding "the other side's" arguments. Although most of us can come up with counterarguments to our own positions, conducting research rather than relying on your own ability to attack your own reasoning and thesis is a better idea. Because counterarguments and refutations are important to your own argument, choose what to refute carefully. To strengthen your own thesis, we think you should refute "the other side's" most common and strongest arguments. By meaningfully engaging with the opposition's *strongest* argument, you increase your *ethos* (and you avoid committing the "straw person" fallacy that would result if you countered only your opposition's *weakest* argument). Because space is limited and time finite, choose one or two of these arguments to refute. For example, if you are arguing for your state to adopt Oregon's Death with Dignity Act, you might consider arguing how medically hastening death does not contradict aspects of the Hippocratic Oath. You may also wish to explore how hospice care already deals with aspects of euthanasia as a way to refute the argument that doctors should kill the pain and not the patient.

6. An optional section on digressions: Cicero argued that digressions could be used tactfully to draw attention away from the more negative aspects of your subject to place the subject in a more favorable light before moving on to the conclusion. If, for instance, you are creating an epideictic argument about a controversial figure (say, defending a corrupt politician), and you know your particular audience loves a certain book (*Harry Potter*) or a specific show (*Law and Order*), you might establish that your client also likes these things as a way of connecting him with the audience. As you might have guessed, this tactic is not really digressive; there is a purpose, one based on establishing unity and good feelings at both a conscious and subconscious level between the subject and audience. Use digressions sparingly, however, as your ethos might be compromised if your audience senses that your digression is merely a form of ingratiation.

7. Conclusion: *Creating a coherent ending to your argument.* No doubt, we can finish our arguments merely by simply stopping our speeches

and papers. As teachers, we have heard our share of "That's it!" when students halt their speeches and leave the lectern. However, mere stoppage tends to confuse audiences who end up asking "That's it?" for speakers who fail to plan an effective conclusion. Effective conclusions are important, but what constitutes a conclusion? For the most part, particularly for the five-paragraph essay, summary statements will suffice because they cue the audience to the end by reinforcing previous arguments. Craft your conclusion wisely based on your audience, purpose, and intention. The conclusion is your final chance to persuade your audience. Although summaries are an effective means to reinforce earlier points, summaries alone hardly constitute a good conclusion. In addition to some summative statements, you might use your conclusion to create a final learning situation for your audience. For instance, in a proposal argument, you might conclude your argument by making some sort of feasible prediction as to what will happen if your proposal is accepted or not accepted. For an analysis argument, you might consider concluding by arguing that more analysis and study are required to better understand the issues and make suggestions as to which areas to study further. And for a persuasion argument, you might consider a call-to-action—asking your audience members to do something by giving them a petition to sign, the names of people to contact, or asking them to join you in some sort of social action.

As scholars Edward Corbett and Richard Leo Enos have pointed out, Cicero argued that the rhetor is free to creatively use this schema to arrange arguments based on the given rhetorical situation. Rhetoric teachers want their students to learn to adapt to varying situations and audiences, so the quickest way to create your own model is to understand existing models. We recommend following this model in an argumentative assignment unless your teacher gives you a different system of organization. Finally, this seven-step process doesn't represent the number of paragraphs in the argument. Rather, these divisions represent the number of rhetorical moves in your argument.

INDUCING CHANGE IN AN ADVERSARIAL AUDIENCE: THE ROGERIAN METHOD

Most people believe that the strength of their arguments alone will persuade people—even their opponents—to their side, thinking that their superior skills in the parry and thrust of combat will win the day. However, more often than not, adversarial audiences will rarely alter their own beliefs, because they are emotionally invested in defending their positions.

Carl Rogers, the American humanist and psychotherapist, stated that the more you argue with your adversaries, the more they will cling to their beliefs. For instance, an audience may go with good intentions to listen to a political candidate from a rival political party, but as soon as this person challenges the audience, many will respond with "I don't like what he is saying" or "I disagree with his point." These reactions are instinctive, but the reason why audiences react this way is because they are evaluating what the person is saying. And in this rush to judgment, *real communication*, Rogers argues, is lost.

For Rogers, real communication occurs when both sides put aside their differences in order to develop an empathic understanding of each other's assumptions, fears, and concerns. Rogers argued that rather than evaluating someone's statements as the first rhetorical move, we should approach these situations with an alternative purpose: "to listen with understanding." For Rogers, an empathic approach could prevent hostilities from occurring because different parties would be trying to find common values and locate common ground rather than defending their arguments.

Rogers formulated a procedure for communicating so adversaries could engage each other to minimize passions. For Rogers, the first step is for the parties to agree to meet, and in their face-to-face meeting, begin a process of stating and restating each person's views until the other person is satisfied. This process of summary, paraphrase, and quoting is meant to clarify statements and understand intentions. This step implies that the most important way to allay hostility is to find common ground. For instance, if rhetor X can satisfactorily restate rhetor Y's argument (and vice versa), then a mutual understanding has been brokered and real communication has been achieved.

Concessions, too, are an important part of finding common ground. When you concede a point, you are affirming something in the other person's argument or point of view that is accurate, positive, or valid. In essence, you are agreeing with some *aspect* of their argument but not their entire argument. Tactically and tactfully, you concede something in order to make a more important point about your argument.

For Rogers, the ultimate goal as an effective communicator is to create an empathic understanding of your adversary's view in order to relieve them of their apprehensions, their defensiveness, and their fears before you can change their hearts and minds. Rogers conceded that such a process is difficult because when people begin to reference the world from their adversary's point of view, they risk changing their views as well. Rogers's hope was that this interpersonal method could work with groups as well.

In a Rogerian-style argument, the way to induce change is different from Cicero's method. For instance, before the rhetor presents his side of the argument, he first has to paraphrase, summarize, and quote from the other person's position. In essence, stating the other person's argument becomes a significant part of your argument. Only after you have stated their side and found common ground can you begin your argument, an approach that contrasts with Cicero's method.

Remember: Rogers was concerned about resolving both personal and social problems, so the Rogerian method is suited specifically for problem-solving assignments. Below is our interpretation of a schema for the Rogerian process of arguing. An example can be found in the appendix. When students approach a Rogerian assignment, they use this method as a preventive model, one designed to keep any kind of hostility from manifesting.

1. **Introducing the Rhetorical Situation**: *Explaining the issue and the problem.* Begin by clarifying and illustrating the rhetorical situation. The introduction should explain the shape and scope of the problem, the reasons for the conflict, and why the conflict persists. Here, as you explain the problem, do so without blaming anyone or anybody. If possible, present the rhetorical situation in a value-neutral way. As you craft the introduction, you should believe that a dialogue between both sides is possible and beneficial. <u>Do not</u> place your thesis in the introduction. You should delay your thesis until you have explained the "other side" first. After all, following a traditional model of placing a thesis in the introduction could stoke fires and raise ires.

2. **Presenting the "Other Side"**: *Building an empathic understanding for your adversary.* Before you state your argument, you must present their view(s) with a thoroughness that would satisfy your opponents. If you are arguing for a conservative position on abortion, then you will present the liberal side here. When you present this information, do so with modesty and good nature; remember: your goal is to create an *empathic understanding* of their position, their argument, their assumptions. To achieve this perspective, you will need to thoroughly research the opposing side.

Summarize, paraphrase and quote their best arguments—and do so with fairness and without any judgment.

3. **Establishing Common Ground**: *Finding common values allays bad feelings, and making concessions builds common ground.* Here, discuss and analyze the common values each side shares. For instance, Republicans and Democrats share common values in many areas; both value the Bill of Rights, the democratic process, strong political leadership, etc. If you cannot find common values in their beliefs or statements, then perhaps you can find commonality in their behaviors and actions. For instance, both pro-choice advocates and abortion opponents are motivated, well-organized, and vocal. There is much to admire about their civic actions. Most ideological opponents spend a lot of time articulating their differences. Your task is to go beyond traditional stances to see what commonalities the two sides possess in order to bring them together. Establishing common ground is an important part of your argument, and one important way to establish common ground is to make valid concessions to their arguments. But before you can concede to anything, you must analyze their position and find some merit in their stances. Once you find merit, your concessions should be credible and persuasive. Your underlying purpose is to illustrate how your own understanding of the issue has been enlarged by some of their most valid points.

4. **Transitioning to Your Side:** *Asking them to concede and negotiating your side.* As you transition from discussing common values and finding common ground, begin to discuss elements of your argument that you think they can agree with. Remember to articulate that their understanding of the issue can be enhanced by comprehending some of your most valid points. When you begin the process of counterarguing, point out the problems with their claims, interpretations, or evidence to show the weaknesses in their arguments.

5. **Explaining Your Side and Making a Stand:** *Presenting your thesis and argument.* Your thesis should be stated clearly, and after stating your thesis, present your research and arguments firmly but modestly. Use quotations, paraphrase, and summaries to

establish your points. Be thorough and concise. Give your audience an opportunity to develop an understanding of your claims and evidence. Solicit agreement with your audience in creative ways (by asking questions) as a means of sustaining good will. Your goal is to allow your adversarial audience to understand your perspective, so you may invite them to contemplate your arguments. Again, use logical arguments to strengthen your case.

6. **Conclusion**: As you conclude your argument, leave your audience on a good note: summarize the common values and emphasize the common ground shared between both sides. You may conclude by reinforcing your own major points and inviting all parties to study the issue further. Rather than merely summarizing your points, try to contemplate the problem and envision a future in which people from opposing sides work together (despite their differences) to resolve this issue. For the Rogerian argument, recall that immediate persuasion is unlikely but cumulative persuasion is probable.

A caveat: These six steps do not represent the number of paragraphs in your argument. Rather, they represent the number of rhetorical moves you should make when organizing your speech or paper. Again, as a rhetor, you are free to interpret Rogers's theories, but consult your teacher if you decide to deviate from this schema. To fully understand Rogers's theories, we recommend reading his essay.

PROPOSAL WRITING

Many teachers will assign a proposal argument—either as an individual or group project—as a means to advocate change. Proposals can be broadly or specifically conceived. For example, a general proposal would be open-ended, directing students to find a social problem in the community or neighborhood to resolve feasibly. Other proposal-based assignments are specific, typically campus-based, aimed at making some facet of the campus better. Teachers may also assign business proposals, ones that are aimed at improving some aspect of business, such as customer service, or a business procedure or product. Regardless of the focus, proposal-based arguments rely on several key factors, such as a valid needs assessment and feasible and desirable solutions.

While students are encouraged to come up with new and expressive ideas related to proposal development, they must follow the rules of the prompt. In proposal writing, because of the competitive nature of the process, following the rules is a necessary condition, for in writing proposals for grant money or other kinds of funds or enhancements, government agencies, private endowment firms and corporations often disqualify applicants on technical grounds (for not following the rules). For these reasons, teachers may want students to really follow the rules of a "request for proposals" (RFP) or "request for applications" (RFA) process to approximate real-world conditions.

When government agencies or corporations put out their RFPs, they create their own forms and rules for submissions. Below is a schema that follows some common practices in the RFP process.

1. **Needs Assessment and Statement:** Most requests begin with an assessment of the community you are attempting to serve. If your proposal is campus-based, a good way to find a legitimate need is to discuss campus-based problems with your class, roommates, or campus-based clubs. A good resource to find problems is to read your campus newspaper or speak to the public safety office. If you are thinking about writing a proposal for your work, ask your customers; if you are trying to improve work relations, ask your peers. Once an issue has been decided upon, students often design their own surveys or questionnaires as a way of finding out the shape and scope of the problem and the most plausible solutions. Once you have discovered these needs and made some choices, you must actually discover what problems can be addressed by your proposal. For instance, if your goal is to argue that campus safety can be enhanced by hiring more officers to develop better relations with students, then you must establish this need; if you believe that there is a legitimate need for an improved recycling solution to your campus's trash problem, then you must state your method of assessment and establish your need here.

2. **The Vision or Mission**: If your proposal is aimed at helping the university community, then one way to support your proposal is to align your request with your university's mission and/or vision statements. Businesses, as well, have mission statements. Mission

statements are the expressed values of a group of people; therefore, arguing that your proposal helps fulfill aspects of your university or business's mission would make your proposal more valid. This kind of contextualization will help focus your proposal. Here, your goal is to establish that the body to which you are appealing (the president's office, admissions office, catering, public safety, etc.) has an ethical responsibility to address your problem.

3. **Problem Statement:** Based on your needs assessment, you must illustrate the problem(s) you wish to resolve. Describe in detail what the problem is, how long it has been a problem, and why it exists and who it affects. If the problem is costing a firm money, then explain how much and project how much more will be lost. If the problem is an efficiency problem, then illustrate how much time is wasted or how productivity is lost as a result of the problem. If the problem is a customer relations problem, then explain how customers are being affected and to what extent. You might consider directly relating your problem-statement to your needs assessment to establish coherency.

4. **Resolution Statement and Sustainability Assessment**: State your resolution(s) here. Your proposal must be viable and feasible. Specific solutions to specific problems have the best chance of succeeding; therefore, your resolution must request that something happen or request that funding be allocated to help address an issue. Explain in some detail how this resolution can be implemented; describe the steps of implementation and provide a feasible timeline. There are, of course, short-term and long-term solutions. If your proposal is for a one-time fix of a problem, then you should concede to this situation. However, if your resolution affects any number of people or groups of people (departments, offices, etc.) over a longer term, then you must explain how your resolution will be sustained over a period of time. What you are trying to resolve may take more time than you might think, but remain optimistic, positive, and clear about your intentions. Your goal is to persuade your audience that your solution is not only feasible and viable but necessary.

If your resolution will cost money, then formulate a feasible budget and itemize as many items (products and services) as you can. The budget is often a realistic assessment of whether or not a proposed solution is feasible. If your proposal seeks more campus police officers to develop better community relations with students who live on campus to prevent crime, then find out how much the university pays an officer (plus benefits) and forecast how many officers your proposal needs.

5. **Assessment**: Most proposals ask the applicant to think about how the proposal should be evaluated. For example, if your proposal is to hire additional community-oriented police officers for your campus, then you should predict that campus-based crime should decrease over time. How would this solution be assessed? By looking at crime reports for the year after hiring the officers. If you are proposing to improve customer relations, then your proposal should predict that customer satisfaction should increase (this assessment would be reflected in customer surveys).

6. **Call to Action**: Though a call to action might not be an official part of the proposal, your teacher may require you to ask your audience to do something to help support your proposal, such as sign a petition, make phone calls or emails, or write letters. This call to action is often the part of the speech when the proposal is presented. At this time the student will ask to have his audience become involved in the proposed solution.

Your goal is not just to come up with a feasible solution; your goal is come up with a desirable solution. It is not unusual for teachers to pass on well-written proposals to the audience your proposal directly affects. For example, we have forwarded excellent proposals to university administrators with good results. Our students have been called to meet with vice presidents and directors of programs to discuss proposals to institute change. Students are genuinely excited to present their ideas to a responsive community that will consider seriously their ideas for making their campuses better.

THE SPEAKING/WRITING CONNECTION: PREPARING AN OUTLINE

Students are strongly encouraged to outline their speeches and papers because the benefits are too numerous to pass up. Whether an outline is turned in or not is based on the requirements of the assignment. However, outlining will keep you on track as a way to organize and focus your paper or speech.

By definition, outlines are a visual framework. For a speech, there are two kinds of outlines. The first is a developing outline. The developing outline is your primary outline, one that is a substantive, coherent representation of your notes and research, one that is shaped and reasoned. Developing outlines have varying degrees, from the initial stages to a more completed product. In this process, you will organize the body of your speech based on the needs of your audience, your purpose, and the requirements of the assignment.

The developing outline is one that you consult (and revise) when you practice and rehearse for your speech. However, when you prepare to give an extemporaneous speech, most speakers prepare a speaking outline for this task. Speaking outlines are a condensed version of your developing outline and serve as an aid to your memory.

To move effectively from your developing outline to your speaking outline, follow these simple rules. Break down your ideas into manageable units and subunits—usually in sentence formatting—and organize them in a consistently helpful visual design. Keep the lines evenly spaced and far enough away to make distinctions between the sections. You might even make the font size big enough to read without too much effort.

Below is an example of a speaking outline for a values speech based on ethos.

The assignment: "Three Words in Three Minutes." The particulars:

Choose *three words* that represent something about you—something meaningful, insightful, perhaps even humorous—to introduce yourself to the class. Now remember, you should speak only about things that you want your audience to understand about you as a person. Your choice of words is entirely up to you, but please choose your words carefully. In the selection process, please avoid synonyms. You may introduce your words in any way effective way; however, we recommend you try to find some apparent or explicit connections between the words you choose. For the first speech, you may choose either manuscript reading, extemporaneous speaking, or a combination of the two.

Sample Speaking Outline

I. Introduce self: name, home, and state a theme based on three words.

II. First word: **love** is family and friends.
    a. Love is community.

III. **Knowledge** is a power we all respect.
    a. Knowledge is community.

IV. **Memory**: without our memories, we wouldn't recall past loves and the great wisdom of our forefathers.
    a. The importance of shared memories.

V. Conclusion: love, knowledge and memory—all are important, but memory is the basis of how we measure the growth of our emotions and intellect. Thank you.

A caveat: Because of nervousness or anxiety, new speakers will often bring to the lectern a developing outline rather than a speaking outline. Although they may fully intend to give an extemporaneous speech, their nerves take over, and they choose to manuscript read from their paper to ensure completing the assignment. This choice is credible because the goal for the first speech is to get through the speech and be faithful to your words. However, if your goal is to improve your delivery with every new assignment, then you must progress to using your speaking outline when the assignment requires extemporaneous delivery only.

FROM WRITING TO SPEAKING

In a combined public speaking and college composition class, many of the speeches are derived from writing assignments. In these situations, your research, analysis and thoughts regarding your subject will often serve both tasks. Most students will choose to arrange their speech and essay in the same manner—with the speech serving as an abbreviated representation of their essay. This approach should work well unless your teacher wants a different approach for your speech. If there is ever a question about arrangement, ask your teacher.

As we discussed in chapter 1, many things are gained and lost in the translation between speaking and writing, but one constant is how you organize each task. Clearly, the depth of your organization is abbreviated when you give a seven-minute speech on an eight-page paper. However, your goals for the speech may be different from your paper, so ask your teacher what the expectations are for each assignment and keep in mind the due dates for these separate assignments.

WORKS CITED

Enos, Richard Leo. "Ciceronian *Dispositio* as an Architect for Creativity in Composition: A Note for the Affirmative." *Rhetoric Review.* 4.1. (September 1985): 108-110.

Rogers, Carl R. *On Becoming a Person.* Boston: Houghton Mifflin, 1961.

SECTION FOUR

Rehearsing and Presenting Your Ideas

CHAPTER 11

Delivery: The Impressions
We Give Our Audience

Every accent, every emphasis, every modulation of voice, was so
perfectly well turned and well placed, that, without being interested
in the subject, one could not help being pleased with the discourse; a
pleasure of much the same kind with that received from an excellent
piece of music. This is an advantage itinerant preachers have over
those who are stationary, as the latter can not well improve their
delivery of a sermon by so many rehearsals.

—Benjamin Franklin

YOUR METHOD OF DELIVERY—how you present your words—is an important area of study. In speech classes, delivery often has two meanings: (1) the method by which a speech is presented, and (2) the non-verbal means by which a speech is supported. Before we study the non-verbal methods of supporting speeches, we must first understand the four methods of delivering a speech. They are: manuscript reading, extemporaneous speaking, memorized speaking, and impromptu.

MANUSCRIPT READING: "TALKING HEADS"

Most professional television broadcasters rarely use their hands when broadcasting the news. They merit the nickname *talking heads* because their task is merely to read the teleprompter in an engaging and compelling way. These broadcasters are not giving public speeches *per se*; they are reading a manuscript.

In a public speaking context, there are times when manuscript reading is appropriate. For instance, a politician or a business leader who wishes to convey a carefully crafted policy message or a scientist who needs to read the findings of an important study will probably have to read from a prepared manuscript. In these circumstances, manuscript reading is perfectly appropriate because the speaker needs to be thorough, careful, and clear. This approach allows the speaker to read a text without laboring to remember the words because these speeches are usually lengthy and require precision. Paraphrasing or speaking "off the script" is not favored in situations that demand manuscript reading, because the speaker may forget important sections of the speech.

EXTEMPORANEOUS SPEAKING: SPEAKING WITH NOTES

In an academic setting, the preferred method of public speaking is the extemporaneous speech (manuscript reading is not the norm). In addition, extemporaneous speaking (the style in which students rely on notes and their knowledge rather than on scripts) is the kind of public speaking that occurs most frequently in business and the civic community.

Politicians often use manuscript reading and extemporaneous speaking together. For instance, public officials will begin with a press conference by reading from a prepared statement and then will open up the process by taking questions from the audience or the media. Media questions prompt extemporaneous responses by public officials who often give rehearsed answers to anticipated questions. In fact, all of us have given extemporaneous responses. In casual conversations, classrooms, or business situations, we've been asked questions and have responded with knowledgeable responses. We've been able to respond because we possess the knowledge and experience that allows us to answer questions intelligently "off the top of our heads."

The reason that manuscript reading is often not preferred is that these speeches do not allow students to think on their feet or react to their audience. Manuscript reading has many other pitfalls: the speaker goes from sentence to sentence, rarely lifting his eyes from the paper; his voice achieves only a monotone, rarely shifting in tone, speed, or volume; and the speaker barely moves his arms and hands to help illustrate his words. The problem is that manuscript readers are tied to their papers, and they do not develop a relationship with their audience beyond merely speaking to them.

Public speaking is much more dynamic; the speaker is supposed to command the attention of the audience by supporting her words with purposeful, physical actions, such as illustrative gesturing. Your audience is there to hear you and see you—even interact with and learn from you.

Your speech is supposed to be a live action performance in which you enlighten, entertain and persuade your audience. And for most students, extemporaneous speaking is the best means of achieving this standard of public speaking.

MEMORIZED SPEAKING: INTERPRETING A TEXT

A memorized speech is, in many ways, similar to manuscript reading. However, the speaker delivers the entire speech without the script in front of him because the script exists in his mind. Memorized speeches are usually brief—lasting a few minutes—such as a toast, an introduction, or a descriptive speech. Students have some experience with memorized speaking. They have been taught to recite old songs and articulate pledges since kindergarten. Later, memorized assignments often mean reciting famous speeches or classical poems—texts written by someone other than the speaker.

In the context of Readers' Theater or other forms of oral interpretation, students will bring the manuscript to indicate the author's presence and will work on their speaking fluency and non-verbal delivery by reading from the manuscript. Readers' Theater is an interpretive reading and speaking activity in which students use their voices, facial expressions, and bodily gestures to interpret the story.

These interpretive assignments usually have two purposes: (1) to revive and perform old speeches for a new audience; and (2) to give practical opportunities for students to train their memories. For these assignments, teachers place an emphasis on how well students recall memorized speeches and deliver poignant or inspirational words. To be successful, you must not merely read the words; you must interpret the text carefully and perform the text appropriately. Reading a text for its overall meaning is an important part of interpretation. As interpreters, we construct meaning not only by reading the text, but also by understanding the context from which this text came.

As a critical reader, your interpretation and performance will often represent the motives (or partial motives) of the original author. Your attempt to revive these words is symbolic and *performative* because the context of this speech is a classroom rather than a battlefield in Gettysburg, Pennsylvania.

As we discussed previously, speeches and arguments are responses to rhetorical situations, and we understand that your representation of these old speeches is done in a different rhetorical context rather than the context of the original speech. For instance, if the rhetorical situation for your memorized performance is your presentation to your academic community, you are analyzing and interpreting the text for your class and your teacher. You use this situation to develop your skills as an interpreter and as a speechmaker.

There is great critical value in studying accomplished speeches: we study them not only to understand their form and structure, but also to understand the underlying arguments and principles. To avoid the artificial or mechanical re-reading of an old speech, you might consider trying this analytical process:

- Study and annotate the text carefully to understand the message or multiple messages.

- This understanding can turn into some kind of personal identification. Our desire to identify with others is a powerful motive in interpreting a text. For instance, when reading or listening to King's *I Have a Dream*, we can identify with King's arguments related to equality and civil rights. When we read a love sonnet, we might consider identifying with the feelings of the poet and relate these feelings to the people we care about.

- This "getting inside of the head" of the author is, on one hand, about understanding the author's feelings and thoughts, and on the other hand, about examining the underlying intentions related to the author's intended audience. This kind of analysis should be a focus of your interpretive act.

- The expression of your interpretation should, then, influence how you read the text aloud. Your voice and pace of reading, in particular, should reflect the tone and pace of the words. For instance, a speech or poem of reverence should be read slowly at key points. A speech of defiance, on the other hand, may be read and performed with fiery passion.

This analytical method of interpretation is an important part of performing the text. For the most part, your interpretation of original intent and understanding of the historical context should influence how you perform your speech.

However, as teachers, we understand that locating original intent may be too difficult and may not even be enough for a modern audience. Therefore, one purpose for performing older texts is to re-examine, re-experience and re-view principles and practices from a contemporary view. Our contemporary view may indicate that we still feel strongly about Lincoln's *Gettysburg Address* and find great value in Martin Luther King Jr.'s *I Have a Dream*. However, our changing views, tastes, or cultural perspectives may also mean that we find some older speeches a bit too distant to appreciate. Nevertheless, interpreting a text from a different era is a helpful way of understanding our past, our audience, and ourselves.

IMPROMPTU SPEAKING: "OFF THE TOP OF YOUR HEAD"

Another dimension of public speaking is the impromptu speech. Quite literally, impromptu means speaking without preparation or rehearsing. Because most speeches are practiced and rehearsed, having to deliver an improvised speech often alarms students. However, truly improvisational speeches are rare in an academic setting. Most teachers will alert students about impromptus and actually instruct them to prepare for and anticipate certain questions.

For instance, teachers will tell students to read campus newspapers, student handbooks, this textbook, watch a specific news show, or follow particular political issues. After some time has passed, the instructor will call the student or students and determine the topic. When this situation occurs, your teacher will ask you to speak about your topic "off the top of your head." But "off the top of your head" does not mean your teacher wants mumbled musings or confusing chatter. Rather, your teacher wants a speech that is focused, directed, and coherent.

To be successful, you have to speak with fluency and deliver your impromptu in a relaxed yet direct manner. Don't let impromptus scare you. If you have a little time to prepare for a specific topic before your impromptu begins, script or jot some notes or bullet points. After all, preparing a quick outline can calm your nerves, help you focus, and help minimize your chances of mumbling or chattering. Other times, a teacher will not allow you to prepare right before the impromptu, saying that you should have been preparing all along.

In either of these circumstances, the key to delivering an effective impromptu speech depends upon how well you understand your subject and how well you organize your points. You can enhance your chances of succeeding by preparing well in advance and anticipating what your teacher expects so that your moment of impromptu goes smoothly.

MANUSCRIPT DELIVERY: HANDING IN YOUR PAPER

Manuscript delivery is important. Your *ethos* as a writer is evaluated not just by the content of your paper but by how well your paper complies with formatting requirements and submission deadlines. Naturally, the standard of acceptability is often a subjective one. Teachers have the freedom to set due dates, assign the papers, and require a certain number of assignments. As a student, your goal is to meet these requirements.

As a matter of practice, teachers will provide an assignment prompt for each writing assignment. This prompt should contain the requirements for completing your paper—items such as due dates, page length, research and resource requirements—and page formatting (MLA, APA, Chicago, etc).

We encourage teachers to be clear about these requirements by providing a checklist, such as the example below, to students, far in advance. Your goal as a student is to comply with the requirements and deliver your paper on time and in the manner in which your teacher wants.

Sample Manuscript Delivery Checklist

Please refer to this checklist when finalizing your papers to turn in to your teacher.

• Did you meet the word count? Manuscript word count: 1,000 words + a citation page.

• Did you follow MLA, APA, or other formatting requirements for your paper as specified by your instructor? The hard copies should be printed on 8.5" x 11" paper, black ink, 12-point font.

• Did you hand in your paper at the beginning of class and email if required?

The Art of Memory

"Memory is the reservoir of all things . . ."
—Cicero, *De Oratore (I, 5)*

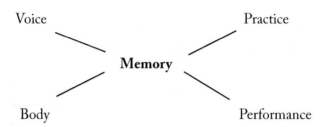

The most important organ in your body is your brain. Right now, your brain is executing billions of interactions, but there is no way you are conscious of these electrochemical processes as they happen. Rarely do we "feel" a thought cross our nerves and membranes like we do when we feel our bodies ache or when our muscles contract, twitch, and spasm. The act of thinking is an elaborate, intricate process that allows us to concentrate on things that interest and bother us and contemplate images or thoughts that pop suddenly into our awareness. As a thinking person, you are able to read these lines, feel the weight and texture of this book, sip your java, and compare what you are reading with your past experiences. One reason why you can do this is your capacity for memory.

On average, our brains weigh a skosh more than two pounds, and this watery, wrinkly organism holds billions of cells and organizes these cells to interact in ways that produce our capacity to think, hope, believe, imagine, and also remember—to learn and recall, even many years later—an old game, a favorite tune, a sad moment, a loving face, or a prepared speech.

But what is memory? A simple chemical reaction? Can we manipulate this chemical process? For instance, can artificial aids—such as writing—improve our natural ability to remember things? The answer is yes, of course. We wrestle with our memories every day. When we are walking down the street, studying for an exam, or gathering with friends, we rely on our memories to function. Psychologists theorize that there are different

YOUR MIND: WHAT STICKS?

Our ears, nose, eyes, and skin capture information simultaneously. Our senses are the means by which we gather external information and interpret the world. Everything that is within the range of our senses is captured in some way as part of our *sensory memory*. According to psychologists, our sensory memory lasts, however, for one or two seconds—just long enough to develop a perception. But these initial perceptions are fleeting things. To preserve important information, we must move whatever information our sensory-memory has captured to our shorter and longer-term memories. We can accomplish this task by two means: *acoustical encoding* and *semantic encoding*. For instance, when your teacher is lecturing, your sensory memory captures his words, and you consciously record this acoustical information as a mental note. Unfortunately, our short-term memories last only for a few seconds longer than our sensory memories. Therefore, this acoustic-based knowledge has a slim chance of encoding itself in your longer-term memory unless there is some kind of emotional meaning attached to the spoken words.

A more surefire way of capturing this information is to write down what you decide is important. By writing your instructor's words, you have already begun the process of moving this acoustic information into your short-term memory. This process of recording acoustic information (information we hear) into written form is called *semantic encoding*. Semantic encoding is an active process that requires selective attention to the material.

Here is a common example: On the first day of class, your teacher asks for a definition of *rhetoric*. He says the word aloud and writes it on the board. Not understanding the word, you write the word, feeling compelled that the word is important. Somehow, the class manages a definition, and you write down the definition. When you encode this information in writing, your chances of remembering what *rhetoric* means by the next day has improved significantly because you wrote down this term and can refer to it many times. Better still, if your teacher assigned a reading describing the significance of rhetoric, the chances of you understanding and remembering the definition of rhetoric have been enhanced further—particularly if written homework was required and you spend the next class session discussing your responses to the reading.

Ordinarily, if these learning habits (reading/writing/speaking) are maintained consistently over a longer period of time, this information has a better chance of staying in your long-term memory. For instance, if the semester-long goal is to study rhetoric, then your chances of understanding and remembering the term *rhetoric* at the end of the semester are greatly improved because you have many weeks of studying this important subject.

However, if this information is not maintained, then your memory will, for the most part, degrade. Details will be lost. Definitions will become blurred. And, in a few months or so after the class has ended, you may forget what the term *rhetoric* means, and you may even forget the name of the teacher who gave you that definition.

kinds of memories, each with a different purpose: sensory memory, which stimulates short-term memory, which can lead to long-term memory.

SENSORY MEMORY → SHORT-TERM MEMORY → LONG-TERM MEMORY

MEMORY TRAINING: REHEARSE, REHEARSE, REHEARSE

Although memory is a natural human function, the development of our memory requires due diligence. We all understand that memory plays an important part in our learning, and we can use artificial instruments such as writing to enhance our memories. Simple recitation and recursive studying practices do strengthen our memories when studying for an exam or composing a speech. Psychologists identify semantic encoding as an important way of affecting our long-term memories. For instance, training your memory follows this process: (1) write down what you need to remember and (2) read what you have written aloud. Then, repeat this process again and again. This dialectical process (writing, reading, speaking) is a good way of preparing yourself for quizzes, tests, essay exams, and speeches—and is an essential part of learning.

This process implies that memory is less a science than it is a skill or an art. For speech preparation, this process is, of course, a simplification of what really happens when composing a speech. For instance, most students acoustically and semantically compose their speeches as they write on a computer or jot down their notes. When we are in the active process of composing and editing, we are using our inner voice and inner ear to ensure that our speech sounds right. By using this voice, we are acoustically encoding this speech, and by writing it down, we are semantically encoding this information in our memories. This relationship is dialectical; our inner voice controls what we write, and our writing influences what we say.

Then, once enough material has been composed either orally or in writing, most students will find a quiet place and will rehearse aloud. This recursive process of reading-writing-speaking is an effective and important way of moving speech information from your short-term memory to your long-term memory. Because we know our memories are imperfect, we must rehearse.

MEMORIZATION

There is some misunderstanding in communication studies regarding the use of memory. With the exception of the occasional memorized speech assignment, most speech teachers shun rote memorization. The act of memorizing a speech line by line, and then delivering the speech without comprehending the speech's context, meaning, and purpose often yields very mechanical performances. You might be asked to memorize someone else's speech, perhaps a famous one, and "perform" it from memory. These living performances require preparation and rehearsal. Delivering classical speeches by Abraham Lincoln or Winston Churchill can be interesting and fun—particularly if you "perform" them.

Most of the time, however, you will be required to deliver speeches of your own making. The key to giving a good speech is to thoroughly understand your subject and become confident in your knowledge about the subject. If you are not used to giving speeches or explaining your point of view over a sustained period of time, the practical steps listed below can help you with delivering a speech. Recitation is a simple way of encoding information into your longer-term memory. Your goal is to internalize the information you think is important in order to control or manage the creation of your speech. Here are a few important ways to further encode your speech into your long-term memory.

> "Knowing is not understanding. There is a great difference between knowing and understanding: you can know a lot about something and not really understand it."
> —Charles Kettering

- Rehearse, rehearse, rehearse. Yes, rehearsing can be tedious even boring. However, rehearsing your speech will help you become more comfortable with your words and become more confident with the act of speaking these words out loud. We recommend five to eight full-blown rehearsals spread out over a period of a few days. The benefits are simple: the more you practice, the better formed, more focused, and intelligible your speech becomes. In this circumstance, giving yourself confidence will heighten your chances of moving your speech from merely repeating your memorized speech to giving an eloquent performance.

- Just as important, we recommend reciting your speeches in less formal situations, such as while showering, walking, or sitting idly in your car. These less than formal circumstances can help you with your confidence. Remember: what is important is not so much remembering your speech but the confidence you gain when you can speak in direct, focused, and substantive ways about your topic.

- Tape record your speech and, as you play back your voice, repeat what you are saying without looking at your notes; this process is often how we learn new songs.

- Videotaping your rehearsals will help you visualize how you perform your speech, but will also, again, help you internalize your speech.

- **Analysis**: One important and fundamental way of internalizing knowledge is to analyze this knowledge rather than merely memorize it. Understanding your speech means being able to analyze your subject from different perspectives and explain this information in coherent ways.

INTERNALIZATION

The result of this process is that your speech—your words—becomes more internalized as you move from "knowing" your words to "understanding" what you are saying. The key distinction between knowing and understanding is realizing that meaning is made in people and not in the words themselves.

Knowing and Understanding: When we put a car key into the ignition, we know the engine should start. Few of us, however, understand the mechanical steps involved in how the combustion engine actually starts.

Certainly, we know our words when we craft our speeches, but we begin to understand the implications of what we are saying when we perform our words, experience our words, and see our words impact our audiences. Internalization is about a personal connection you gain when you create meaning from writing and understanding how written and spoken words impact your learning. In short, knowing is about having intuitive knowledge about something; understanding a subject means you possess an analytical understanding of your topic.

BENEFITS TO INTERNALIZATION

The benefits to internalization are simple: understanding the subject of your speech will free your eyes to look at your audience and enable your hands, arms, shoulders, and body to interact with your words. We cannot emphasize this factor enough: *internalizing your speech is a key component in allowing your body to help support your speech.* Learning how to trust your memory is a key factor in moving you away from a public reading of a text to delivering a bona fide speech. Below are some of the best practices from our students.

TIPS ON REHEARSING

- We recommend rehearsing your speeches a minimum of five to eight times before presenting your speech.

- We recommend rehearsing in front of other people to help you deal with certain performance-related problems, such as working with visual aids or relying on technology, and perhaps take the edge off your nervousness about performing in front of people.

- We encourage you to solicit feedback from your roommates, friends, or speech tutors as a means of gaining confidence and dealing with issues of clarity. Speaking in front of a small group can help you prepare for a larger venue.

NON-VERBAL DELIVERY AND PERFORMANCE: LOOKING AT YOUR AUDIENCE

Internalization will free your eyes from your manuscript or notes so you can look at your audience. However, sometimes tension, fear, and anxiety can prevent you from engaging your audience with your eyes. Many speech teachers will emphasize the importance of engaging your audience by looking directly at them. This principle is both valuable and effective. You can instill confidence in your audience and build a credible *ethos* by looking at your audience rather than staring at your notes. However, if you are too nervous to look directly into their eyes, then don't look at them directly (please see chapter 4 on speech-related anxieties). Merely pretend that you are.

Abstract Looks: We tell our inexperienced speakers to begin by looking at the back wall; then, look at the heads or shoulders of people; and look at the spaces between people: their desks, hands, chest or foreheads. This tactic helps new speakers acclimate themselves to public speaking because students are acting like they are looking at their audience when, in fact, they are merely pretending that they are. A gradual approach is most helpful for nervous students. As you grow more comfortable giving speeches, your abstract looks should grow into more direct or focused looks at your audience. Your teacher will expect your skills to grow as you give more speeches, so you should demonstrate your growth by looking directly at your audience as you gain more experience. Here is some more advice about looking at your audience:

- Avoid "tunnel vision;" some students ignore the sides of the class by looking look straight down the middle of the class.

- Spread your gaze evenly; move your head left to right as you give your speech.

- Strategy: pick three people in class (sitting in different places) to look at and spend an even amount of time with them. This tactic will help spread your look throughout the class.

- If you are nearsighted and can read your notes without your glasses, try taking off your corrective lenses so that you can "pretend" to look directly at your audience. The fact that the audience is blurry (but your notes are not) may help you overcome your nervousness. But remember: put your glasses back on at the end of your speech if you have to field some questions.

- A seasoned speaker will look directly into the eyes of an audience member without losing her train of thought; however, new speakers can lose their place when catching sight of even a friendly pair of eyes looking directly at them. After your first speech, we recommend pushing yourself to try looking at one person in their eyes—perhaps your teacher, or perhaps someone sitting away from you. This step can help you become more accustomed to looking directly at people as you give more and more speeches.

NON-VERBAL DELIVERY AND BODY LANGUAGE

Stop reading for a moment and look at yourself. Are you hunched over this book as you read these words? How is your posture? If possible, look around you. How are other people sitting? Standing? Do they look relaxed? How do you know they are relaxed? Our non-verbal actions—our stance, how we tilt our heads, our varying facial expressions, our "body language"—are subject to interpretation. Sometimes, our body language yields obvious signs. Our state of mind causes us to twiddle our thumbs, furrow our brows, and pace nervously. Though these non-verbal cues are helpful in interpreting how our bodies communicate different mental or emotional states, non-verbal signals are just too ambiguous of an action to rely on because they are non-linguistic in nature. We do not know for certain what people are thinking when we try to interpret their physical actions.

Thankfully, public speaking requires speaking, and most successful public speakers lend their bodies to support their verbal expressions; the right kind of physical cue can help your audience better understand your points and remember your performance. We believe an effective speech incorporates your whole being—not just your thoughts as expressed through your words, but your body as expressed through your hands, arms, shoulders, head, face, and posture.

New public speakers often fail to incorporate these important characteristics because they are caught in the grips of tension, nerves, or anxiety. Most speeches are delivered when standing, and students should stand upright with both heels firmly planted on the floor. Here is a brief list of things you can do to help support your speech.

SPEECH-RELATED NON-VERBALS:

- Stand upright; avoid drooping your shoulders or slouching on the lectern.

- Avoid rocking back and forth between your feet.

- Avoid putting hands in pockets or playing with your hair.

- For the most part, consider not using the lectern because the lectern often blocks you from your audience.

Be purposeful and intentional. A good posture will open up the rest of your upper body and allow you to incorporate your hands, arms, shoulders and legs.

Don't be afraid, however, to move your legs. Effective speakers will move during their speeches when appropriate. If, for instance, you are using PowerPoint for a visual aid, don't be afraid to move to the screen in order to point out an important statistic or move closer to your audience when you are finished making that point. You may also wish to move within your allotted space if your particular speech is meant to be motivational or is thematically tied to some sort of action, such as sports-related topics.

Yet, as most college students can attest, a dry recitation of the facts can make for a very boring lecture, one on which the audience is likely to tune out (or go to sleep). Therefore, to give a successful informative presentation, the speaker ought to present facts in a lively, engaging manner—and that usually means using visual aids.

In print, we generally think of visuals as charts, graphs, diagrams, tables, artist's illustrations, photographs. However, a very important, and often neglected, method of increasing audience interest with visuals is document design—using the "white space" on the page. The white spaces, too, carry a message. Headlines, bullet points, bold or italic type, and inset margins are all devices that can be used to emphasize the purpose of your report and help the audience understand your meaning.

Similarly, there are many visual devices that speakers can use to make a report more interesting—charts, slides, overhead transparencies, models, artifacts. Recent technology, however, has supplanted most of these with video and sound clips and, especially, with presentation programs such as PowerPoint. Just as an example, it has entirely changed the way some of us teach. Depending on the subject, we used to make outline handouts of lectures, flip through overhead transparencies, show a carousel of slides, or have artifacts out on a display table. Now we plug our laptops into the projection devices and have not only our notes, but the entire world of the internet at our fingertips, as well as charts, graphs, diagrams, tables, artist's illustrations, and photographs. In other words, the advent of technology has eroded the wall between oral and written uses of visual aids to inform. Now the images of the printed page can be presented to a vast real-time audience, and the images presented during a speech may be captured on the printed page—yet another example of convergence.

CHIRONOMIA OR THE ART OF SPEAKING WITH HANDS, ARMS, AND SHOULDERS

All of us have used our hands to help illustrate a point. If you are giving someone directions to your campus bookstore, you will tell them to walk two blocks and go west until they reach the large brown building. More than likely, you will also use your hands to point that person in the proper direction. In this circumstance, using your hands will probably help the person better understand your directions and, perhaps, may help him remember your words.

In a more relaxed environment, most of us use our hands and arms when we are engaging in casual conversation among close friends and family. Sometimes we're not aware that our hands our moving as we emphasize certain points or when we are engaged within the passions of a debate. But, what, exactly, is the natural expression of our hands? We instinctively know that supportive physical gestures are meant to promote continuity with our linguistic messages.

One reason why gestures are important is because this action was our first means of communication. When human beings created language, verbal expressions became an easier and clearer way of categorizing the world and communicating ideas. When we are asked to speak in less than ordinary circumstances, our natural instincts often freeze. Our nervousness often precludes us from being our normal selves. Therefore, we have to work hard to overcome this nervousness by rehearsing and preparing.

Professional communicators often use their shoulders, arms, and hands to give shape to their work. Quite often, professional orators, such as pastors and politicians, employ gestures frequently to emphasize their points. In practical terms, you should make some earnest attempts to use your hands and arms—so long as your gestures appear natural rather than mechanical. You should not commit misdemeanors of the hands by being overly theatrical in your presentation because even the most relaxed of audiences can spot mechanical moves, and these gestures can be painful to watch. However, the last image you wish to project is that of a statue. Rather than merely standing behind the lectern, practice specific moves to help your movements become more fluid and supportive. Even if you fail to make your gestures to appear natural, we think your teacher will appreciate the fact that you tried to support your words rather than not try at all.

Practitioners of sign language understand the skill of communicating with hands and arms. This facility allows for manual communication for people in deaf communities. In this community, bodily movements have specific meanings. People outside of deaf communities also use gestures to convey messages. Mimes, gymnasts, martial artists, and spokesmodels understand the concept of *chironomia*, the art of gesturing. They often take special care in communicating grace, elegance, and force in their gestures. For amateur and even seasoned speakers, we know that there should be a limited yet effective number of gestures to help us in our elocutions, but what gestures should you use? When?

In the past, gestures were rigidly prescribed. Now, however, gestures are more informal and spontaneous.

Throughout history, teachers have taught non-verbal techniques as a means of supporting spoken words. In a modern context, natural hand gestures are expected in a speech. Rarely, however, does the contemporary student set about planning and choosing their gestures ahead of time. Modern students are more likely to allow their bodies to go with the flow of their speeches. But in earlier eras of learning, students learned to match specific gestures with specific kinds of argumentative points. Gilbert Austen's techniques emphasized a normalized process of physical expression in which orators would place their arms, hands and fingers (and even their heads and chins) in specific positions as a means of supporting the character and tenor of their orations. We recommend plotting your movements ahead of time. Rehearse these movements in order to take the mechanical or artificial edge off of them.

DEFIANCE OR PROTEST

From time to time, students will give speeches of defiance. These circumstances are rare in the classroom, but they do occur on campus. If you are delivering a speech of defiance inside or outside the context of the classroom, we say your defiance must be directed ethically and responsibly. You must, at all times, remain in control of your emotions. Your defiance (whether aimed at some political or academic policy, politician, or issue of social justice) may be expressed with mild forms of hand slapping or finger tapping on the lectern. However, don't hurt yourself and don't frighten your audience. If the purpose of defiance is to initiate some sort of social action, then anger must be focused on task-oriented directions, such as signing petitions, organizing a march, or some other means of pro-social action.

Voice and Vocal Delivery

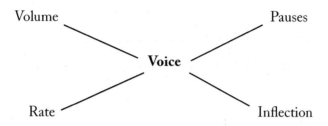

Your voice is an extraordinary instrument. You give life to your thoughts and ideas by speaking aloud and focusing your attention on your audience. Your voice is extraordinary because it is uniquely yours. For instance, have you ever called someone and the person on the other end identifies you before you finished saying "Hello?" Have you ever identified someone by merely hearing her voice as it echoed in conversation while she was walking down the hall? Yes, people have identifiable voices because our voices are unique, and a trained ear can make simple acoustic distinctions. This situation makes your voice personal.

Yet few of us have full control over our voices. There is little we can do about our physical attributes. People have different vocal chords, tongues, lips and teeth. Some vocal chords are thicker than others. Some people have deep voices; some have higher ones. Some people have nasal afflictions or breathing problems that influence their voice. With the exception of choir students or professional actors, students rarely are initiated in the process of vocal production, but developing vocal habits and breathing patterns can help you in your delivery. The diagram above illustrates the four aspects of voice that can be improved through practice.

VOCAL PRODUCTION

Your voice is nothing but air—a column of air that is produced, shaped, and controlled by you. The good news is that because you are in control, you can work on improving your voice by practicing some very simple, yet important, techniques that are really more about anatomy and physics than rhetoric.

Breathing: First, you must learn to breathe. But wait, you say, we all know how to breathe, or we could not live. True, but how many of you know how to breathe correctly? You used to—when you were a baby. We all breathed correctly. Somehow, though, most of us have abandoned correct breathing. Have you ever wondered how an actor can make a "stage whisper" heard in the back rows of an auditorium, or how an opera singer can sing a complicated farewell aria while lying on her deathbed, apparently dying? The secret is that they know how to breathe from the diaphragm. Like them, we must develop the technique of breathing from the diaphragm.

The diaphragm is a thin sheet of muscle that lies approximately under your lungs and on top of your stomach. It supports that column of air and helps your voice carry to all parts of the room. Try this:

Sit in a chair as you normally do and breathe. Place your left hand on your chest about where your lungs are located, and the right hand about where your stomach is. Now breathe in and out a few times. If you are like most of us, you can feel the left hand move, but the right hand will remain stationery. You are breathing from your chest, which gives no support at all to the voice.

Now try this (preferably when no one else is around). Lay on your back on the floor (a hard surface is important). Now put your right hand on your stomach again and breathe. Can you feel it move? If not, try saying "Ha!" out loud several times. The movement you feel means that you are breathing from your diaphragm. Now just lay there and breathe for about a minute or two. Try to see how it feels to be breathing correctly. Try saying a few words, reciting a poem, or going over the grocery list aloud. Can you hear any difference in your voice? Chances are you will notice a slight difference. It may sound firmer, stronger, less nasal, less shrill. Now get up off the floor and see if you can recapture the same breathing and voice quality while standing and sitting. Congratulations! You are now in control of the first step in voice production.

Shaping. You can now breathe correctly, but your breath is not voice. Without shaping the breath, all you can make is the hoarse rasping sounds that are so familiar as the evil sounds of Darth Vader. First that column of air passes through the trachea, or windpipe, then through the larynx, the box that contains the vocal cords. These cords must be set to vibrate to produce recognizable sound. Try this—again, to avoid looking slightly silly we suggest making sure no one else is around:

Breathe through your mouth as you normally would. Now, without changing the shape of your mouth, say "Ahhh." Can you feel the difference? Those are your vocals cords in action.

Now, say the following without stopping: "Ahhhh, uhhhhh, eeeeee, iii (as in 'it'), ohhhhhh, oooh." Notice that only your lips move when you change from one sound to the next. These are commonly known as the vowel sounds—*a,e,i,o,u.*

Next, discover the role that lips, tongue, and teeth play in sound production to form consonant sounds. First the lips: say the following "wuh, wuh wuh, puh puh, puh, buh, buh, buh." "Ummm," the sound of */m/* is also made with the lips only, by pursing them tightly together.

By adding the teeth to the lip sounds, we can make the sounds of */t/,* */p/, /f/,* and */v/.* Try "tuh, tuh, tuh, puh, puh, puh, off, off, off, uvv, uvv."

By getting the tongue involved, in relation to the lips and/or palate (or roof of the mouth), you can make the sounds of */k/, /g/, /j/, /l/* and */r/.* Try "kuh, guh, juh, llllll, rrrrr."

The point of all this silliness is that you can indeed control the shape of the sounds you make, and that is called articulation. In order to be understood, you must shape the sounds correctly and separate them rather than running together in phrases such as "wadjageter" ("What did you get her?"). If you have trouble with this, it might not hurt to practice some tongue twisters; it not only helps with articulation, it can be a lot of fun.

For example, if you have a problem with "swallowing" your */r/*s, try this:

Round and round the rugged rock the ragged rascal ran.

For distinguishing between the sounds of */s/* and */sh/,* try:

She sells sea shells by the sea shore.

And if sloppy */p/* sounds are your problem, there's the ever-popular nursery rhyme: "Peter Piper picked a peck of pickled peppers; a peck of pickled peppers did Peter Piper pick."

There are literally hundreds of these tongue twisters that have been devised over the years. You might want to look up collections of them on the internet and see if you can find one that addresses whatever problem you might be having with clear articulation.

Vocal Control. This is the area of vocal production that deals with volume, pace, tone and pitch, and inflection; we often lump these factors together under the heading *vocal variety*.

Volume is perhaps the easiest to control. You need to make sure that everyone in the room can hear you without being so loud that it makes people uncomfortable. Your volume is largely based on the amount of air you breathe. There are a few tricks that can help you. Especially if you are nervous, the tendency is to speak too softly. This may be because you assume that if you speak only to the people directly in front of you it won't expose any weaknesses you might have. Instead, look at the people in the back of the room and pretend you are speaking directly to them. We don't understand why this works, but it does. Somehow you will psychologically adjust the volume to the right level so that you can be heard.

If, on the other hand, you tend to speak too loudly, try having a friend in the back of the room give you a subtle hand signal when your volume increases. Soon you will become aware of the difference and be able to make the adjustment yourself.

A word about microphones: if you are going to have to use a microphone, there are several precautions you should take. First, be familiar with the equipment. Know how to raise and lower it, if possible, how to turn it off or on, and how to adjust the volume (usually by standing closer or further away). If you will have someone else available to run the sound system, make sure to test your normal speaking volume with them. You should be prepared to adjust to room conditions, as well. Sometimes rooms with high ceilings, hard walls, or metal furniture can create echoes and delays that might distract you.

It is always a good idea to practice your entire speech with the microphone before you give it.

By the way, there may be an occasion where you will have the opportunity to read your speech from a teleprompter. Please remember this rule: Never trust the teleprompter! Always have a manuscript copy of the speech in front of you so that if something happens to the projected script you can refer to your own copy.

Pace is the speed at which you speak. Here again, nervousness can be a problem because if you are nervous you tend to speak too fast, and often get faster and faster as you go. In a one-to-one conversation, speed may not be a problem, but if you are speaking to a group, very rapid speech may be lost as the words become jumbled together.

The pace must also be adjusted to the size of the room, especially if you are using a microphone. Sound waves are non-directional. As soon as a sound leaves your mouth it begins to spread in all directions. In a large room it takes sound longer to travel from you to the listeners in the back. If you speak too rapidly, your words will be lost to them as sounds bounce back and forth from wall to wall and ceiling to floor. Again, practicing the speech in the room you will give it is a great help.

Tone and Pitch. We have included these two qualities together because they are somewhat related. Tone is a way of thinking about the evocative qualities of a voice, and pitch relates to the bass-treble scale. These operate together to create what we might call a pleasant voice.

Now think for a moment about some of the words used to describe people's voices. A shrill voice is nasal, high-pitched, and makes us uncomfortable, kind of like fingernails on a blackboard. A romantic voice is low-pitched, soft, melodic. A business-like voice is firm and does not display great emotion. A boring voice is robotic, devoid of variations in volume and tone. You can undoubtedly think of other possibilities. The point is that these are all qualities that are closely linked to our tastes and emotional associations, and they can all be manipulated.

Try this: Tell the story of the three bears. Practice using a deep voice with a firm tone for Papa Bear, a lilting, sweet voice for Mama Bear, and a high-pitched whiny voice for Baby Bear.

Where did you learn to do this? We don't know—it's something we've all picked up listening to people around us and from experimenting with voice and tone. Of course, you can develop this talent by dramatic training and theater experience. But wherever you've learned it, you must agree it definitely makes the three bears more interesting characters when you tell the story.

You can work on improving your tone—it is entirely a matter of art and practice. Your best ally is a tape recorder. Listen to yourself—see what words you would use to describe your tone. If it is nasal or shrill, you may be breathing incorrectly. Try some of those exercises at the beginning of this section. If your tone is monotonous, practice adding some changes in inflection. If your tone tends toward either melodic or businesslike, don't do anything. A voice that falls somewhere in between those two descriptors will be both pleasant to listen to and will carry some authority, which will add to your *ethos*.

Pitch, however, is not as easy for you to control because it is partly determined by an inherited anatomical factor—the thickness of your vocal cords. The thicker the cords, the more slowly they vibrate and the lower your pitch will be, and conversely, the thinner the cords, the faster the vibrations and the higher the pitch. However, you can do two things to change your pitch somewhat. The first is—you guessed it—breathe correctly; provide a good column of air. The second is easy to say, but often hard to do—Relax! If you are tense, your vocal cords will be tense, they will vibrate faster, and your pitch will go up. Think of a guitar string. The tighter it is stretched, the higher the note. If this is a problem for you, we suggest you go back and read chapter 4, on Communication Anxiety, to help you learn some techniques for relaxation.

Finally, these techniques may not turn you into a golden-voiced radio announcer, but they can help you be happier about putting yourself in front of an audience.

PAUSING AND STRETCHING

The techniques you learn in vocal production can enhance your vocal performance. In our ordinary conversations with friends and loved ones, we raise and lower our voices at will. Indeed, we inflect words (str-e-t-ch-ing words, for example) for emphasis and even pause between our words in order to illustrate our points. These same principles are important in our informal and formal speeches. Whatever the speech, there should be moments when you s-l-o-w t-h-i-n-g-s down. Speakers should rarely mumble or slur their words because the goal for every speech is to be heard and understood. If you have a habit of speaking very fast, then purposely slow your speaking down so your audience can comprehend your points.

VOLUME AND FREQUENCY

Adjusting your volume depends on a few things, such as the room, the size of your audience, and the noise level of your environment. Of course, we left out the most important thing: the normal volume of your voice. If your voice carries well, then a normal speaking volume should suffice. However, if you are soft-spoken, then a slightly elevated speaking voice is probably enough to be heard by your class. However, for larger rooms or a noisy event, microphones may be necessary. When using a microphone, the volume of your speech should be at a conversational level, because if you raise your frequency while using a microphone, you are liable to be a bit too loud.

For most speeches, you will not need a microphone. But when the rain is pelting your classroom window and the wind is howling outside, you may have to raise your voice in order to be heard. Here's a good rule of thumb: speak to the back of the class. Speak so that the farthest person away can hear you. One important principle of vocal variety is to vary your pitch. Raise your voice slightly and vary your tone when making emphatic, critical points and lower your voice when making reflective points. Why? Pitch is reflective of your mood and presents a discernible tone for your speech. This kind of variance gives your voice a vocal variety.

"THE WIZARD OF UHS . . . "

Quite often, nervous students will inadvertently pepper their speeches with copious amounts of *uhs* or *ums*. Our record for this verbal transgression is 26 times in a three minute speech. For the audience, this expression is distracting, one in which the audience begins to anticipate the *uh* rather than pay attention to the content of the speech.

For the speaker, this verbal expression often signifies an inner tension or anxiety, one in which the speaker feels compelled to speak constantly throughout his speech. This verbalism often appears in impromptu or extemporaneous speeches. In these instances, the *uh* becomes a delaying mechanism in which the student searches his mind for the next word, the next line, the next idea.

One way to remedy this problem is to pause between transitions. Building in pauses will not only slow your presentation but might make you concentrate better on articulating your points. This kind of control is a good way to fight off the unintentional urge to say *uh*.

LANGUAGE AND SOCIAL POWER: DIALECTS AND ACCENTS

Each one of us has an accent. Our accent is a product of our familial speech patterns and our social environments. In America, there are a variety of accents, from New York (or "New Yahwk"), Boston, and other east coast accents to other distinct southern ones, such as Tennessee, and southwestern ones, such as Texas. Though western residents (Arizona, California, Nevada, Oregon, and Washington) often claim to have no accents, they just have to travel east to understand that they do. Most of us rarely recognize that we have accents until we venture outside of our regions and speak in areas where different accents are dominant. Unfortunately, prejudices and stereotypes regarding accents often surface. Terms such as *hicks, yokels, lazy,* and *dumb* are often associated with accents other than our own. Many ideological opponents of President George W. Bush questioned his intelligence based on his malapropisms and his accent.

There is no direct correlation between accents and intelligence. However, there is an implicit perception in many Americans that associates smarts with accented speech. For instance, if you happen to drop your *g* in *ing* or say, "How ya' doin'?"—this style of speaking can potentially harm your chances of getting a job. Recent research indicates that heavy accents can impede a job applicant from getting hired because of the stigma attached to certain accents. Conversely, having a less identifiable accent can enhance an applicant's potential of getting hired (Cukor-Avila and Markley).

In other cases, dialects can impede an understanding of Standard English. For instance, many linguists recognize Black English as a dialect of Standard English. Black English Vernacular, also called African-American Vernacular (AAVE), is largely an oral-based, urban phenomenon characterized by a different inventory of sounds, structures, and tenses. When students whose oral dialect is different from Standard English begin writing in an academic setting, a significant amount of their orality often appears in their writing. Simple tasks such as writing a sentence in Standard English become complex mixture of standard and non-standard spelling, syntax, and sounds.

Students who are proficient in their dialect should use their dialect based on audience and purpose. If your community expects a certain way of speaking, then you should use your knowledge and skill to speak to this particular audience. But we also say that mastering the language of the academic community allows students to communicate with another audience, particularly because an academic audience often demands Standard English. Mastering the linguistic and rhetorical conventions of academic discourse is one way to become a contributing member of this community.

SPEECH DISFLUENCY

Though there is no direct correlation between dialects, accents, and intelligence, people tend to associate accents with intellectual ability. These prejudices are often, unfortunately, transferred to speakers who lack normal speech fluency. There are different speech disfluencies; some are caused by genetics while others are caused by environmental factors, illness, or injury. The cause of childhood stuttering is often unknown. Though there have been numerous studies to discover its causes, no definitive knowledge exists to explain why stuttering happens. Quite interestingly, half of all children who stutter as preschoolers overcome this disfluency by the age of seven, but boys tend to recover less often. In a world in which social relationships are often created by the spoken word, the spoken word is often seen differently by the stutterer. Quite often, the person who stutters may feel a strong anxiety toward speaking situations and may explicitly avoid public speaking altogether.

There are other instances when disfluency is caused by injury or illness, such as a stroke, brain tumor, or dementia. Neurological diseases, such as cerebral palsy, amyotrophic lateral sclerosis (also known as Lou Gehrig's Disease), and Parkinson's Disease, often impede speech fluency. Brain and larynx surgery, as well, may also cause speech disfluency. Swallowing disorders and language disorders are, unfortunately, common, and hearing disorders may create speech-related problems.

As listeners, we must be attentive and patient toward disfluent speakers in and outside of class and give them the same courtesy and respect we do with non-disfluent speakers. Our public role as listeners is to listen to understand their message and make them feel as comfortable as a classroom allows.

TOUCH AND PHYSICAL CONTACT

As public speakers, most students rarely venture out into their audience. Bold students and advanced speaking students will sometimes walk up to their audience and even stroll up and down the aisles and tap their audience's shoulders to further engage their listeners in an interactive speech. A more likely occurrence is when speakers invite audience members up to the lectern to help with their presentations. Most public speaking courses rarely discuss—perhaps even shun for good reasons—a discussion of the boundaries of touching as a means of supporting public speeches. As a general rule, avoid touching members of your audience. There are, however, some acceptable forms of physical interaction.

In competitions, for example, speakers will shake the hands of opponents or judges in order to communicate sincerity and formality. These kinds of gestures can be viewed as polite as long as the judges are within proximity of your speaking area. In more complicated scenarios, students have given definitional speeches on their physiology (brain, heart), speeches on the sport of arm-wrestling and talks on self-defense. In these situations when student speakers were giving demonstrations with the help of other students, contact among students was a thematic and demonstrative part of their speeches.

We recall, however, when one particular student gave a speech on the personal and social benefits of hugging. After citing some encouraging studies that connected parental hugging with the wellness of infants, the student concluded her speech with questions from the audience. In a humorous gesture, one student raised his hand and requested a hug. In this situation, touching wasn't a thematic part of the speech, so the speaker gracefully and smartly declined his request arguing that, after all, she was neither his parent nor was he an infant. In these circumstances, you must be careful. In North American culture, social contact is more appropriate for women than men. However, shaking hands or including someone in a demonstration can be an effective way of thematically supporting your speech.

HOW TO BE GOOD AT THE FRONT OF THE CLASS

Giving a good speech begins with a vision. We envision ourselves speaking in front of an audience, stirring them with our words, compelling them to contemplate our thoughts, and inciting them to some kind of action. Our thoughts of success are often based on seeing good speeches given by motivational speakers, politicians, teachers, or exceptional students. We are roused by a good speech and imagine ourselves doing the same things. This kind of positive modeling is an essential starting point when planning your speech.

As teachers, we believe that a lot of work goes into turning that vision into reality. Truth be told, most students have many strengths on which to capitalize. Students know what their strengths are and what their challenges are. And if they don't, their teachers will tell them.

We wish to underscore two important points. The key to succeeding as a successful communicator is understanding both your topic and your strengths as a communicator. Having tension, anxiety, or fear is an important part of being human, and working through these varying states of emotion is also a very important human endeavor. Using your resources is an important part of working through potential barriers (both internal and external ones). If your school has speech tutors, then consult with them; if your teacher is willing to meet with you to discuss your speech, then meet with your teacher before and after your speech.

Preparation, forethought, intentionality, purposefulness, and internalization are key components of a good regimen for succeeding in front of the class. Not planning ahead of time or waiting until the last minute to plan and rehearse your speech can lead to poor execution and a minimalist performance.

GROUP PROJECTS: PLANNING AND PROBLEM-SOLVING

Collaborative and cooperative projects are quite normative in academic contexts. Group writing and speaking projects do occur in your composition and speech courses. Our rule of thumb is simple: keep the group members for your collaborative project between three and five people. Any more creates too many potential problems to manage. There are other principles that are worth applying as your project is conceived and developed.

Many groups get a late start because of the varying nature of their schedules outside of class. Work out your schedules ahead of time. Early on in the process, sit down with your group, bring your planners or calendars, and plan the production of your speech or essay week by week. Set goals and stick to them. Even though your group may make honest attempts at staying on task, problems will occur, but problems and problem-solving are a normal part of the group learning process. Be patient. Keep the lines of communication open. And these lines of communication also include your instructor.

Two potential problems are related to "group chemistry" and varying work ethics. Though creating a group composed of similar personalities is often beneficial, such aims aren't practically realistic—unless your group consists of two people. However, if your group runs into personality or chemistry-related issues, one way to resolve this issue is to focus on common objectives and goals as a way of unifying your group. Again, staying on task and meeting deadlines is a good way to move the project along. Although different students have different work ethics and pace of work, most of the time, the group dynamic will compel the slower students to keep pace, as long as deadlines are made clear ahead of time and group members are in constant contact with each other.

Good communication protocols should also include your instructor. If a student isn't producing in a timely manner for whatever reason, then make sure you contact your instructor well before the due date to involve the teacher in helping resolve this issue.

Instructors who assign group projects have confronted group problems before. But remember: involve your teacher in the process when problems seem to come to an impasse. Don't wait until the night before the speech or paper is due before you tell the instructor. Finally, instructors tend to grade group projects holistically, so make sure you understand how your group project will be graded is made clear early in the process.

COOPERATION AND COLLABORATION: WRITING TOGETHER

Group projects can be done cooperatively or collaboratively. Cooperative projects involve each student taking her piece of the assignment, retreating to her private space, and reappearing at the appropriate time with her portion of the product. Then, the group coordinates the sections in an attempt to unify the disparate writing styles, edit redundancies, smooth out rough patches and add transitions. This process is probably the most practical and efficient way of executing a group project because this kind of work can be achieved with less interference. But, in the long run, this process is also the most problematic because it does not always produce the best results.

Creating a group project that speaks with one voice is difficult if the project is conceived and executed cooperatively or independently of each other. One way to address this problem at the front end is to write a collaborative rather than a cooperative paper.

Collaborative writing projects involve your group dividing the project equally. Once the parts have been divided, collaboration means sitting, brainstorming and composing together as a group. This process is, as you might guess, time consuming and often difficult. Having your group sit together in front of a computer seems impractical, but groups have managed to sit together and craft their ideas into a draft as they discuss and analyze what they are writing. When groups commit to writing collaboratively, they manage to compose a reflective draft that speaks in a unified voice. This kind of unity can be created at the front end and maintained as the paper or presentation evolve. Quite often, redundancies and overlap are eliminated as the project moves along.

Teachers will often dedicate class time for group projects, but most successful groups do not wait to work together in class. The key is working together more frequently—whether outside of class in a computer lab or in a more social setting—and reading each other's writing as the paper develops. Constant feedback and revision are essential in order to have the different parts develop into a more cohesive and cogent whole.

GROUP SPEECHES AND DELIVERY

In most public speaking situations, groups should present different sections of the project equally and uniformly. What is most important is to present the different parts of your paper with great continuity. First is the time issue. If your group cooperatively composed a paper, then each person will speak about her own section. If your group collaboratively wrote your project, then each person should choose a part about which she feels most strongly. Either way, please ensure each group member shares the time equally in front of the class.

Second is the issue of delivery. Successful group speeches promote uniformity of delivery and continuity of message. To better achieve this continuity, your group should avoid disparate delivery styles. For instance, all group members should agree to use one form of delivery rather than using varied styles. Having one person deliver from memory, another extemporaneously, and another manuscript reading often results in an inconsistent performance.

As your group presents its speech, make sure your group executes good transitions between members. Too many groups get hung up on not knowing when the next member is going to speak because of a lack of rehearsal time. This situation creates uneasy gaps between speakers and brief moments of confusion for the audience. One way to avoid this lack of fluidity is, again, to rehearse often enough so that members understand when to transition. Good transitions create a nice continuity among the group members and keep the information coming at a nice, steady pace. Again, this kind of continuity best occurs when your group gets together to rehearse and problem-solve when developing the speech.

WORKS CITED

Austin, Gilbert. *Chironomia (or, a Treatise on Rhetorical Delivery)*. Eds. Mary Margaret Robb and Lester Thonssem. Carbondale, IL: Southern Illinois P, 1966.

Cukor-Avila, Patricia and Dianne Markley. "Employers show bias against accent, study says." *University of North Texas News Service*. 7 July 2000. <http://web2.unt.edu/news/story.cfm?story=7775>.

Social Norms, Language, and an Academic Style

Never offend people with style when you can offend them with substance.

—Sam Brown, *Washington Post*

In matters of style, swim with the current; in matters of principle, stand like a rock.

—Thomas Jefferson

Audience, Purpose, and Choice

Ey, wassup?
Hi. How are you?
Greetings.

THE THREE GREETINGS above give us some insight into the relationship between the communicator and his audience. The first greeting is very casual and slangy, typically oral-based, and implies a peer-based familiarity between the speaker and listener. The degree of formality increases in the second greeting as if the speaker were being introduced to a friend of his parents or a stranger. The final greeting might be used for a very formal e-mail inquiring about a job opening. All greetings are appropriate based on varying rhetorical situations.

Most of us can move between these three styles without much effort. In many ways, a particular style is an outgrowth of our personality and character. Other times, a certain style exists outside of us. When necessary, we adopt a particular style to best meet a particular situation. We shift our word choice and employ different ways of communicating based on our audience, purpose, and environment. How come we use different words to say, essentially, the same thing? The answer is simple: we wish to be understood and to have our greetings accepted.

We do understand, however, that the three greetings *do not* say exactly the same thing. With language comes values, and by shifting our word choice, we are also shifting our message to meet the expectations of different audiences. The reason why we shift our word choice is because different audiences have different values. Understanding this variance helps us build our *ethos* as credible communicators. To a large extent (and more than we realize), our *ethos* depends on our style of communication. As communicators, our goal is to understand the expectations of our audience so we can fit in, and we achieve this by speaking and writing in such a way that our audience accepts us.

Although prescriptive grammarians may cringe at "Ey, wassup?" as rhetoricians, we do not. We realize that a looser, freer style of communicating is probably best when working in peer groups. Because different groups and communities have different expectations regarding the style of communication, style contributes to the overall meaning of our messages. When we alter our style, we alter our message. As Cicero argued, there is no separating style from content or content from style. To fully understand this point, try using "Ey, wassup?" as you walk into your white-collar job interview. How do you think your greeting will be accepted?

The purpose of this chapter is not just to illustrate the stylistic boundaries of speaking and writing, but to reveal the reasons and strategies behind this style of communicating we call an *academic style*. This style is one that predominates in the range of formal writing teachers expect in most classes. Our purpose is to give the most useful information, so students can profit from our clear-cut advice.

PRINCIPLES OF STYLE

Style pertains to more than greeting people. The reason style is important is because it represents our own ethical attitude, emotional state, and logical position. For instance, we speak slowly and softly—perhaps even repetitively—when speaking to very young children; we speak casually and quickly to our friends; we speak in familiar and semi-respectful patterns to parents; and we are polite and cautious when greeting potential employers.

When shifting our style of speech, we dip into our rhetorical register to vary the way we communicate. This register is a place in our minds where our conscious and subconscious thoughts decide on which language and approach is most appropriate. When students enter the university, they are often unsure about what constitutes good writing and speaking. When asked the question, "What is good writing?" students often answer instinctively: "Good writing is clear writing." And when students read professional and student essays, they often critique the writing with impressionism: "Those sentences are good" or "That paragraph flowed nicely" are common observations.

Of course, impressionism is a good start, but as teachers, our goal is to turn whatever instincts and knowledge each student possesses into a reliable skill based on understanding many things, particularly style. With some selective practice and understanding, students can compose their speeches and essays by making some good and reliable choices related to purpose and audience. But what is our definition of an effective academic style? Let's begin with a brief analogy.

STYLE AND SOCIAL NORMS

When someone says, "He has style," or "She has great fashion sense," what do these expressions mean? When we comment about a person's style of dress (from beach wear to formal wear), what are we describing or evaluating? Certainly, we understand that our style of dress is often dictated by many factors: our personalities, character, mood, budget, and occasion. For instance, when we attend a backyard barbecue, we neither dress in our favorite Armani suit nor our Jessica McClintock ball gown (if such things can be afforded). After all, if we show up either over- or under-dressed according to specific social occasions, most of us would feel rather self-conscious or foolish. Why? Social norms and group expectations often dictate our choice of apparel. For pool parties and barbecues, we dress in casual wear and swimsuits for practical reasons.

Conversely, when we are in a wedding party, we dress formally, probably in tuxedoes or dresses. Outside of traditional ceremonies, there are different degrees of formal wear. In a business environment, the corporate culture expects a heightened degree of professionalism in dress and behavior. There are explicit exceptions to this norm, but these social and professional expectations apply to the BMW car salesperson and the legal secretary. In addition, police officers, nurses and others have professional attire because their uniforms send explicit social messages regarding their professional duties and codes of conduct. We assume, however, that their professional demeanor shifts to a more casual attitude or familial tone when these folks go home or interact with friends and loved ones.

As we know, dress is a matter of choice and occasion. Formulating our wardrobe is an expression of our inner desires. Sometimes our desire is to stand out, be different. More frequently, we dress to fit in—to conform to the situation and the customs that govern group behavior. We understand that there is a degree of correctness and propriety related to our clothes and language. Though we must never lose sight of the human in the clothes, we must recognize that people make stylistic choices with an idea related to audience, purpose and the situation at hand.

We also believe that one style of clothing is not inherently better than another. For instance, your most expensive dress suit is not inherently better than your favorite pair of jeans. The point is simple: your suit is more appropriate for some occasions while your jeans are more suitable for others. But what is the relationship between style of apparel and style of language? Social norms govern language as well.

The purpose of this chapter is to help you look beyond the surface of language and understand that language is composed of choices. We understand that there are different styles of speech and writing. If you are young, then you speak a certain way to your friends; this casual style (perhaps slangy) is different than speaking to your teachers; furthermore, you probably elevate your style of speech when speaking to your parents' bosses. This shift in style illustrates our point—that you are rhetorically sensitive to your audience because your personality and character have many sides; this richness and complexity show that you have a communicative strategy, one predicated on being understood and fitting in.

In this chapter, the goal is to learn to understand this rhetorical shift and communicate effectively within your own academic community.

ACADEMIC DISCOURSE

As communicators, we make many choices in formulating and presenting our beliefs and arguments. Therefore, we believe that writing and speaking should be composed by genuine choice rather than accident or instinct. The goal of most speech and writing classes is to initiate students into communicating within acceptable academic standards—or, as academics regularly say, "entering academic discourse." Academic discourse is based on diversity. Your business professor, for instance, would argue that writing memos and business letters requires clarity, concision, formality, and some degree of elegance. On the other hand, your poetry teacher may argue that poetic expressions have a broader license of self-expression where ambiguity may even be desired. In other words, there are different kinds of academic discourse.

However, there are some basic styles of expression and common techniques that cross disciplines—in both written and spoken forms—that you could profit from learning well. Because the university is a community in which you plan to prosper, we propose to teach a style of speaking and writing as an important norm for communicating in academia, a style we believe that most university teachers (not all) would find acceptable and desirable. This common, formal standard of expression is the style of expression written for this chapter.

THE IMPORTANCE OF AN ACADEMIC STYLE

This academic style possesses many features, but it is ultimately persuasive. What makes a speech or essay persuasive is not just the argument and proofs it employs but the language in which these important characteristics are presented. By our definition, this academic style is cohesive, fluid, almost always correct, mature, formal, and persuasive. This style is appropriate for a college audience of listeners as well as an audience that reads newspapers and magazines. Clearly stated, these principles have specific forms and techniques, most of which can be easily identified once students understand the terminology and examples. To better understand the virtues and boundaries of this style, we must pay close attention to other styles of expression.

Because the study of style is an enormous undertaking, we divide style into three comprehensible parts. These are: the *grand style*, academic style, and the *plain style*. A reminder: before we examine the different styles, we acknowledge that one style is not inherently superior to another. Rather, one style of expression is better suited for specific audiences than others.

LEVELS OF STYLE

Before we begin our analysis of academic style, let's read the following passage, a text written in what is called the grand style. This style is lofty and elegant, but sometimes hard to grasp:

> Among the innumerable mortifications that waylay human arrogance on every side may well be reckoned our ignorance of the most common objects and effects, a defect of which we become more sensible by every attempt to supply it. Vulgar and inactive minds confound familiarity with knowledge, and conceive themselves informed of the whole nature of things when they are shown their form or told of their use; but the *speculatist*, who is not content with superficial views, harasses himself with fruitless curiosity, and still as he inquires more perceives only that he knows less.
>
> —from *The Idler*

The features of grand style are elevated diction framed in longer sentences. Although there is an engaging rhythm, the readability of this text may hamper a modern audience because of a few unfamiliar words. Clearly, this style is one that stands apart from most of us, the kind of style, however, that is suitable for analysis in a literature class. Your literature professor would probably have you labor over this excerpt to understand the subtleties and nuance of the prose. The above passage is composed in grand style because Samuel Johnson, the writer, was not writing for a twenty-first century college audience. Rather, he was composing this piece for a nineteenth-century audience.

AN ACADEMIC STYLE

Because this style is concerned with persuasion, clarity and comprehension play key parts. If you wish to persuade your audience with your arguments, you must also convince them that you can write and speak effectively. To clarify the features of this style, here is a revision of Johnson's passage in a less grand but still dignified academic style:

> What strikes fear in the hearts of the arrogant is their ignorance of everyday things and ordinary feelings. These vulgar and lazy people think they know-it-all when they speak of the inconsequential things that fill their lives. But those other people, the visionaries and the pioneers, are quietly contemplative and self-reflective because they are not merely content with the *status quo*; they push themselves in their mental playgrounds with their boundless curiosities and dream-filled aspirations and realize that the more they learn, the more they realize they need to learn more, for they are never satisfied with whom they are and desire to be more than what they are.

Analysis: Isn't this passage more accessible? Although this revision is still composed by lengthy sentences, the readability of this text has been improved significantly by a shift in words and syntax. Clearly, an academic style is characterized by a style that is fluid, clear, dignified and forceful. One way to fully appreciate this kind of academic style is to contrast it with two other styles, one based on plainer language, and one based on a more youthful, oral style.

THE PLAIN STYLE

The features of the *plain style* are its ordinary diction, simple sentences, and a lack of stylistic variation. Quite often, however, the plain style doesn't quite develop enough substance or provoke enough interest to move beyond making a few general points.

> Conceited people are afraid when they think about their own lives. These people think they know it all. But the quieter people, in their own way of thinking, are really different. They use their imaginations to work harder and reach above themselves to change who they are.

Analysis: The plain style achieves clarity, but this style often lacks weight and traction. Why? The language is somewhat minimal and general, so the argument descends into simplicity. Notice the fewer words and shorter sentences? The language of the plain style often sounds like the language of ordinary conversations. There are, of course, variations on style. Many students find themselves somewhere between the plain style and the academic style when they begin college.

SLANG

In addition to the styles we have listed above, there is another style of expression, one that our students have called slang or lingo; the technical term is *argot*. This style is adopted by certain groups, particularly young people, or at particular times, and it serves as a sort of code; it identifies those who are members of the group or those who are reflective of the time period. During the 1920s, flappers could be heard uttering phrases such as "Twenty-three skidoo" or "It's the bee's knees." In the 1940s, bebop was common—"cool cats" or "jivin'" in a "Zoot suit." The hippie movement of the 1960s gave us "groovy," "far out," and "man," as in "Peace, man." In the 1990s, Valley Girl talk was "you know, like, soooo hot." Today, with the advent of hip-hop, rap, and such television programs as *Def Comedy Jam* and the popularity of *Def Poetry Jam*, a slang-filled style has taken center stage as the argot of this generation.

It is worth repeating that one style is not inherently better than the other. However, one style may be more suitable than others depending on communicator, message, and audience.

EXERCISE AND DIRECTIONS

Here is one example of grand style. Revise this passage into academic style. Then compare your academic style revision with the grand style text. In your analysis, discuss the process by which you revised the text and note if your revision gained or lost anything.

THE GRAND STYLE

> How alarming, therefore, for any honest critic who should undertake this later subject of Coleridge, to recollect that, after pursuing him through a zodiac of splendours corresponding to those of Milton in kind, however failing in degree—after weighing him as a poet, as a philosophic politician, as a scholar—he will have to wheel after him into another orbit: into the unfathomable nimbus of transcendental metaphysics! Weigh him the critic must in the golden balance of philosophy the most abstruse—a balance which even itself requires weighing previously—or he will have done nothing that can be received for an estimate of the composite Coleridge.
> —Thomas De Quincey, "Coleridge and Opium-Eating."

GROWING PAINS, PLAYING IT SAFE, AND CHALLENGING YOURSELF

If you recognize that your style of writing fits into the plain style, then your teacher will more than likely challenge you to grow. If you continue to write in the plain style (simple words, short sentences), then you're playing it safe. If your modes of expression do not grow, more than likely your ideas will not grow either. However, if you take some principled risks with your writing and speaking, then you will learn from this experience. But there are dangers. If you begin to vary your techniques, you might begin to lose grip of your points. Moving from simple sentences to compound-complex sentences may prove to be difficult. Your teacher will guide you through this process, but you will have to make this effort as a matter of choice, so push yourself.

ACADEMIC STYLE: SOME CLARIFICATION

Given our argument that most teachers appreciate and want similar things, we must clarify the components of academic style. Below is a list of the features favored in this style.

- *Prefer the active voice:* To achieve active voice, place the active agent in the subject position (e.g., "I threw the ball," as opposed to "The ball was thrown by me"). There are some exceptions to this rule, however. The sciences and social sciences, for instance, often prefer third-person passive voice to express specific actions in which the agent is not as important (e.g., instead of writing "I heated the chemical solution to 300 degrees," it would be more appropriate to write: "The chemical solution was heated to 300 degrees"). Again, academic styles are varied, but active voice is most often preferred.

- *Varied diction*: Effective rhetors must understand the diversity and power of words. The diction of this style should rarely baffle an academic audience but should sufficiently challenge them. Academic writing effectively mixes denotative and connotative words as well as abstract and concrete words. Each discourse has its terminology and jargon, and your effectiveness as a communicator is often measured by how well you relate terminology (and theory) within your own acts of communicating.

- *Sentence variety*: Use different kinds of sentences for different ideas. Moving from simple sentences to compound and compound-complex sentences is an important feature of academic style. The sentence choices of this text book use disjunction, coordination, and subordination.

- *Transitions*: Connect ideas logically, cue the reader, make sentences "flow." Make sure your transitions are logical (use *however, therefore,* etc.). But strongly consider using more organic transitions (such as anadiplosis or antithesis) to make your prose and ideas coherent.

- *Tying your ideas together:* Most western audiences tend to favor a cause and effect sequence in their sentences. For example, the sentence: "The malfunctioning traffic light caused several accidents." This sentence, in active voice, places the cause in the subject position and the effect in the predicate.

- *Use limited contractions:* Spell out *do not* before writing *don't.* Use *is not* instead of *isn't.*

- *Eliminate first and second person references, such as* I *and* you— unless you are composing a first-person narrative or directly addressing an audience (such as in this sentence). Do not make frequent use of the general pronoun *it* as either a subject or object, for *it* introduces vagueness into your writing. Choose clearer nouns for subjects and objects.

There are, of course, more features, but remember: these features are meant to achieve concision, clarity, and persuasiveness. For an example of a paper written in an effective kind of academic style, please refer to the student essay in our appendix.

BUILDING YOUR STYLISTIC MUSCLES: *COPIA* AND *BREVITA*

Here, our goal is to explain the boundaries of undergraduate writing and speaking. We believe that students can learn these boundaries quickly, but we also argue that there is no substitute for working hard at prospering within these boundaries. Erasmus (1466–1536), the rhetorician and theologian, argued that students needed to learn *copia* ("abundance") in order to move effectively between audiences. For instance, he challenged his students to revise this sentence one hundred different ways:

> Your letter pleases me very much.

To prove his own deftness at *copia*, he then proceeded to list variations on this sentence, such as: "Your letter delighted me very much. In a wonderful way, your letter has delighted me . . . In an unusually wonderful way your letter has delighted me . . . By your letter I have been greatly delighted" (38–42).

Erasmus wanted his students to understand the stylistic range of communicating effectively. In order to understand variance, one must learn how to extend and elaborate based on audience and purpose. Furthermore, Erasmus argues that training in *copia* will aid students in their extemporaneous deliveries, for exercises in *copia* will help speakers in their verbal fluency (17).

Exercise: Try adding to this exercise. Here are our own in both grand style and slang: "I received intimate pleasure perusing your epistle" to "Your IM was wicked cool." How many more can you come up with?

BUILDING YOUR STYLISTIC MUSCLES II:
READING THE SPEAKING/WRITING CONNECTION: A RHETORIC

Compare chapters 1 and 4 of this book. Are the writing styles different? If so, why? Theorize why the authors would approach composing these chapters differently.

Understanding the Features of the Academic Style: Disjunction, Coordination, and Subordination

One way to understand an academic style of communicating is to study the different stylistic approaches that serve different purposes. The Academic Style generally uses three different techniques to express ideas: disjunction, coordination, and subordination. These methods appear frequently at different times in the prose of skilled (done purposefully) and unskilled rhetors (done randomly or accidentally).

CORRECTNESS AND CREDIBILITY

Our definition of an Academic Style favors conciseness, coherence, and persuasiveness. Beneath this statement is a belief in grammatical correctness. Certainly, there are times when using a well-placed fragment within a forest of well-written sentences can be effective. Really? Yes, really. A fragment often draws attention to itself because of the choppy nature of its expression, so use fragments sparingly. OK? But, for the most part, students must understand the norms of language and the expectations of their teachers for the sake of their own credibility as communicators.

DISJUNCTION

Disjunction means a lack of coordination or connection between sentences. For example, Julius Caesar's famous saying, "I came. I saw. I conquered," shows no coordination between his sentences. The sentences exist side by side. Another example: most athletes and sports commentators say, "Game. Set. Match," not "Game, set, *and* match." Although these words do not constitute sentences (they are fragments), tennis players shun coordination among the words. How come? For swiftness and forcefulness, that's why.

The disjunctive style is perfectly fine for certain situations, such as listmaking or direction-giving. Quite often, when we are giving directions over the phone, we may say:

> Go down Golden Gate St. Turn right on Hyde. Get in the left lane. Go down five lights to 10th Street. Make a left on Wilson. We live in the third house on the right.

In the hands of the skilled rhetor, disjunction could lead to many benefits, such as clarity, swiftness, and forcefulness. Disjunction can be used smartly when a rhetor is expressing some kind of action. For example, consider this portion of Winston Churchill's speech:

> We shall fight on the beaches. We shall fight on the landing-grounds. We shall fight in the fields *and* in the streets. We shall fight in the hills. We shall never surrender.

In thirty-two words, Churchill uses one coordinator: *and.* Notice the extended parallelism that connects Churchill's words (repetition of the same words at the beginning of successive sentences is called *anaphora*), but also realize that Churchill's words are framed by a disjunctive style that relies on rhythm, cadence, and speed for force. Quite often, this method appears in defiant political speeches. But be careful. Too many short sentences is destined to be ineffectual. Notice how the skilled communicator, Abraham Lincoln, uses disjunction at the beginning of this portion of the *Gettysburg Address* but moves on to other patterns:

> ... in a larger sense, we cannot dedicate. We cannot consecrate. We cannot hallow this ground. The brave men, living and dead, who struggled here have consecrated it, far above our poor power to add or detract. The world will little note, nor long remember, what we say here, but it can never forget what

they did here. It is for us the living, rather, to be dedicated here to the unfinished work which they who fought here have thus far so nobly advanced. It is rather for us to be here dedicated to the great task remaining before us that from these honored dead we take increased devotion to that cause for which they gave the last full measure of devotion that we here highly resolve that these dead shall not have died in vain that this nation, under God, shall have a new birth of freedom and that government of the people, by the people, for the people shall not perish from this earth.

Analysis and Question: Interestingly, this passage begins with disjunction but thereafter makes effective use of some of the coordinators (from FANBOYS: *for, and, nor, but, or, yet, so*), choices that lead to a more coordinated style. Lincoln then uses disjunction to create a forceful rhythm. Why do you think he chose to compose this as one long sentence (82 words)?

COORDINATION: THE ADDITIVE CHOICE

The antithesis of disjunction is coordination. Whereas disjunction often rejects using coordinators, coordination is concerned mainly with tying ideas together. For example, "I crawled slowly away from the explosion, *and* then I felt my face for any blood." This sentence has two independent clauses connected by the coordinator *and*. Most often, writers use coordinators such as *for, and, nor, but, or, yet, so* (FANBOYS) to link sentences. These conjunctions are the most frequent means of bringing relationships into clear view. For example:

1. Ms. Layne was nice *but* tough.

2. Odysseus was a skilled tactician *and* a savvy rhetorician.

3. Her next campaign speech will determine whether she wins *or* loses the election.

The sentences above do several things. First, each sentences presents an idea ("Ms. Layne was nice..."; then, it adds a second idea in relation to the first ("but tough"). In these sentences, the writer relates these ideas as a way to extend and develop the sentence.

As writers expand their sentences, observe this simple rule of punctuation: Place a comma between the coordinator that separates the two <u>independent</u> clauses (a clause possesses a subject and a verb) as demonstrated below:

4. Faith once lived in a mansion, *yet* now she lives in an empty apartment.

5. Nicco wanted to live closer to nature, *so* he built himself a cabin in the Colorado mountains.

6. Ms. Holmes was a tough writing teacher, *but* she was the nicest speech coach I ever had.

7. Brian and Grace bought an expensive hybrid, *for* they wanted a cheaper commute.

8. Neither Laura nor Mark liked Steven Spielberg's film, *Saving Private Ryan.*

Coordination works well because it imposes a logical coherence and a sharp clarity to your ideas. Using the additive style in parallel forms can give your words an elegance, grace, and force. Below is another passage that really emphasizes coordination:

> *And* God said, "Let the earth bring forth living creatures according to their kinds: cattle *and* creeping things *and* beasts of the earth according to their kinds." *And* it was so. *And* God made the beasts of the earth according to their kinds *and* the cattle according to their kinds *and* everything that creeps upon the ground according to its kind. *And* God saw that it was good.
>
> —Genesis, I:24-25

In this example from scripture, the repetition of *and* (called *polysyndeton*) suggests an oral style of using additive transitions, one based on repetitiveness. One explanation for this kind of additive style is that scripture was originally composed orally (before the advent of writing), and one feature of an oral style is the abundant use of additive transitions, a style meant to be heard rather than read.

In this respect, one should use coordination in concert with other choices, for if this sort of approach were to appear in paragraph after paragraph in your essay or speech, the forceful repetition would quickly become tiresome. However, this passage does follow one important rule: the conjunction *and* must be used to compare equally important words or

FANBOYS

for introduces a "because" statement

and links phrases and clauses of equal value

nor used to introduce alternatives; typically with *neither*, as in *neither/ nor*

but introduces contrary statements or opposing viewpoints

or used to coordinate two or more alternatives; often, the first choice is introduced by *either*, as in *either/or*

yet introduces a nevertheless sequence or used to introduce irony

so indicates a consequence, reason or result

concepts. When using *and*, the writer is stating that the compared words or phrases <u>are equally important</u>. For example:

1. Keegan hit it big as a theater actress, *and* Nolan, her brother, directed her in a production of *Hamlet*.

2. Diane began the race cautiously, and she ended the race quickly.

These sentences indicate that both ideas are equally important in each of the clauses. Because *and* is used only to *express equally important concepts.* If you understand this rule, then, what is problematic with the following sentence?

3. Dillon ran for the cab, *and* he found an expensive diamond ring.

The problem is that there are two ideas, and one, you could argue, is more important than the other. We tend to believe that finding the diamond ring is more important than running for the cab. One way to make important ideas more distinct than ordinary ideas is to subordinate the lesser idea in a phrase.

SUBORDINATION

Though disjunction and coordination emphasize different things, subordination achieves a level of emphasis that forces ideas to stand apart from others. The techniques of subordination are so diverse that they give sentences a rich and varied maturity and allow you to emphasize important ideas over lesser ones. For instance, you may *subordinate* lesser ideas in prepositional, appositive, or participial phrases and, consequently, express the more important ideas in the main clause (clauses have a subject and a verb). Here are revisions for sentence three using subordination:

SUBORDINATE PHRASE   MAIN CLAUSE
As Dillon ran to catch the cab, he found a diamond ring.

SUBORDINATE PHRASE   MAIN CLAUSE
While running for the cab, Dillon found a diamond ring.

These revisions show a conciseness and a more fluid cause-and-effect relationship when the lesser idea is expressed through a subordinate construction (such as introductory appositives, prepositional, and participial phrases) and the main idea is expressed through the main clause (s+v). When using subordination, remember to place the main idea in the main clause.

SUBORDINATING IDEAS IN PARTICIPLES

In academic writing, effective communicators distinguish between *main ideas* and *subordinate ideas*. The sentence below has two ideas: one is cast in a participial phrase (that modifies the subject) and the other is an idea expressed through the main clause.

PARTICIPIAL PHRASE   MAIN CLAUSE
1. *Spraying insecticide,* Yvette walked through the garden.

Then, examine this revision:

PARTICIPIAL PHRASE   MAIN CLAUSE
2. *Walking through the garden,* Yvette sprayed insecticide.

The problem with sentence one is that the writer is saying that "walking" is more important than "spraying insecticide" because the idea of walking is expressed in the main clause (subject+verb). In the second sentence, the writer is arguing that spraying insecticide is more important than walking through the garden.

Below are more examples of sentences that misplace the emphasis of meaning.

3. *Feeding the squirrels,* a man walked through the park.

4. *Denouncing all of her enemies, the* mayor stood on the podium.

5. *Laughing himself into a heart attack,* Mr. Sanford sat in his chair.

The third through fifth sentences, although grammatically correct, may sound funny or odd because the main idea (the most important idea) is expressed through a subordinate phrase. Remember: when using subordination, you must place the main idea in the main clause. The lesser idea, for the most part, must be expressed in some variation of a phrase (appositive, absolute phrase, participial phrase, etc.). In the third sentence, the writer is telling us that the man's stroll through the park is more important than his murderous act—in the fourth, the mayor's posture is more important than her speech—and in the fifth, that Mr. Sanford's sedentariness is more important than his heart attack.

As readers and listeners, we may argue that killing squirrels, denouncing enemies, and heart attacks are too important to leave in a participial phrase. The main idea should be expressed in the main clause. Look at these revisions:

3. Walking through the park, a man fed the squirrels.

4. Standing on the podium, the mayor denounced all of her enemies.

5. Sitting in his chair, Mr. Sanford laughed himself into a heart attack.

These revisions are more effective. As rhetors, you may place these participial phrases in different places, such as the beginning of the sentence (as in sentence three) to show cause and effect relationship and also add more information. Here is one sentence with three important ideas:

> Crawling through the attic, Yvette sprayed insecticide, killing the mosquitoes.

Although adding information is a good way of expanding the meaning of the sentence, be careful. Many readers will find the chronological sequence unsatisfying. An alert student may argue that "killing the mosquitoes" is more important than the previous two ideas. Hence, this student's suggested revision may go like this:

> Spraying insecticide, Yvette killed the mosquitoes, crawling through the attic.

> or

> Crawling through the attic and spraying insecticide, Yvette killed the mosquitoes.

These revisions effectively follow the rule of putting the most important information in the main clause and subordinating the less important information in subordinating phrases. As we have written a few times, writing is about making good choices, so make informed choices that best communicate your points.

Academic Style: Figures of Speech

After reading about disjunction, coordination, and subordination, you may have figured out that an academic style favors a variety of techniques. Below is a brief list of tropes and schemes that skilled writers use to make more stylistic choices. These strategies—when used appropriately—add great vitality to your writing. When skilled writers revise their papers, they often consciously incorporate these strategies to achieve a style that propels their writing from the soggy bogs of ordinariness into the broader range of aesthetic elegance and persuasive power. There are many strategies. Here are a few of the most practiced:

1. **Anadiplosis** ("doubling back"): A transitional device in which the beginning of one word group uses the last word (or a close synonym) or nearly the last word of the preceding clause:

> His favorite television show is *Law and Order. Law and Order* has spawned three spin-offs.

> The teacher's favorite rhetorical device is *anadiplosis,* yet *this transitional scheme* was despised by her students because it made writing too easy.

> Victor was in *perpetual trouble. This scofflaw* has been arrested 19 times in four years.

Anadiplosis is often used to join sentences and paragraphs. By using this organizational scheme, you can create organic (rather than additive) transitions between your ideas. However, using this device too frequently can prove tiresome. Use this device carefully in your papers and speeches.

2. **Anaphora**: Repetition of the same word or group of words at the beginning of successive clauses or phrases. Anaphora is a form of parallel structure (where grammatical forms match or parallel each other in different sentences or different parts of the same sentence). In extended parallel structures, this device is meant to create rhythm, cadence, and eloquence. This device is the characteristic of religious leaders, politicians, and prose stylists.

> We shall fight on the beaches. We shall fight on the landing-grounds. We shall fight in the fields and in the streets. We shall fight in the hills. We shall never surrender.
> —Winston Churchill

Again, use sparingly. Churchill uses anaphora to create an emphatic point about the ceaseless spirits of Britons. If you are making a motivational speech or a call to action, try using this forceful device as a way of creating momentum and forcefulness, particularly in your conclusion. Notice that Churchill omits, for the most part, coordination among the sentences.

3. **Antithesis:** An important device: the pairing of contrasting words or ideas—usually presented in parallel structure. For example:

> It was the *best* of times, it was the *worst* of times, it was the age of *wisdom,* it was the age of *foolishness,* it was the epoch of *belief,* it was the epoch of *incredulity,* it was the season of *Light,* it was the season of *Darkness,* it was the spring of hope, it was the *winter of despair. . .*

This passage, from Charles Dickens's *A Tale of Two Cities,* swirls with antithesis and parallelism. Here are others:

> *Copia* is the antithesis of *brevitas*.

> Even the *blind* can *see*.

> The boss's *loose work ethic* contrasts sharply with his statements about *working hard*.

> The politician's argument for more *accountability* in legislative affairs conflicts with his own personal life, a life of *philandering, tax evasion, and backstabbing*.

> "What keeps the <u>Fantastic Four</u> franchise alive is *the Human Torch's emotional fire* and *the Silver Surfer's melancholy ice*."
> —Michael Sragow, *Baltimore Sun*

A great device. Students often use antithesis in separate sentences, but try making contrasting points within one sentence (indicated above). Some students use this figure to transition between paragraphs. For example, as one paragraph about the benefits of a higher minimum wage ends, the next paragraph begins with the problems of raising this wage.

4. Apothegm: a curt or terse statement embedded within longer sentences. This effective device usually captures the main point by pointing out an emphatic anger, contempt, or joy. For example:

> Dan told me that if I studied hard, got plenty of rest, and spoke to my teachers regularly, I would be at absolutely no risk of failure. *Dan was wrong*. Last semester, I spent four excruciating months on academic probation for plagiarizing a paper.

5. Appositives (a device of subordination) are phrases or words (usually nouns, sometimes adjectives) that rename or give more information about the subject or object. Appositives can be used before or after the noun they modify. For example:

> *Boldness, courage, toughness*—these are the hallmarks of Greek warriors.

> Michael Josephson, *a highly respected councilman*, was appointed as Dean of Public Administration.

> The vice president publicly praised his student interns—
> *Angela, Janet, and Kelly*—for working hard during the
> summer.
>
> Chris Rock, *the edgy comic,* is appearing tonight at the
> Memorial Auditorium.
>
> Richard Belzer, *the stand-up comedian,* has played Lt.
> John Munch in at least seven different television shows:
> *Homicide: Life on the Streets, Law and Order, Law and
> Order: SVU, Law and Order: Trial by Jury, the Simpsons,
> Arrested Development* and *the X-Files.*

Use appositives liberally but responsibly. Appositives are a good way of extending your ideas by adding more information to your sentences.

6. Chiasmus ("criss-cross"): The deliberate reversal of grammatical patterns in successive phrases or clauses. Also, a deliberate rejection of parallel structure. For instance, here is a sentence that honors parallel structure: "By day, we study, and, by night, we frolic." Here are examples of *chiasmus*:

> By day, we study, and we frolic by night.
>
> It is very hard to make money, but spending it is quite
> easy.
>
> He exalts his enemies; his friends, he destroys.

Teachers enjoy parallel structure. However, deliberately rejecting parallelism from time to time is a way of making the idea (which isn't expressed in parallel form) stand out.

7. Parallel Structure: Introduced earlier, this device adds strength and rhythm to your writing by deliberately using matching grammatical forms. Here, the idea is to create symmetry in your writing by crafting forms that match. For example:

> As a businessman, I work hard to provide for my
> customers, but as a consumer, I shop diligently to save
> for my family.

Notice the matching forms of "as a businessman" and "as a consumer." Further, "I work hard…" is grammatically matched with "I shop diligently…" Parallelism can be used in many ways. Notice how parallelism appears in doublet and triplet form.

8. Doublet: A pair of grammatically parallel words combined with a conjunction. This simple device is economical because it reveals more information about the object of the doublet:

> Terrence is an *insightful* and *talented* artist.

> Natalie was *smart* and *funny*. Roger was *quiet* yet *bold*. Together, they were an *adventurous* yet *sensitive* couple.

> We found the film repulsive and offensive; and we thought it was insulting and embarrassing.

Using doublets shows control and intent. Again, the pace of reading quickens when using this form of parallelism. Use doublets for emphasis and as a way of adding more information to your points.

9. Triplet: An extension of the doublet; a parallel series of three terms (usually adjectives, sometimes nouns) or three successive phrases:

> "The perfect summer movie, that is if you're eight years old or under. For the rest of us, the sequel to the first <u>Fantastic Four</u> that miraculously amassed more than $150 million in 2005, is a *plotless, brainless, witless* bore."
> — Pete Travers, *Rolling Stone*

> Our team must be *courageous, brave,* and *determined* if we are to defeat our opponent.

Skilled writers often extend this parallelism to achieve a triplet within a triplet:

> Our team must be *courageous, brave,* and *determined,* if we are to *win this game, earn this set,* and *defeat our opponent.*

In this example, three phrases are expressed in parallel form:

> Gary was *an excellent dribbler, a speedy passer,* and *a proficient shooter.*

In this respect, parallel structure can be used deliberately as a means of creating longer sentences and extending your ideas.

10. Rhetorical Question: Asking a question not for the sake of eliciting an answer but for the purpose of asserting or denying something.

It is an effective device to draw your readers and listeners into your essay or speech. But do not overuse the device! Use it sparingly at a key moment to solicit agreement from your audience or to retort a position.

> If you prick us, do we not bleed? If you tickle us, do we not laugh? If you poison us, do we not die? And if you wrong us, shall we not seek revenge?
> —Shakespeare, *The Merchant of Venice*

USING TROPES AND SCHEMES

Recall that a trope produces an artful deviation in the ordinary *meaning* of words (such as metaphor and simile)—while a scheme produces an artful deviation from the ordinary *arrangement* of words. Below is Max Shulman's opening line from his short story, "Love is a Fallacy." Read this passage and explain how Shulman uses these devices to sharpen his prose.

> Cool was I and logical. Keen, calculating, perspicacious, acute and astute—I was all of these. My brain was as powerful as a dynamo, precise as a chemist's scales, as penetrating as a scalpel. And—think of it!—I was only eighteen.

READING AND ANALYZING STYLE

1. In the final paragraph of this chapter, "A Final Word (or two) About Style," we deliberately use parallel structure to help craft our points. Task: locate the parallel examples and explain how this use of parallelism affects our thematic points.

2. One of the most moving speeches in American history is Sojourner Truth's "Ain't I a Woman?" Truth, born a slave in 1797, was later freed and became active in the abolitionist movement. This speech was delivered in 1851 at the Women's Convention in Akron, Ohio. Observe her use of rhetorical questions and her ability to create eloquence in spite of the plain style.

Ain't I a Woman?

Well, children, where there is so much racket there must be something out of kilter. I think that 'twixt the negroes of the South and the women at the North, all talking about rights, the white men will be in a fix pretty soon. But what's all this here talking about?

That man over there says that women need to be helped into carriages, and lifted over ditches, and to have the best place everywhere. Nobody ever helps me into carriages, or over mud-puddles, or gives me any best place! And ain't I a woman? Look at me! Look at my arm! I have ploughed and planted, and gathered into barns, and no man could head me! And ain't I a woman? I could work as much and eat as much as a man—when I could get it—and bear the lash as well! And ain't I a woman? I have borne thirteen children, and seen most all sold off to slavery, and when I cried out with my mother's grief, none but Jesus heard me! And ain't I a woman?

Then they talk about this thing in the head; what's this they call it? [member of audience whispers, "intellect"] That's it, honey. What's that got to do with women's rights or negroes' rights? If my cup won't hold but a pint, and yours holds a quart, wouldn't you be mean not to let me have my little half measure full?

Then that little man in black there, he says women can't have as much rights as men, 'cause Christ wasn't a woman! Where did your Christ come from? Where did your Christ come from? From God and a woman! Man had nothing to do with Him.

If the first woman God ever made was strong enough to turn the world upside down all alone, these women together ought to be able to turn it back, and get it right side up again! And now they is asking to do it, the men better let them.

Obliged to you for hearing me, and now old Sojourner ain't got nothing more to say.

More Examples

Below are some effective examples worth studying. After learning the terminology and the purposes of style, writers and speakers work to intertwine these organizational patterns in their thoughts and ideas to bring more force to their points. By forging their ideas with these devices, these rhetors develop a stronger academic style that favors concision, clarity, and persuasion. The benefit is that rhetors also begin to shape further their own "voices," their own styles of writing and speaking. Here, the examples incorporate many more tropes and schemes than we have room to discuss.

RHETORICAL QUESTION AND APOTHEGM

I guess the ban was lifted because I was able to read the book in my high school English class. Because high school students have not reached adulthood, school boards shield them from great and controversial works of literature. *Denying the students the right to read a book? A ridiculous policy!* I do not understand why <u>Catcher in the Rye</u> was ever banned.

USING ANTITHESIS AS A TRANSITION AND TO MAKE EMPHATIC POINTS

Nancy Benoit was *living* a *dream. Her death,* and that of her son, last week has thrown into sharp focus the *nightmare* that can result if pro wrestlers get lost between *fact* and *fantasy.*
—Elizabeth Merrill, espn.go.com

PARALLEL SUBJECTS, DOUBLET, APPOSITIVE, APOTHEGM, AND ANAPHORA WITH ASYNDETON

When student newspapers are involved in freedom of the press controversies, the *news media* leap to their defense. *Local and national* exposure usually forces a publicity-shy high school administration to retreat. But the *news media* apparently were slumbering when high school journalism was downsized into oblivion. Administrators, *wary of public censorship battles,* simply got rid of the newspaper the old-fashioned way—through the purse. *And that was that! No more* potential problems. *No more* embarrassing questions. *No more* negative publicity.

ANADIPLOSIS, ANAPHORA, DOUBLET, ANAPHORA, DOUBLET WITHIN AN APPOSITIVE, ANAPHORA/PARALLEL STRUCTURE/ANTITHESIS, AND RHETORICAL QUESTION

The only reason why I could not be so quick to pull the plug is because of a word called *"Hope."* Hope gives me the feeling that this person could soon rise again. *Hope* may also eliminate the *facts and reality* of my loved one—*the reality that* there will never be any actual life for this person on this earth—*the reality that* this person is deteriorating daily and should be moved on to the afterlife. The word *"Hope"* will, again, tell me that there will soon be a cure for a loved one, a much *beloved and cherished* human being. *What would I do? What would you do?*

DOUBLETS, ANADIPLOSIS, ANTITHESIS (WITHIN A DOUBLET), TRIPLET, APOTHEGM, MILD ANAPHORA, AND TERMINAL ANTITHESIS

Everyday, hundreds of thousands of people suffer unbearable *physical and emotional* pain as they face *illness*. *Illness* can attack even the strongest person and render them *mentally and physically* ill. In many cases, death is imminent. Ailments such as *cancer, leukemia, and AIDS* can cause *long and painful lives* before imminent <u>death</u>. If these battles with incurable afflictions are already lost, then why must the suffering victims continue to fight? *What is there to win?* Unfortunately, *we* are forced *to live. We* do not have the right *to die.*

ANAPHORA, ANTITHESIS WITH PARALLEL STRUCTURE, ANAPHORA WITH PARALLEL STRUCTURE, AND DOUBLETS

"...would it be better for students to be subject to no censorship by their school administrators under any circumstances, or *would it be better for* high school students that school administrators have the legal right to censor their high school newspapers? Addressing these questions can help reach a negotiated settlement between *the practice of free speech without any regulation* and *the practice of free speech with some kind of regulation* to ensure its proper usage. There is no doubt that *the group of individuals arguing against censorship* and *that the group of individuals arguing for censorship* want to provide *students* and *student presses* with the best system which allows them *to develop and to deal* with *the issues* and *problems* they face."

A Final Word (or two) About Style

We believe that the study of grammar and style can greatly benefit students. However, studying language is often uncongenial and difficult. Our students often say that studying grammar and style is like eating broccoli and bell peppers. Though most of our students don't necessarily enjoy the experience, they understand the benefits of a good diet of green vegetables.

Our expectation is that you will learn and apply these choices with good intent. When students begin to deliberately craft tropes and schemes into their own language, they begin to expand their stylistic choices and develop their ideas (as in the above examples). In this respect, teachers appreciate and welcome this effort, for writing and speaking teachers would rather see their students try parallelism with antithesis than not see students try these devices at all. Remember: when your teacher teaches style and grammar, she expects you to incorporate what you are learning in your speeches and essays.

But get started early. When students wait until the day (or a few days) before to begin their papers or speeches, they tend to forget about developing a sharper prose style. We recommend starting and completing a draft sooner rather than later, for if you start sooner, there is more time to spend on revising your claims, proofs, and prose style.

WORKS CITED

De Quincey, Thomas. "Coleridge and Opium-Eating." *The Collected Writings of Thomas De Quincey: Biographies and Biographical Sketches.* Ed. David Masson. Edinburgh: A & C Black, Vol. 5: 182.

Erasmus, Desiderius. *On Copia of Words and Ideas.* Milwaukee, WI: Marquette UP, 1963.

Johnson, Samuel. "The Idler." *Samuel Johnson: Selected Writings.* Ed. Patrick Cuttwell. New York: Penguin, 1984.

Sragow, Michael. "Less than fantastic: 'Silver Surfer' lacks the spark of its predecessor although the Human Torch ignites." *Baltimore Sun.* 15 June 2007. 23 June 2007. <http://www.baltimoresun.com/entertainment/movies/bal-to.four15jun15,0,4126812.story?coll=bal-movies-utility>.

Travers, Peter. "Fantastic Four: Rise of the Silver Surfer." *Rolling Stone.* 13 June 2007. Web. <http://www.rollingstone.com/reviews/ movie/8653930/review/15096583/fantastic_four_rise_of_the_ silver_surfer>.

Truth, Sojourner. "Ain't I A Woman?" *AmericanRhetoric.com.* 5 July 2007. Web. <www.americanrhetoric.com>.

CHAPTER
13

Rhetorical Analysis and Criticism

Rhetoric is the master art of the trivium, for it presupposes and makes use of grammar and logic; it is the art of communicating through symbols ideas about reality.

—Sr. Miriam Joseph, C.S.C.

C ALLING RHETORIC the *master* art is audacious, a bold move intended to convey just how important we believe rhetoric is to all areas of study. We think this audacity is justified by what you have learned so far about writing, speaking, language, research skills, argument, persuasion, and ethics; these are the very components of education. In this chapter, we will apply all of those skills to the essential academic purposes of analysis and criticism.

ANALYSIS AND SYNTHESIS

Analysis and synthesis are high-order skills, and are, not coincidentally, two of the most valuable skills demanded of college students. In analysis, we look at the components of a text or artifact in order to discover more about its nature. The botanist looks at a leaf through a microscope to discover information about possible diseases within its cells; an art historian analyzes paint chips to determine the age of a painting; and rhetoricians analyze the parts of a speech or essay to determine how the communicator attempts to convince an audience. In each of these scenarios, the researchers are looking for specific information, to the exclusion of other information. We might say they are looking through a frame.

A *frame*, as we use it in this book, is a viewpoint or standpoint from which the researcher operates. Some frames are intentional, as in the examples above; the scope and amount of information is limited so the researcher can focus on a particular problem. However, there are also *unintentional* frames—these are the identities, values, and beliefs that shape everything we do. They frame our worldview. If you are a student, you see education somewhat differently than a teacher does, but that frame will change if you should become a teacher. Most residents of the United States see the world through the frame of democracy, often leading to misunderstanding other cultures and forms of government, which suggests that frames are also culturally formed. Finally, frames are intellectual constructs based on theory—in our case, rhetorical theory.

The values of frames is that once we can identify the frames through which we and others see the world, we can communicate more effectively because we become aware of the biases, values, and culture of our audience. We can also advance understanding by publicly identifying the frames through which we view the world, and, for this textbook, the texts and communicative acts that we seek to analyze.

ANALYTICAL FRAMES

In the academic world, there are a number of generally accepted frames that are used to analyze texts, each of which suggests certain critical questions that, like research questions, guide and focus our analysis. This list is by no means exhaustive, but we do hope to give you some ideas for ways to approach speeches, essays, images, media, and other communication acts you encounter.

The first frame is what we might call the *classical* or *Aristotelian* frame. Grounded solidly in the tenets of classical rhetoric, this frame looks at such issues as an author's awareness of audience and purpose; use of *logos*, *ethos*, and *pathos*; the use of syllogisms and enthymemes; and the adherence to the canons of classical rhetoric, including style. Critical questions might include: How does the speaker use *pathos* to establish common ground with the audience? What are the distinguishing features of the author's style, and does the style suit both audience and purpose?

Another frame that you might use to analyze a piece is *fact-checking*. This frame is particularly useful in analyzing political speeches and advertisements. The issue at hand in fact-checking is whether the claims are truthful and the evidence credible and accurate. Critical questions in this frame might ask: Where did the statistical data come from, and is it accurate? What survey questions were asked and how were they phrased? Does the evidence support the communicator's claim?

A third useful frame, especially for classes in literature, is the *literary* frame. Here you look carefully at the plot, character development, use of literary devices such as irony and satire, author's point-of-view, or genre expectations. Questions here could include: Are the characters static or dynamic? Is the plot believable? If this was meant to be a satire, does it succeed?

Linguistic analysis, on the other hand, looks at the grammar, syntax, and word choice that a speaker or writer uses. For example, are the sentences simple or complex; does the author use Standard Written English, or is there an attempt to use nonstandard English to achieve a particular effect? Does the vocabulary show anything about the author's assumptions about power?

Clearly, the *cultural* frame is very important. We are products of our culture, and we tend to see all that is around us, including texts, from our own cultural viewpoint. In fact, most of us cannot help being so heavily influenced by our own culture that we show a bias in favor of that culture. You will notice, for example, that we have included nothing in this book about non-Western rhetoric. That is because our training, our bias, and our cultural heritage have formed our conception of rhetoric. One might certainly say that this omission is a character flaw on our part, but the truth is that we cannot escape the cultural assumptions that have shaped us. When we hear "rhetoric," we think "Aristotle, Isocrates, Protagoras." Protagoras once said, by the way, that "man is the measure of all things." By this he meant that we tend to measure or evaluate everything by that which is known to us, and that is precisely the point we make here. We tend to evaluate everything according to our own culturally formed standards. The critical questions here are more subtle and often more personal: How does the author's culture influence his or her point of view? What cultural biases can be discerned from the speech or text?

Unlike the cultural frame, the *political/ideological* frame is not inherited, but is adopted. No one is born a Democrat or Libertarian or Marxist; political ideology is a product of values and beliefs that are adopted over the course of time as one experiences life. Politics and ideology can change. It is not at all unusual to find someone who might have been influenced as a young person to support a liberal, or even revolutionary, agenda but who has adopted a more conservative ideology in middle age. The reverse is also true. It is hard to imagine that Senator Hillary Clinton was, when she was in high school, a "Goldwater Girl" who supported the 1964 presidential bid of the very conservative senator from Arizona, Barry Goldwater, but there are pictures to prove it. Questions from a political frame might include:

What impact will this speech or editorial have on the next election? Does a given piece of legislation conform with a candidate's views? How does the author's ideological bias affect his or her stance on the war?

Any of these frames can furnish a valuable approach to academic analysis and criticism. The last frame we're going to discuss, however, does not. This is the *self-referential* frame. You will recognize this frame immediately if you think about high school book reports—"I liked the book. It was interesting;" "I hated this book because it was so boring." In the private sphere, there is nothing wrong with using a self-referential frame, but in the public and technical spheres—especially the academic sphere—it is inappropriate, and is generally considered a sign of immature writing and thinking. When you are tempted to lapse into personal taste and reflection, keep in mind the following phrase: "It's not *about* you!" If you liked the book, you need to be able to spell out the strengths you found; if you hated the book, you need to point out where the author fell short of your expectations. Were the characters flat? Was the plot too far-fetched? You also need to give, as you do in all analysis, specific passages that support your argument.

DOING ANALYSIS

Now that you have considered possible frames and decided on the questions, it is time to analyze. The steps you will need to take are deciding on a frame, selecting the analytical question or questions that you will address, forming a claim, developing the analysis, doing the research, and providing support. Except that the word *analysis* keeps cropping up in this list, you should see that this process is much like the process for developing any other speech or essay that we have discussed in this book.

First, after reading the text to be analyzed, you must decide on a specific frame and make the frame implicit to your audience. To an audience not composed of fellow rhetoricians (and at this point in the book, we consider *you* a rhetorician) you will need to explain the implications of your choice. For example, if you are doing a literary analysis, you should tell your audience, either in your introduction or your claim, why you chose this frame and what you will include. Examples:

[*introduction*]
"In this analysis of *The Great Gatsby* I will focus on Fitzgerald's use of visual metaphor, specifically the spectacles and the green light."

or

[*claim*]
"When Barbara Jordan delivered the keynote address
to the 1976 Democratic convention, she used the
Aristotelian device of the enthymeme to draw the
audience into her argument."

Next you need to research the rhetorical situation. Who was the audience
or audiences? What was the occasion? What is the intended purpose? In
most cases, you should also consider the historical context. What were the
prevalent social attitudes in the 1920s when Fitzgerald wrote *The Great
Gatsby*? What were the issues and historical events surrounding the 1976
Democratic convention? The rhetorical and historical contexts of an event
or text are crucial to understanding the text itself.

Moving forward, you should now reread the text you are analyzing
(more than once), keeping in mind both your chosen frame and the context.
Perform a careful, annotated reading, carefully underlining, making
marginal notes, and highlighting sections you find to be particularly
relevant to your frame. For instance, if you are using a linguistic frame,
be particularly careful to note the words the author or speaker chooses
and the way in which the sentences are structured. Do the words have
connotative meanings that reveal something about the author's point of
view? As an example, why do you suppose we chose the word *perform* in
the second sentence of this paragraph rather than a more common word
such as *do*? Maybe it has something to do with the fact that we consider
reading, writing, thinking, and speaking as performances that demonstrate
knowledge.

Another important set of questions to ask in a linguistic frame is about
sentence structure. Are sentences simple or complex—what does that say
about the intended audience? What position does the subject hold? Is the
sentence construction passive or active voice?

Once you have a thorough grasp of the text itself, you should begin
to formulate your analytical questions. Refer to the discussions of frames
above, and see what kinds of questions your particular frame suggests.
Make a list of the questions and think about which you would be most
interested in pursuing, but also select the question that will fulfill your
assignment and have some significance for your audience.

Naturally, after you ask the question, you have to answer the question,
and that answer will form the structure of your main claim, or thesis
statement. Again, we refer to the sentence above: "When Barbara Jordan

delivered the keynote address to the 1976 Democratic convention, she used the Aristotelian device of the enthymeme to draw the audience into her argument." There's something missing here though—the "So what?" statement. Who cares if she used the enthymeme? Probably no one, unless you tell them why they should. The "so what" statement depends heavily on your audience. To your classmates or perhaps to a group of political consultants, the "so what" may be that your speech or paper demonstrates a rhetorical device (the enthymeme) and shows how it can be applied to make papers and speeches better. To an audience of rhetorical scholars, the "so what" may be to uncover an unusual use of the enthymeme or to see how it can be applied in certain arguments. Outside these specialized audiences, however, we suggest that not too many people will be fascinated by a discussion of enthymemes. Perhaps for these audiences you might consider a different analytical question such as how (or if) Jordan used humor in crafting the speech.

The next step is finding support for your analytical claim. First, of course, you want to map out your argument with a series of subclaims and use solid reasoning to connect the subclaims to your main claim. We've discussed this process at length in chapter 8, so we won't repeat ourselves here except to remind you that this mapping is always important when you're writing and speaking, especially when you are performing a higher-level academic task such as analysis.

After you've mapped the argument, you need to support the reasoning with evidence, and this is where analysis departs from a traditional research paper. One of the distinguishing features of analysis is that, except perhaps for the introduction, almost all of the evidence comes from the text you are analyzing itself—we call it *textual evidence*. Here the dictum "Show; don't tell" is very useful. Show examples from the text that support your claim and subclaims, and use reasoning to show exactly how the evidence supports your argument. Both individual quotations from the text itself and summaries of ideas in the text can be used to support your arguments, but we recommend avoiding paraphrases in textual analysis—it is better to deal with the words of the author than with your version of them.

You are aware by this point that there is more than one theory of rhetoric—all of the frames we presented in this chapter are drawn from various theories of rhetoric. There is the Aristotelian frame, the Marxist frame, the linguistic frame, and so forth. Partly because we do not have time or space to tell you about even a small portion of the theories, and selfishly because the Aristotelian or classical frame is the one we use most often, that is what we will use in this chapter.

The ultimate question in a rhetorical analysis is this: "Is this text persuasive?" If it is not, it fails rhetorically since persuasion is the goal of rhetoric. But this is not a simple "yes" or "no" question. How can you determine if the text is persuasive? First you need to consider the fundamental rhetorical concepts you have learned in this text. Let's go down the list:

- Audience
- Purpose
- Ethics
- Argument
- Evidence
- Arrangement
- Delivery
- Style

The first two considerations, audience and purpose, are essential for any rhetorical analysis for a very simple reason. How can you evaluate whether a text was persuasive unless you know *who* the author is trying to persuade, and *what* the author's purpose is? For example, a great leader might give a very stirring patriotic speech using grand style in hopes of making the nation take up arms against an enemy. (If this sounds familiar, it is the very description of Pericles's *Funeral Oration* to which we referred in chapter 5.) To an audience of Athenian (male) citizens who wanted to protect their city-state and their rights and privileges, this was a compelling speech. However, if his audience had been composed of women whose husbands had been killed in the wars, we might judge Pericles's persuasive strategies as being somewhat less effective.

You also need to evaluate the speech to see if any there are any ethical violations. Does the writer or speaker appear to be biased? Has he or she committed any errors in reasoning?

A very important part of your analysis is the argument and evidence. What argument is the speaker trying to make? Does the writer follow the rules of formal or informal logic as we have learned them? Is the reasoning sound and the evidence credible? How does the author use the Aristotelian proofs—*logos, ethos, pathos*?

Another set of questions has to do with arrangement—how is the speech or essay organized? Does the author use inductive or deductive reasoning? Is the thesis stated at the beginning or at the end, and what does that tell you about the text? Is the thesis implied or overt?

Delivery, either oral or written, is crucial to any analysis. In speeches, the delivery plays a huge part in persuasiveness, of course, but it plays an important role in written texts as well.

If you are analyzing the persuasive effect of a speech, you want to pay attention to voice, gesture, vocal variety, eye contact, expression, and fluency. In writing, consider the appearance of the manuscript—neatness does count! So does the use of white space, headings, fonts. Above all, consider the mechanics—grammar, spelling, punctuation, capitalization. What do these say about the author's *ethos*?

Finally, analyze the style. Did the author choose grand, academic or plain style? Were the words carefully chosen? Did the author or speaker use metaphor, figures of speech, or tropes, and did these devices add to or detract from the meaning? Is the text so convoluted as to be indecipherable, or is it plain, simple, and easy to understand?

SYNTHESIS: THE BRIDGE FROM ANALYSIS TO CRITICISM

We wrote earlier in this chapter about those self-referential junior high school book reports you and your friends probably wrote, generally the night before they were due, often after only a cursory reading of the book in question.

> I really liked this book because it was interesting. It had a good plot. The characters were cool.

> I didn't like this book; it was boring and the people in it were dumb. I couldn't understand it.

Believe it or not, as unsophisticated as the writing appears to you now, those book reports were your first attempts at criticism. "But wait," you say. "I liked the first book, so I wasn't critical of it; only the second report should be called criticism." Aha! We have the same problem here as we had with definition of argument; the definition of criticism used in academic discourse is different than the common definition. When you, and most people, hear the word *criticism*, you think of it as negative feedback, often nagging or picking. That is not what it really means—*criticism*, as we use it, is evaluation.

To help you understand this point, think of movie reviews. The journalists and writers who prepare movie reviews are called *critics*, yet they praise good movies as often (well, almost as often) as they pan bad movies. You read the reviews to decide which movies to see, which means you are looking for positive criticism. Further, you also generally look for reviews by critics whose reviews have been helpful in the past because their tastes appear to be similar to yours. For example, some critics dislike horror movies; you would probably not seek their advice for a scary movie to watch on Halloween. You have learned, to some extent, the frame through which that particular critic views film.

Criticism is merely evaluation according to a set of criteria, and the criteria are determined by the particular frame through which the text is viewed. Remember that list of frames at the beginning of this chapter? We used them to select an analytical framework. Good criticism begins with analysis. In the case of rhetorical analysis, rhetorical theory becomes our frame.

Unless you're writing a 40- or 50-page paper, you're simply not going to be able to use all of the elements you've analyzed. We suggest you pick one or two—such as style and arrangement, or delivery, or perhaps argument—to focus on. You can even be more specific—focus not just on argument, but on the use of the enthymeme to make the argument. We gave you an example of that earlier. There are several examples on our website that can give you further ideas and assistance.

Once you've completed the analysis, you will synthesize your information—"put the text back together again"—and examine it as a whole. When you're doing a rhetorical criticism, here's the bottom line: Is this text or speech persuasive? Why or why not? That is the critical question, and your answer to that forms the basis of your critical claim—the thesis for your paper or speech. Examples:

- Barbara Jordan's 1976 Democratic keynote address succeeded because she involved the audience in her own experiences through the use of the enthymeme. *(Aristotelian analysis)*

- The Simpsons has dramatically changed America's view of the family. *(Cultural analysis)*

> • John Edwards's speech "The Two Americas" has mobilized the working classes by emphasizing the advantages of the bourgeoisie. *(Marxist analysis)*

Simply making the claim, of course, isn't enough. Just as you supported your analysis with textual evidence, you also need to support your critical arguments. This involves outside research. The first step you probably ought to take is looking for resources that will help explain your frame. Rhetorical theory textbooks are your number one choice here, and there are dozens of them. Your school library undoubtedly has some, or you can ask your instructor to recommend something. Next, look for other critics' evaluations of the text. The best sources here are the scholarly publications such as *Rhetoric Review, Quarterly Journal of Speech, College English,* or *The Rhetoric Society Quarterly.* Do *they* think it is persuasive? What do they have to say about the text, particularly in light of your frame? Don't ignore less scholarly works, either, particularly if you are analyzing and critiquing a speech, movie, or book. Look at the reviews. They give you an excellent insight into that key question, "Was the text persuasive?" Think about the reviewer, too; that can be very telling. (Of course, that means you will have to do more research, doesn't it?) Who is this person and what does he know? What are her biases? For example, if you listen to the "instant analysis" of a candidate's speech, you will discover that the Republican and Democratic analysts seem not to have even heard the same speech. Who should you believe—the one you agree with? That's not a very good way to decide, is it? You need to check out the credentials of both analysts before you assess their credibility.

Finally, you will put the analysis and criticism together—you will synthesize. You will draft your paper or plan your speech. But before you stagger off to bed exhausted, before you run that last draft through the printer, you must do one more thing. You must conclude. Bring your concepts together and tell the audience why it matters.

It matters because every day we are bombarded with information: news broadcasts, advertising, pictures, music, speeches, books, magazines, newspapers, web sites, blogs. Unless each of us is capable of analyzing and critiquing, and communicating our analysis to others, the thousands of bits of information that constantly assault our ears, our eyes, and our minds, we will stumble through life letting others control our fates and our fortunes.

And following our own advice, that's what we intend to do now. Conclude. We have written much; we hope you have learned much, and maybe even laughed a little. Why does all this matter? Because, as Thomas Jefferson reminds us:

"An informed citizenry is the bulwark of a free nation."

✦ IDEAS FOR FURTHER EXPLORATION

1. To see the difference that a frame can make, do a little experiment in visual rhetoric. On Google Images, or a similar visual search engine, enter the term "Manzanar," a Northern California site where United States citizens of Japanese ancestry were interned (many say imprisoned) during World War II because our government felt they posed a security threat. Look first for the photos of Manzanar taken by Ansel Adams, then find and compare them with the photos by Dorothea Lange. What differences do you see between the two? What frame do you think each photographer constructed for the work at Manzanar? Does one set seem more negative, one more positive? What might account for this difference?

2. Analyze the rhetorical appeals of an advertisement in a magazine or on television. How many rhetorical elements can you identify?

3. Watch a movie or television show and write a critique of it as though you were writing for your local newspaper. Consider your audience.

WORKS CITED

Fitzgerald, F. Scott. *The Great Gatsby*. New York: Scribners, 1925, 1953.

Jordan, Barbara. "Keynote Address to the 1976 Democratic National Convention." *AmericanRhetoric.com* 2007. 2 Aug. 2007. Web. <www.americanrhetoric.com>.

Joseph, Sr. Miriam, C.S.C. *The Trivium: The Liberal Arts of Logic, Grammar, and Rhetoric*. Ed. Marguerite McGlinn. Philadelphia: Paul Dry Books, 2002.

Murphy, James J. and Richard A. Katula. *A Synoptic History of Classical Rhetoric*. 3rd ed. Mahweh, NJ: Lawrence Erlbaum Associates, 2003.

Appendix

This student essay is prefaced by a note from Jillian Ramos, the student writer, and her instructor, Professor David Holler. The essay is followed by Jillian's speech outline, one derived from her paper.

WRITER'S COMMENTS

It is a sad reality that only certain events in history ever make it to the general conscience of the masses. It is even more unfortunate that the untold stories of the past are often those that need to be remembered the most. This is certainly no exception for the Filipinos who served under the United States flag during World War II. In exploring their nearly seventy-year plight for justice and equity, I have discovered that these veterans not only deserve legislative action: they deserve to be a part of America's conscious memory. I was able to effectively voice my opinion on this issue in Professor Holler's Written and Oral Communication course at the University of San Francisco—by challenging us to create a policy change on current legislation, I was given an outlet to write on a social justice issue of which I am extremely passionate. It is my hope that this essay would, at the very least, make its readers realize what is missing in their history textbooks and daily headlines. Moreover, I hope that it would encourage others to advocate for the unheard—change is, after all, better late than never.

—*Jillian Ramos*

INSTRUCTOR'S COMMENTS

Perhaps the most challenging aspect of writing a Rogerian argument is the control of tone. How, despite guarding a passionately held belief, can one engage with opposition meaningfully—without condescension or indeed anger (and anger is certainly warranted when considering the unjust treatment of Filipino veterans after the war). Jillian does here what she managed to do for me all year—she maintains her composure and opts instead to allow her detailed and even-handed research to emerge as her trump card. Pausing over Jillian's research a bit more, note how it is *not* procrustean (i.e., it does not truncate complicating evidence about the costs of repaying veterans' families despite our nation's present preoccupation with "austerity"). Indeed, she uses the financial information provided by the VA and other government sources to make her case even stronger. I'd also like to note that Jillian presented the material printed here in USF's Spring 2011 Speakers' Showcase, and by all accounts, it was a masterful speech. I am proud to have had Jillian in my midst for a yearlong Written and Oral Communication class and I predict great things for her—both on pages and stages—here at USF and beyond.

—David Holler, Department of Rhetoric and Language,
University of San Francisco

Jillian Ramos

Prof. Holler

RHET 130

10 May 2011

In Honor of the Forgotten:

A Search for Equity for

Filipino-American World War II Veterans

Abstract

Approximately 200,000 Filipinos served in the United States military during World War II. However, the 1946 Rescission Act retracted most of the benefits these soldiers were entitled to—the law stated that because they were not citizens at the time of the war, they were not eligible to receive them. It was not until President Obama signed the American Recovery and Reinvestment Act of 2009 that some Filipinos were finally able to receive lump-sums of either $15,000 as citizens or $9,000 as non-citizens. But there are still several flaws within the legislation that must be taken into consideration. Therefore, I propose for these benefits to be paid back in the full value that was promised them (accounting for inflation) and be made accessible to the veterans' widows and family members; determining the eligibility of these soldiers should also be more efficient and fair. I also advocate for a greater emphasis of past Filipino-American relations in history curricula throughout the United States in order to pay tribute to these veterans and to ensure that the injustices they had undergone do not go untold in the future.

Introduction

It has been nearly seventy years since World War II has passed: since the grueling Bataan Death March; since Filipino soldiers suffered inhuman concentration camps under brutal Japanese control; since the Filipinos fought under the United States flag. But it took nearly seventy years before America finally granted these war veterans *some* of the rights were entitled to. "At the time of recruitment," notes U.S. Representative and Chairman of the Asian Pacific American Caucus, Michael Honda, "the U.S. government promised that ... Filipino soldiers would be treated as U.S. veterans and entitled to full benefits" (Honda 193). But the problem is far from over. Filipinos have become a forgotten part of American past; it is time that they are given what is due them.

American Colonialism and Racism

American involvement in the Philippines dates as far back as 1899 during the Philippine-American War, which was "a result of the Philippine Revolution [against their previous colonizer, Spain] and U.S. involvement with Spain's other major colony, Cuba" (Dumindin 1). The war left the Philippines with approximately 220,000 dead and a new era of colonial rule under the United States—the entire nation became radically Americanized, from education to cultural norms. And yet, this event is hardly considered common knowledge in American history. New York University adjunct professor of Asian Pacific American Studies, Luis Francia, notes:

> How convenient (and necessary) that it be forgotten for the sake of upholding the self-spun myth of a freedom-fighting giant! Here is a war that lasted for a decade, cost so much more money than the Spanish-American War, reduced in scale and intensity to a nonevent. Such has been the fervent aim of a nation of apologists (including not a few scholars whose allegiance seems more to pre-serving America's aw-shucks good-guy image rather than to the facts). (Francia and Shaw 23)

However, even after they migrated to the United States, Filipinos faced racism similar to that which African Americans had undergone prior to the Civil Rights Era. For instance, "in California in the 1920s and 1930s, Filipinos faced de facto segregation": several facilities prohibited Filipinos from entering at all costs; they were reduced to working in agricultural fields for menial wages; Filipino men were forbidden to be seen anywhere near white women; and in the U.S. Navy, they were limited to serving only as busboys and musicians. But most of all, Filipinos were not granted citizenship "despite their ability as U.S. nationals to move freely" (Posadas 20-24). Still, as with many aspects of Filipino-American history, these events remain unknown to the general American public.

Filipino Involvement in World War II

The role of the Filipino changed dramatically during World War II, however. Commissioner to the Federal Council on the Aging, Alice P. Bulos, notes that on July 26, 1941, "President Franklin Delano Roosevelt ordered the induction of the Philippine Army into the United States Armed Forces in the Far East (USAFFE) under the command of General Douglas MacArthur"—less than five months before the Japanese bombing on Pearl Harbor (Bulos qtd. in Alabado 117). Because the Philippine Army was under American command, young Filipino men were automatically drafted into the Army to fight off the Japanese in the Pacific theater—notably, the Philippines.

But on April 9, 1942, "90,000 to 100,000 American and Filipino prisoners of war captured by the Japanese" were "force-marched 55 miles (88 km) to San Fernando, then taken by rail to Capas, from where they walked the final 8 miles (13 km) to Camp O'Donnell … only 54,000 reached the camp" ("Bataan Death March" 1). These soldiers suffered from severe mistreatment by the Japanese—including, but not limited to, abuse, starvation, and disease caused by lack of proper sanitation—in what came to be known as the Bataan Death March. To those who were fortunate enough to survive its terrors, this event marked just the beginning of the plight of the Filipino in service of the United States.

According to Paul Daniel Rivera, J.D. Candidate of the University of California, Hastings College of Law, "these veterans …[engaged] in some of the Pacific's bloodiest combat and were crucial in helping America take the Pacific back from the Japanese" (Rivera 449). As a reward for their bravery and their willingness to fight under the American flag, the Filipino soldiers were promised equal benefits to any American soldier. However, not long after the end of the war, these Filipinos faced a most gruesome form of racism. In 1946, Congress passed the Rescission Act, which stated that "service in the organized forces of the Government of the Commonwealth of the Philippines ... shall not be deemed to be or to have been active service in the military or naval forces of the United States for purposes ... of conferring rights, privileges [and] benefits (Bulos qtd. in Alabado 118). The law basically denied Philippine soldiers who fought for the Pacific theater "all non-service-connected U.S. veterans' benefits"; the legislation also "reduced ... payments [for benefits regarding service-connected disabilities] to the rate of fifty cents for each dollar to account for the lower standard of living in the Philippines" (Rivera 457). In an open letter to Congress, Atty. Corban K. Alabado, a retired 3rd Lieutenant of the USAFFE and member of Veterans of Foreign Wars, pled:

> Was it not in the active service that we went to Bataan ... and fought side by side with our American brothers? Were we not in the uniform of the USAFFE when the United States Military High Command gave us orders to surrender on April 9, 1942? Were we not taken prisoners of war and made to walk the many kilometers of the brutal Death March? ... As soon as we had recovered from

malaria and dysentery, many of us joined the resistance under-
ground movement [against the Japanese]. When the Americans returned to the Philippines, we returned to military control ... what
of the above services are not 'active' as described by the Rescission Act? (Alabado 114)

The Philippine war veterans (or *veteranos*) thus found themselves in a
state of inequality that brought their status back to where they were prior
to the war. Little did they know that they would still be fighting six decades
later.

The Rescission Act, Justified

The American government was hesitant to give such benefits to the Filipino soldiers because, according to Rivera, "so few of these veterans lived
in the United States" (458). And because most of these Filipino soldiers
were fighting only as U.S. nationals, Congress argued that they should
not be entitled to the same benefits as every other U.S. citizen. In *Harris
v. Rosario* (1980), the Supreme Court "relied upon Congress' broad powers under the Territory Clause of the Constitution," which gave Congress
the right to "treat [Territories] differently from States so long as there is a
rational basis" (460). Since the Philippines was still not independent at the
time of the war, Congress was thus technically able to pass the Rescission
Act while still staying within the confines of the Constitution. Furthermore, while the Philippines was a territory of the United States, it was

never taxed—therefore, "that community ... has never contributed to the funding of U.S. veterans' benefits" (460). This notion further led Congress to believe that giving Filipino veterans equal benefits would be unjust for American taxpayers, particularly citizens who also served in the war.

The American government also makes a valid claim when justifying why Filipinos are only entitled to half the payment amount than what American veterans receive. Because the standard of living is much lower in the Philippines than it is in the United States, it would only make sense to adjust their benefits according to where they live—it would certainly create a sense of imbalance if one country receives more benefits relative to another country, in terms of the exchange rate. If Filipinos were to receive the same dollar amount in benefits as American veterans, they would technically be receiving more than their American counterparts, provided that they stay in the Philippines. Those in favor of the Rescission Act may argue that this would be an injustice towards American-born soldiers.

Steps Toward Equity

Initially, the 1946 legislation may have been well-justified and easily supported; however, since 1993, activists have frequently attempted to pass a bill that would give the *veteranos* the benefits they were promised before enlisting for the war. But according to attorneys Sara Fargnoli, Rebecca Feinberg, and Adriane Turnipseed of the Department of Veterans Affairs, Board of Veterans' Appeals, "every version of the bill died in committee until 2008." And even when the Filipino Veterans Fairness Act passed through the House of Representatives in 2008, "no further action was taken thereon" (Fargnoli, Feinberg, and Turnipseed 272).

It was not until February 17, 2009, when President Obama signed the American Recovery and Reinvestment Act, which, according to the U.S. Department of Veterans Affairs, appropriated $198 million in order to pay "eligible World War II (WWII) Philippine Veterans" a "one-time, lump payment." If eligible, veterans would be given $15,000 if they were U.S. citizens and $9,000 if not ("What's New in Compensation & Pension Benefits" 1). However, Rivera argues that this act passed because it was "buried amidst hundreds of pages and billions of dollars funded by the [stimulus] bill"—because efforts to pass a bill solely addressing Filipino veterans' rights have failed in the past, it was finally inserted into a much larger bill, one that the Obama administration fervently pushed to pass (Rivera 447). Still, even with this rather unfortunate truth, the fact that this act finally passed through was a major triumph for the Filipino community.

The American Recovery and Reinvestment Act of 2009 could literally not help every *veterano* who fought for the United States during World War II, however. Because it came into effect several decades after the war, the legislation unfortunately came far too late for most of the veterans. According to an article by *San Francisco Chronicle* staff writer, Bob Egelko, out of the approximately 200,000 Filipinos who served the United States, only about 18,000 men are alive today (Egelko 1). But the untimely passing of this bill is not the only problem: the fight for the Filipinos is far from over.

"Full Equity Now"

Had the legislation been completely fair to the *veteranos*, it probably would not have garnered nearly as much backlash from the Filipino community. However, because of its restrictive provisions, two lawsuits in the Bay Area "challenged the government's treatment" of the Filipino veterans as of October 2010 (1). It is clear that the new law must be modified in order to ensure full equity for the Filipinos who served under the United States during World War II. Therefore, I advocate for veterans' benefits to be paid back in the full value that was promised these Filipinos, accounting for inflation rates. These benefits must also be made available for the widows and families of these veterans. In addition, I propose a fairer means of determining eligibility for the veterans rather than relying solely on one "federal registry of military personnel" (1). Finally, in order to educate future American generations of this lesser-known past, I suggest that the United States as a whole should implement greater emphasis on American relations with the Philippines in its elementary and secondary school U.S. history curriculum.

In Honor of the Forgotten

If taken at face value, the new legislation may seem like a huge step toward equity for the Filipino veterans. While this may be true to some degree, it must also be considered that the current stipend is nowhere near enough what the veterans truly deserve. According to Commissioner Alice P. Bulos, the Rescission Act "rescinded the Filipino WWII veterans' $3.2 billion claim for unpaid salaries during the duration of the war" (Alabado 118). Accounting for the approximately 200,000 soldiers who fought during the war, each *veterano* was entitled to about $16,000 in salaries in 1946, which is still more than what current veterans get now, even after several decades of waiting. Therefore, I propose that the United States should pay back each veteran—citizen or non-citizen—the $16,000 they were promised, but adjusted for inflation rates. The U.S. Bureau of Labor Statistics Consumer Price Index reveals that $16,000 in 1946 equates to about $183,357.54 in 2011 ("CPI Inflation Calculator 1"). This hefty jump from the $15,000/$9,000 currently being given to the eligible veterans seems only fair: after all, this proposal only seeks to adjust nothing more than the original promised value. After over sixty years of waiting, the least the United States could do is pay these veterans back in full value.

The current legislation also has several limitations that prevent it from being as equitable as it needs to be. For instance, during the 2010 Bay Area lawsuits, one of the most sought-after revisions was to "make the widows of Filipino soldiers who died before the benefits [be] approved eligible to receive their husbands' share" ("RP war vets sue U.S. gov't over benefits" 1). This argument only makes sense—the deaths of the veterans and the passing of this legislation are not in the hands of the widows. "To put it to the test," argues Rivera, "this would mean that the spouses who were widowed just one day before the legislation passed cannot receive the lump-sum payment" (Rivera 481). Congress should not be able to put one widow over another simply because one's husband died prior to February 2009—especially when Congress itself took so long to pass the bill in the first place.

Furthermore, there are benefits that are still withheld from these veterans, even if they are eligible. For instance, the legislation does not include education and home loan guarantees for these veterans (475-76). In terms of the veterans themselves, these two benefits are not very applicable in the first place: after all, they are most likely not going to be concerned with higher education and buying homes at over eighty years of age (not to mention many of them lack sufficient sources of income to begin with). Therefore, in agreement with Rivera, I propose that these benefits should instead be extended to the families of these veterans, particularly the children and grandchildren. The "thirty-six months of education benefits," as well as the home loans, that the VA provides would no doubt be useful for the younger members of the veteran's family (476). If these benefits are impractical for the veterans now, the least the government can do is pass them over to the later generations who can make good use of them. In this way, the United States can still honor these veterans through their families.

The method of determining which applicants are eligible for benefits is also rather flawed in many ways. Some veterans whose applications were denied argued that their documentation was "burned in a 1973 fire ...

at NPRC (National Personnel Records Center)"—the Department of Veterans Affairs, however, claims that "in most instances the service department can verify New Philippine Scout service using alternative methods" ("News Flash – Center for Minority Veterans" 1). But the numbers suggest just how effective these "alternative methods" are: the VA reveals that, as of December 23, 2010, 23,442 claims were denied out of the total 41,234 claims completed (see Table 1). Felino Punsalan, a 92-year-old *veterano*, was one of the many who were denied because "his name is not on the [NPRC] database" despite having "forwarded a copy of his discharge papers" (Egelko 1). The solution to this problem is simple: allow the denied applicants a chance to file their claim again with any sort of proof they may have of their service—even something as simple as their uniforms should be able to verify their claims. If this law were truly equitable, the amount of denials should not have exceeded the amount of granted claims: these veterans have the right to use anything that may prove their service, especially if their files were destroyed by a fire that was beyond their control. Approving more veterans' claims, as well as allowing more widows to file for their late husbands' benefits, would greatly reduce the gap between denials and grants.

But these Filipinos deserve more than monetary gains and short-lived public acknowledgements. Perhaps the greatest way to pay tribute to the *veteranos* is by letting their legacy live on in future generations. As a nation, the United States must not only recognize, but remember, the sacrifices that these Filipino veterans have made both on and off the battlefield. Therefore, I urge for all states to extend their history curriculum to include greater details of U.S.-Philippine relations, with a particular emphasis on World War II and the veterans' fight for equity. These additions should be made starting at the elementary level. But in order to truly understand the depths of their tragic history, more emphasis must be made in secondary school. While this last suggestion may not directly benefit the *veteranos*, it is still crucial in preserving their dignity within the United States. According to Rep. Honda, for decades, "many members of Congress, unaware of the history of Filipino contributions and sacrifices during World War II, seemed unmoved by appeals to make good our country's broken promise to these veterans" (Honda 195). Had these congressional representatives been given adequate education on the true struggles of these veterans, the fight for equity could have been drastically reduced or even avoided altogether. And while it is impossible to turn back the clock and fix this error, the least the United States could do is to make sure similar tragedies would not happen again in the future—for Filipinos, or for any minority group.

Conclusion

It is a shame that the American government has neglected the *active* service of these Filipino veterans during World War II; it would be an even greater shame if we let these aging heroes settle for less than what they deserve. While the United States has taken some steps to further their cause, it is imperative that we continue to fight for their sake, just as they fought for us. In closing his letter to Congress, Ret. Lt. Alabado writes, "our thoughts are happiest when we think we had done our duty, but sad, that we have been discarded like an old useless rag ... we still look forward though to the day when through your help and support the injustices brought about the Rescission Act are corrected ... restore our dignity and respect" (Alabado 116). It has been nearly seventy years since World War II has passed—it is about time that the United States listens to the *veteranos*.

Appendix

Status	Number
Pending Claims	1,366
Claims Granted ($9.000)	8,878
Claims Granted ($15,000)	8,914
Claims Denied	23,442
Claims Completed	41,234

Table 1.
Out of the 41,234 claims completed for the Filipino veterans benefits (as of December 23, 2010), the VA reveals that many more claims were actually denied than were granted.

Source: "As of 12/23/2010." Table. *News Flash*. U.S. Department of Veterans Affairs. 30 Dec. 2010. Web. 21 Apr. 2011.

Works Cited

Alabado, Corbin K. *Bataan Death March, Capas.* San Francisco: Sulu

Books, 1995. Print.

"Bataan Death March." *Encyclopædia Britannica Online.* Encyclopædia

Britannica, 2011. Web. 24 Apr. 2011.

"CPI Inflation Calculator." U.S. Bureau of Labor Statistics. 2011. Web.

23 April 2011.

Dumindin, Arnaldo. "Background: The Philippine Revolution and the

Spanish-American War." *Philippine American War.* 2006. Web. 15

Apr. 2011.

Egelko, Bob. "Filipino WWII veterans sue over benefits." *SFGate.* 09

Oct. 2010. Web. 24 Mar. 2011.

Fargnoli, Sara, Rebecca Feinberg, and Adriane Turnipseed. "Trend

toward Equality? Noncitizen Veterans in the Administration of

Post-Service Benefits." *Veterans Law Review* 2 (2010). Web. 14 Apr.

2011.

"Filipino American World War II Vets Seek Equal Benefits." *Pacific

Citizen.* 04 March 2011. Web. 24 Mar. 2011.

Francia, Luis and Angel Velasco Shaw. *Vestiges of War: The Philippine-

American War and the Aftermath of an Imperial Dream, 1899-1999.*

New York: New York University Press, 2002. Print.

Honda, Michael. "Justice for Filipino Veterans, at Long Last." *Asian American Law Journal* 16.1 (2009): 193-196. Web. 24 Mar. 2011.

"News Flash – Center for Minority Veterans." United States Dept. of Veteran Affairs. 30 Dec. 2010. Web. 24 Mar. 2011.

Posadas, Barbara Mercedes. *The Filipino Americans.* Westport, CT: Greenwood Press, 1999. Print.

Rice, Mark. "His Name was Don Francisco Muro: Reconstructing an Image of American Imperialism." *American Quarterly* 62.1 (2010): 49-76. Web. 24 Mar. 2011.

Rivera, Paul Daniel. "We've Been Waiting a Long Time." *Hastings Race and Poverty Law Journal* 7.2 (2010): 447-482. Web. 24 Mar. 2011.

"RP war vets sue U.S. gov't over benefits." *The Philippine Inquirer*. 11 Oct. 2010. Web. 24 Mar. 2011.

Vestiges of War: The Philippine-American War and the Aftermath of an Imperial Dream. Eds. Angel Velasco Shaw and Luis H. Francia. New York: New York UP, 2003. Print.

"What's New in Compensation & Pension Benefits." United States Dept. of Veteran Affairs. 03 Mar. 2010. Web. 24 Mar. 2011.

Jillian Ramos
Professor Holler
RHET 131 – 04
27 April 2011

Outline: Filipino American Veterans' Benefits

Thesis: <u>I advocate for Filipino veterans' benefits to be paid back in the full value that was promised these soldiers, accounting for inflation rates. These benefits must also be made available for the widows and families of these veterans. In addition, I propose a fairer means of determining eligibility for the veterans rather than relying solely on one "federal registry of military personnel" (Egelko 1). Finally, in order to educate future American generations of this lesser-known past, I suggest that the United States as a whole should implement greater emphasis on American relations with the Philippines in its elementary and secondary school U.S. history curriculum.</u>

I. Introduction
   a. Nearly seventy years since WWII: Bataan Death March, concentration camps under brutal Japanese control, Filipinos under U.S. Military command
   b. Quote: "At the time of recruitment, the U.S. government promised that these Filipino soldiers would be treated as U.S. veterans and entitled to full benefits." – U.S. Representative Michael Honda, Chairman of the Congressional Asian Pacific American Caucus
   c. Filipino American veterans still fighting to this day for WWII benefits
   d. Road map: history of WWII/aftermath; current status on fight for equity; proposed solution
II. World War II
   a. Philippines: U.S. colony at the time of WWII
   b. April 9, 1942: "90,000 to 100,000 American and Filipino prisoners of war captured by the Japanese" were "force-marched 55 miles (88 km) to San Fernando, then taken by rail to Capas, from where they walked the final 8 miles (13 km) to Camp O'Donnell…only 54,000 reached the camp" ("Bataan Death March" 1) – Encyclopedia Britannica
      i. Reduced to starvation, abuse, and disease (malaria, dysentery, etc.) under the Japanese
   c. Continued to fight even when released from

concentration camps—American victory in Pacific heavily due to Filipino efforts

    d. Rescission Act of 1946

        i. Revoked promise to grant Filipinos full benefits because they were not considered to have been in "active service"

        ii. Justifications:

            1. Not U.S. citizens = not paying taxes that go toward benefits—U.S. Constitution gives Congress right to treat territories differently from States

            2. Full benefits deemed unfair due to lower living standards in the Philippines (if accounting for exchange rates)

III. Steps toward Equity

    a. Feb. 17, 2009: American Recovery and Reinvestment Act

        i. $198 million appropriated to *veteranos*: $15,000 per eligible U.S. citizen, $9,000 per eligible non-U.S. citizens

        ii. Arguably passed only because it was part of Obama's stimulus bill

        iii. Only about 18,000 of approx. 200,000 veterans survived to see bill pass

IV. Thesis

V. Paying back the veterans

    a. Commissioner Alice P. Bulos: Rescission Act "rescinded the Filipino WWII veterans $3.2 billion claim for unpaid salaries during the duration of the war"

        i. Solution: divide $3.2 billion by 200,000 (# of soldiers) to get each soldiers' due salary—adjusted for inflation = $183, 357.54 (U.S. Bureau of Labor Statistics)

    b. Education/home loan guarantees: extend to widows and family members (since these denied benefits would not be useful to veterans)

VI. Fairer determination of eligibility

    a. Currently only using one federal registry

    b. U.S. Dept. of Veterans Affairs: claims to have alt. suggestions—still denied 23,442 claims out of 41,234 total (either due to widows applying for deceased husbands' benefits or being denied altogether)

VII. Extending U.S. history curriculum to include greater detail of U.S.-Philippines relations

       a.   Particularly in secondary school for greater depth—so as not to have story go forgotten

VIII.   Conclusion

       a.   Cannot forget the *active* service of these men: "Our thoughts are happiest when we think we had done our duty, but sad, that we have been discarded like an old useless rag … restore our dignity and respect." – Corban K. Alabado, 3rd Lt. USAFFE (ret.), letter to Congress

Index